PERFORMING FEMINISMS

IN CONTEMPORARY IRELAND

W/0

PERFORMING FEMINISMS

IN CONTEMPORARY IRELAND

EDITED BY LISA FITZPATRICK

CARYSFORT PRESS

A Carysfort Press Book

Performing Feminisms in Contemporary Ireland
Edited by Lisa Fitzpatrick

First published in Ireland in 2013 as a paperback original by

Carysfort Press, 58 Woodfield, Scholarstown Road

Dublin 16, Ireland

ISBN 978-1-904505-62-4
©2013 Copyright remains with the authors

Typeset by Carysfort Press

Cover design by eprint limited
Printed and bound by eprint limited
Unit 35
Coolmine Industrial Estate
Dublin 15
Ireland

This book is published with the financial assistance of
The Arts Council (An Chomhairle Ealaíon) Dublin, Ireland

CONTENTS

ACKNOWLEDGEMENTS

I would like to thank the many people who contributed to this project, which began with a panel at the International Association for the Study of Irish Literatures conference in Maynooth in 2010, with papers from Mária Kurdi and Tina O'Toole and a rigorous and productive discussion from the delegates who attended. I would like to thank all the contributors for their hard work and generosity with their scholarship, and Eamonn Jordan, Dan Farrelly and Lilian Chambers of Carysfort Press.

I would also like to thank Ruth McCarthy, Jacsail McBicycle and HOMOCULT for permission to use their images in the essay 'Le Monkey Homosexual'; the National Library of Ireland; Chris McCallion, and my colleagues in the School of Creative Arts at the University of Ulster.

List of Illustrations

Introduction: Performing Feminisms

Lisa Fitzpatrick

The idea for this collection of essays begins with an image from Linda Connolly and Tina O'Toole's *Documenting Irish Feminisms*: a joyful photograph of young women in the 1970s holding up the banner of the Irish Women's Liberation Movement, the woman in the centre with her fist raised in a salute. While I was reading their book it struck me how very different this image of Irish women was to many of the images propagated in popular culture throughout the twentieth century. It is as if these women are performing a new idea of Irish womanhood as active, challenging, and taking control: they are trying on a possible new social role, demonstrating it publicly, and in so doing making it possible for other women to explore roles and behaviour that were previously prohibited. It is in this sense that this collection uses the term 'performance', to include the performances of everyday life that mark and shape identities, reshape and adorn the body, tell stories and shape our experience and our place in and of the world around us. This collection seeks to explore some of the debates, old and new, that shape and delimit the performance of gender and sexuality in contemporary Ireland, and to consider the ways in which feminism is 'performed' in everyday life by ordinary women, who may not identify themselves as feminist but who, increasingly, move through the social, cultural and political matrices of everyday life with a sense of their own status and dignity, and a belief in their equality as full citizens.

The 1971 'contraceptive train' (as it became known), the event captured in the image, performs a kind of revolution by staging Irish women as sexual agents, in control of their bodies and their fertility. On 22nd May 1971, a group of approximately forty young women took the train to Belfast from Dublin, purchased contraceptives there, and brought them back to the Republic, challenging the customs officials to arrest them. Listening to Nell McCafferty's account[1] of that day it is astonishing now to hear that most of the women had never seen a contraceptive; that some of the unmarried activists refused to take part because they felt contraceptives should only be available to married women, and that all those involved were worried about what their parents would say! It is difficult to imagine in the largely secular Irish Republic of the early 21st century that it was only in 1985 that the Health (Family Planning) (Amendment) Act lifted restrictions on the sale of condoms; prior to that time, outside of Dublin, contraceptives were not always readily obtainable, giving rise to urban legends about the efficacy of clingfilm as a substitute. Without wishing to reduce the Women's Movement to the single issue of contraception, it is undeniable that the availability of safe and reliable contraceptives has been a very significant factor in broadening the choices available to women in their daily lives, and in freeing women from unchosen pregnancies and family duties.

Although this collection explores various facets of the Women's Movement over the past forty years, it is important as well to recognize that the Irish Housewives Association (IHA) and the Irish Countrywomen's Association (ICA) had developed a network of women's groups around the country by the middle of the twentieth century, a network which still exists under various names and in various forms today. Indeed the ICA is still in existence and currently has its own reality TV series, *ICA Bootcamp*, on Radio Telifís Éireann, the Irish national broadcasting company. Through their history these organizations exerted a considerable force for change by linking women together and providing a sense of community and belonging for women who were often isolated in the home or on the farm. Linda Connolly argues that this was 'the direct catalyst' for the establishment of the ad hoc committee on women's rights in 1968, leading to the First Commission on the Status of Women two years later (2002: 105). But it is the explosion of activity that begins in 1970 that takes the demands for social change into the public forum that is the focus of this collection.

In the decades since then, 'performances' of feminism in its many guises have reshaped the cultural and social landscape, working sometimes at the peripheries and margins, and sometimes in the

---

[1] BBC World Service
http://www.bbc.co.uk/iplayer/episode/p00gnl35/Witness_The_Irish_cont raceptive_train/.

mainstream. This radical reordering is apparent in almost every area of Irish society, albeit as part of an ongoing struggle: it is apparent in the roles that women perform in the workplace, in women's space and place and freedom to move about in the public world; in the extraordinary changes to family structures, attitudes to sexuality and personal identity, and in education and the expectation that today's children have of equal access to resources and opportunities, unhindered by gender.

The demands of the Irish Women's Liberation Movement, launched in its manifesto *Chains or Change* on the *Late Late Show* in March 1971, were deceptively simple. The manifesto listed equal pay for equal work; equality before the law; equal access to education; access to contraception, and justice for deserted wives, unmarried mothers and widows. Judged from this distance, the simplicity of the manifesto and its naïveté is apparent. The demands seem discrete and readily addressed, assuming that the will exists to address them. But in fact they are not discrete, and the progress towards meeting them over the past forty-plus years has demonstrated the radical, profound change they demand. Equal access to education has meant well-educated and highly skilled women emerging from schools and universities and expecting a place in the workforce and a career structure that reflects their ambitions and abilities. The recent data from the 2010 Census in the Republic of Ireland suggests further change in the near future: women under 40 are increasingly likely to earn more than their male partners. The expectation of a satisfactory career also shapes women's personal relationships, and most women's belief that it is possible and desirable to combine a family with a career. The ability to earn a living wage has radically altered women's experiences of marriage and motherhood, with increasing numbers of women entering, and remaining in the workforce throughout their adult lives; and with the benefit of economic independence comes a greater reluctance to tolerate unsatisfactory marriages. Access to contraception has allowed women to be sexually active without the fear of unwanted or multiple pregnancies, and social support for deserted wives, widows and unmarried mothers has not only allowed women to cope financially with difficult family circumstances but has also had the effect of making those circumstances visible, and giving them a place in the social discourse. This has had a profound impact in a society that, in the early 1970s (and for many years after) was still incarcerating pregnant single women in Magdalene Laundries and forcing them to yield up their 'illegitimate' babies for adoption, and hiding evidence of anything that contradicted Catholic social teaching. The haunting performance *Laundry* at the 2011 Dublin Theatre Festival, for example, reminds us that these places remained open until the mid-1990s.

The changes in the status of women are inextricable from other profound social changes in Ireland such as the processes of economic globalization, the rise of information technology which has made it nearly impossible for countries to censor information, and particularly the diminishing status of the Roman Catholic Church and the falling away from traditional religious beliefs and practices. The challenge that the 'contraceptive train' issued was not only political; it was also a profound challenge to the Catholic Church in Ireland. It proclaimed a willingness to defy Catholic teaching, and asserted the primacy of personal choice in matters of private morality. To a lesser extent, the foundation of refuges for victims of domestic abuse and the establishment of the Rape Crisis Centres across the island of Ireland challenged the primacy of the family unit, insisting that breaches of the law and of individual rights within the family had to be addressed publicly rather than being concealed as private, or shameful. Dealing with abuse within the family tended to place the responsibility with the victims rather than the perpetrator, making the victims' silence the price of public respectability. By forcing the issue into the public domain and into the public consciousness, the founders of these services asserted that the shame lay with the perpetrator.

Although the difficulties women faced in Northern Ireland and the Republic of Ireland differed to some extent, most obviously in the explicitly violent, polarized and militarized situation of Northern Ireland, many of the underlying issues were essentially the same. The Reformed Churches held similarly traditional views on gender and sexuality to those of the Roman Catholic Church. Furthermore, the civil violence in Northern Ireland was frequently prioritized by the police and security forces over 'domestic' incidents, sexual violence, or homophobic violence, all of which were less threatening to the security of the state, as Eileen Evason argues in her work on gender and violence.[2] And, as Fiona Bloomer points out in her essay in this collection, British legislation on women's rights does not always extend to Northern Ireland.

The feminist movement in Ireland, in its various guises, has changed the workplace, the social space of the cities and towns, and the domestic

---

[2] Eileen Evason, Hidden Violence (Farset Cooperative Press, 1982) and Against the Grain: the Contemporary Women's Movement in Northern Ireland (Dublin: Attic Press, 1991)

space. It has joined forces with various local and community initiatives and civil rights movements, most obviously with the campaign for Lesbian, Gay, Bisexual and Transsexual (LGBT) Rights, the rights of ethnic minorities, and the defence of the poorest members of society. The main aim of this book is to consider how these new ideas and possibilities of living as a woman in Ireland have emerged and how they are reflected in the literature and in the arts, as well as in daily life. The Irish Women's Liberation Movement may have begun in 1970 as a single identifiable movement, but it has become part of the fabric of our everyday lives.

The first paper in the collection is Sara Keating's report on women playwrights, directors and performers in the 2011 Dublin Theatre Festival. She notes that out of fifteen Irish productions, 'nine were directed by women, five were written or 'authored' by women and women's experiences of historical or contemporary cultural repression was at the heart of several of the pieces.' The work that Keating describes reflects many of the recurring issues in this volume: concerns with sexuality, maternity, and the tensions between tradition and a changing society.

Susanne Colleary's discussion of comedian Maeve Higgins is titled 'Eating Tiny Cakes in the Dark', a quotation from one of Higgins's best-known sets. Higgins is a Cork-born performer who began working as a stand-up in 2004 and is known for her television work on *Naked Camera* and *Fancy Vittles*. Colleary describes Higgins's distinctive style as 'deceptively charming', analysing how she 'undercuts the surface of her whimsical persona with darker stories and material' to create a subtly anarchic, subversive version of femininity while seeming to conform to popular cultural stereotypes of women as domestic and romantic. Drawing on Higgins's *Thin Means Good Person* set, Colleary connects her mockery of slimming groups and social attitudes to body size and shape to a feminist analysis that identifies persistent, lingering cultural anxieties about women's physicality in contemporary attitudes to weight. Higgins subverts the expected, self-deprecating narrative however to make fun of the slimming clubs and the implicit connection between success in professional and personal life, and control of one's weight. Colleary also explores the performed self-deprecation of many female comics, arguing for the need to examine the roots of such behaviour, the apparent requirement or expectation that women working in the aggressive world of stand-up should present themselves as unthreatening to male dominance and authority.

Brenda Donohue's essay on Marina Carr's work – especially her 2009 play *Marble* – argues that writing for theatre is a feminist act in itself. Donohue considers the marginalization of women playwrights in the Irish theatre and suggests that, in this context, Carr's work asserts and inserts a woman's voice into the repertory. *Marble*, she points out, was the only new play by a woman to be staged in the Abbey that year. John Countryman and Charlotte Headrick, in their essay 'Damned if You Do, Damned if You Don't', offer an American perspective on the reception of Irish women's writing internationally. Their paper charts the absences of plays by women from anthologies of Irish drama, and the lack of attention paid by critics and scholars to women's writing, to argue that part of the problem for theatres and directors is that they have limited access to the material. They continue, to argue that work that unsettles comfortable or conventional images of Ireland, Irish life, or Irish femininity is often regarded by theatres as too risky to produce. They point to the highly recognizable, Bórd Fáilte images of Ireland that shape international conceptions of the island and discuss the ways in which these images shape audiences' expectations of, and responses to, Irish drama. Women's writing often unsettles these expectations – as is evident from the controversy surrounding the presentation of Marina Carr's *On Raftery's Hill* at the Arts from Ireland festival in Washington in 2000, or the 2001 production by Pittsburgh Irish and Classical Theatre Company of the same author's *Portia Coughlan* in 2001 as described by Melissa Sihra.[3]

Tom Maguire and Carole-Anne Upton's essay, 'Myth and Gender in Irish Drama', discusses two productions of plays by women that attempt to engage critically with the representation of women in Irish mythology. Their essay considers ways in which the audience resists this revised reading, holding instead to the received understanding of the texts with their conventional representation of gender. Like Headrick and Countryman's essay, theirs engages with the struggle between conflicting meanings, as older tropes become obsolete while the new are not yet fully formed. Eavan Boland's discussion of the woman poet in the national tradition comes irresistibly to mind: she describes her realization, as a young poet, that 'as a poet I could not easily do without the idea of a nation ... On the other hand, as a woman I could not accept the nation formulated for me by Irish poetry and its traditions'. Most of the poets in the Irish tradition 'used women to

---

3 Melissa Sihra, 'Marina Carr in the US: Perception, Conflict and Culture in Irish Theatre Abroad' *Irish Theatre on Tour* eds Nicholas Grene and Chris Morash (Dublin: Carysfort, 2005): 179-192.

explore their own ideas about Irishness', but: 'I did not recognize these women. Their images could never be a starting point for mine'.[4]

Steve Wilmer and Mary Caulfield address the question of representing women from another perspective: their paper investigates attitudes towards women's place in the nation's history through an analysis of public monuments in Dublin. Identifying Constance Markievicz as their key example, they explore the tensions between the iconographic representations of Ireland as feminine, revolutionary figures like Markievicz, and conventional models of femininity. The essay also considers Markievicz's plays, which also attempt to overturn simplistic identifications of woman with nation and man with the warrior-saviour. The plays are never performed and are clearly at odds with received ideas about gender and nation. Evidence of these tensions is threaded through the essays on women and representation in its various forms.

This marginalization of writing by women and their struggle to find a voice is discussed further in Megan Buckley and Julia Walther's essay about the writing workshops, community writing initiatives and feminist presses that sprang up in the 1970s. Buckley and Walther read the feminist potential of such initiatives and their role in fostering and promoting women's writing, calling them 'midwives to creativity'. These initiatives provided practical as well as moral support: classes and workshops were supported with crèches in recognition of the reality of women's lives and responsibilities. Like Donohue, Buckley and Walther argue that in its social and cultural context this act of writing was a feminist act: a deliberate entry into the public/published world; the assertion of a woman's voice and viewpoint within a male-dominated professional space. What emerges clearly from this essay, and that of Headrick and Countryman, is the sense in which women's marginalization is incidental rather than deliberate. Quoting Ingman, the authors draw attention to the correlation between the fact that most publishers are male, and a reluctance to publish work that did not 'speak' to them, or which perhaps they judged to be unrealistic or unbelievable as it unsettled conventional ideas about gender and the world.

Lisa McGonigle offers a feminist reading of Marian Keyes' novels as offering a culturally specific engagement with the experiences of contemporary Irish women. Keyes' work, and the popular fiction of other women writers, is often disparaged while, as Keyes herself points

---

[4] Eavan Boland, 'The Woman Poet in the National Tradition' *Studies: An Irish Quarterly Review* Vol. 76 No.302 (Summer 1987): 148-158.

out, 'male writers are vaunted for their work within a similar emotional range, 'oh you silly little woman with your little fluffy stories about shoes and romance ... as if men have the monopoly on intellectual criticism'.' McGonigle argues that Keyes re-appropriates the 'chick-lit tag' to write popular fiction that charts both the possibilities open to women in modern Ireland and the continuing reality of sexism and discrimination, in its exploration of sexual relationships, domestic violence, rape, unwanted pregnancy and abortion. Her novels are deceptively radical, in much the same way as Maeve Higgins's stand-up is: it appears to reiterate conventional gender stereotypes while actually undercutting them. McGonigle pays particular attention to Keyes's critique of Irish Catholicism, especially its effects in limiting the opportunities and ambitions of earlier generations of women.

These ideas are reflective of two of the strands that run through the collection: the marginalization of women together with the mythological and conservative representations of gender in Irish culture and the conservative impact of audience reception on the one hand, with acts of resistance both large and small on the other hand. Much of the most effective resistance was at grass-roots level and is concerned with providing spaces within which women could speak about their experiences, record them, and bring them into the public space – making those experiences visible and audible on stage, in writing, in daily life – and asserting the multiplicity of ways to be a woman in Ireland. Quoting Anne Stopper, Buckley and Walther note that 'a successful movement is the point of intersection between personal and social change' and identify writing workshops and community writing initiatives as one element of the movement.

The mother-daughter relationship is of central importance to women's lives, and it is unsurprising that it should be a key concern of female artists. Yet until recently, it rarely found a place on the Irish stage. As recently as 1998, Victoria White wrote of the difficulties for women writers in a theatre tradition that valued 'great national themes', when women 'had no history of national power' and 'could not find a way to make their psychological journeys symbolize those of the tribe. I think I had read and seen so many accounts of the father-son relationships that I thought I had one myself'.[5] In her essay, Mária Kurdi examines the mother-daughter relationship as it is depicted in a number of plays by Irish women, including Miriam Gallagher's *Shyllag* (1993), Gina Moxley's *Danti-Dan* (1995), Stella Feehily's *Duck* (2003)

---

[5] Victoria White, 'Women Writers Finally Take Centre Stage' *The Irish Times* 15 October 1998.

and Marina Carr's *Portia Coughlan* (1996) and *On Raftery's Hill* (2000). Kurdi draws on Irigaray and Chodorow, as well as the work of a range of Irish theatre scholars, to consider the tangled, often painful relationships of mothers and daughters. Carr's exploration of the mother-daughter relationship, though almost unrelentingly grim, might be read as feminist in its determination to plumb the depths of that struggle for power and autonomy; to follow Donohue's argument one might say that the very act of writing and publicly performing this relationship is an act of feminism.

The mother-daughter relationship is a foundational one in all sorts of ways, as Jacinta Byrne-Doran's work on intergenerational influences on mothers working outside the home reveals. Byrne-Doran's essay draws upon her recent qualitative study of maternal employment in Ireland, focusing in particular on the post-'Celtic Tiger' period – to consider the value of work in the lives of mothers and the significance of their mothers' lived examples. Her interviewees reflect on the ways their relationships with their mothers have shaped their own attitudes to work and motherhood, and on the support their mothers now often provide as care-givers to both their daughters and their grandchildren.

One of the values of an interdisciplinary collection, I would suggest, is that it can point to startling differences between disciplinary assumptions and approaches. Byrne-Doran's study reflects the practical, everyday experience of a younger generation of mothers as they negotiate the range of their everyday roles, often with invaluable support from their own mothers. The lives of the two generations of women, separated in time by the Women's Movement, are often very different but there is plenty of space for identification and for shared experience. The contrast with the representation of motherhood in drama and theatre could scarcely be greater. Why is this? Where are the loving and supportive mothers in Irish theatre, particularly theatre by women? While male playwrights like Sean O'Casey may create warm and resilient female characters like Juno, that cherish their children, it seems that Irish women's representation of motherhood is often darker and more fraught with a sense of rejection and longing.

My own essay in the collection looks at the representation of violence in a number of plays by Irish women, focusing in particular on sexual violence on the Irish stage and strategies that women use to represent this intimate form of violence.

Aideen Kerr's essay examines three recent Irish productions of Oscar Wilde's *Importance of Being Earnest* and *An Ideal Husband* to trace Wilde's feminist sympathies and to consider the staging of gender and sexuality in this very popular play. The productions under discussion are those of *Earnest* by Conall Morrison for the Abbey (2005) and Rough Magic for the Gaiety Theatre (2010), and Neil Bartlett's production of *An Ideal Husband* also for the Abbey (2008). Morrison's is notable for being an all-male production (there was a near-simultaneous all-male, two-hander production by Ridiculusmus). Kerr's reading of Wilde's work draws out his comic subversion of Victorian heteronormativity and considers ways in which these three productions used gender to explore contemporary gender politics.

The subversion of heteronormative assumptions is also the focus of Alyson Campbell and Suzanne Patman's essay on lesbian zines in Northern Ireland, which includes an interview with the artist and activist, Ruth McCarthy. McCarthy is co-founder and artistic director of OUTburst Queer Arts Festival, and producer of two queerzines: *Muffmonsters on Prozac* (1996-'98) and *Howl* (2001-'04). Over the past twenty years she has been at the forefront of the LGBT Rights movement in Belfast. Her creation, 'Le Monkey Homosexuel' who is a character in her zines, is a trickster figure that encourages readers to engage with 'disruptive imagination' (Hyde, 1998) as a way to imagine new cultural conditions.

Fiona Bloomer's essay reports on the issue of abortion rights and the campaign to extend the British 1967 Abortion Act to Northern Ireland. Detailing the work for the Alliance for Choice, Bloomer notes that since its foundation in 1996 the organization has attempted to focus the debate on the area of women's rights and social justice, rather than the current emphasis on abortion as a religious question. Bloomer's essay details some of the activities of the Alliance for Choice as they perform both the dominant image of Northern Irish women as contented mothers and wives, and displace that image by drawing attention to the suffering and inequalities obscured by it.

Motherhood, which is such a central experience in most women's lives, runs thematically through the collection whether it is depicted on stage, captured in literary writing, or subjected to sociological study. And the essays also find much to celebrate in contemporary life in Ireland – particularly the wealth of artistic and scholarly interventions by women, the subversive, humorous resistance to conventional and received conceptions of gender and womanhood, and an ability on the part of artists and ordinary women to exploit and take ownership of the tensions between traditional tropes and new understandings of gender that are being formed and performed in Irish culture and society.

1 | Women in the Dublin Theatre Festival 2011

Sara Keating

The Irish element of the Dublin Theatre Festival programme in 2011 was notable for the emphasis on site-specific work, suggesting an interesting evolution in contemporary Irish performance; the unshackling of theatre from the play text and the rise of the role of the director. What was especially significant was the prominence of women within this new dynamic. Out of fifteen Irish productions, nine were directed by women, five were written or 'authored' by women, and women's experience of historical or contemporary cultural repression was at the heart of several of the pieces. Traditionally, Irish theatre has been associated with the patriarchal narrative: from the privilege of male playwrights within the canon to the automatic association made between theatre and the twentieth-century state. However, the volume of work performed at the festival this year that challenges this narrative suggests the emergence of an alternative version of Irish history, a more progressive social reality, and a more egalitarian theatre culture in the new millennium.

Director Louise Lowe contributed two remarkable performance pieces that directly engaged with the history of Irish women's experience and redirected the narrative of institutional abuse in twentieth-century Ireland by raising important questions of societal complicity in the repression of female sexuality. In *World's End Lane* and *Laundry,* Lowe used oral history to complement her immersive site-specific aesthetic; what she defines as a 'geographical response' to the inner city Dublin in which she was born and reared. On the one hand, the two pieces were deeply personal responses to a specific place: audiences were guided through the performances by individual cast members, who gave us access to their most private experiences – in

World's End Lane, a prostitute undresses for us as if we are a client; in *Laundry,* we help a woman as she prepares to bathe. However, in these uncomfortably intimate transactions, the nature of personal responsibility is extrapolated outwards. How the audience behaves – how we passively accept or recoil from the various encounters and enactments of cruelty – becomes the key to the performance.

World's End Lane unfolded in the minimalist exhibition space of the LAB on Foley Street. Tucked away on a back street off Talbot Street, the building's function is both transparent – the main exhibition space is visible from the street – and opaque – what else is housed in its four stories? *World's End Lane* exposed the building's hidden life, both its contemporary secrets as it brought the performance out onto the street, and its historical mysteries: Foley Street was once the heart of the infamous Monto – Dublin's red-light district – and we meet the pimps, peddlers and passers-by that lived in and frequented the area.

On entering the LAB the audience of three was immediately split into its individual members, and introduced by turns to one of the prostitutes, her regular client, and a stern-faced madam, who, in a reversal of expected gender politics, is the architect of female oppression. A young contemporary, meanwhile, informs us that the area's secret history of sexual exploitation is still evolving, as she points out the newly built apartments that house the Eastern European brothels that have become an unsung part of the city's fabric. In one particular scene the juxtaposition of religious iconography with perversity (statues of the Virgin Mary are filled with methylated spirits which the prostitutes use to medicate themselves) foreshadows the fate of the women Lowe introduces us to: the area was closed down after the intervention of the clergy and the prostitutes were rehoused in the local Magdalene Laundry on Gloucester Street (now Sean McDermott Street). It is in the abandoned laundry that the second instalment of Lowe's historical indictment takes place and *Laundry* builds on the intimacy offered in *World's End Lane* on a larger, and ultimately more successful, scale.

Entering the Gloucester Street Magdalene Laundry in groups of three, the audience is again immediately separated. Although we witness the same scenes in different order, Lowe is interested in exploring individual experience: both the subjective experience of the individual audience member and the individual stories of the various Maggies – as the inmates were known – who we meet on our journey through the abandoned building.

The scenes we witness are enacted in closed, cell-like spaces, and the stories themselves reflect harrowing breaches of personal and physical autonomy. The effect is often distressing but never gratuitously so. *Laundry* is not an act of public disclosure but of social questioning. By placing us in such close proximity to history, Lowe is inviting us to question our own complicity. Should you reach out to comfort the young woman who genuflects in front of you so closely that her head almost touches your knees? Should you help the fragile young woman out of the bath, bind her breasts for her again when she invites you to? Should you stay to protect her when the supervising nun forces you out? And do you agree to help the ghostly girl who hides behind the mirror, a palimpsest upon your disturbed reflection, begging for intervention?

In this deliberately undefined theatrical situation, the audience is unsure of its role, is afraid to breach convention, while within the confines of the dramatic illusion we are also made aware of how little power we wield: the story will unfold no matter what we do. For the most part, the church authorities who are confining the women, abusing the women, remain invisible, and it is *our* lack of action that appears to condemn the women to this life of slavery, just as it was an unspoken social collusion that enabled the Magdalene Laundries – among the other dysfunctional Catholic institutions – to remain open into the late twentieth century. If Lowe appears to shirk from direct political engagement with the systemic failures of the Catholic institutions, she effectively reminds us that its dysfunction did not exist in a vacuum; a whole repressed society enabled and perpetuated its abuses.

Landmark Theatre's production of *Testament,* a new play by novelist Colm Tóibín, also engaged with the history and legacy of the Catholic tradition, by offering an alternative perspective on one of the bible's foundational stories: the death and resurrection of Christ. In his novels, Tóibín has offered sensitive versions of love and sexuality from both homosexual and female perspectives: in *The Blackwater Lightship,* a young man lies dying from AIDS; in *Brooklyn,* a naïve Irish emigrant defies her Catholic upbringing when she falls in love with a man from outside her community. *Testament* continues this interest in exploring a worldview through the eyes of traditionally marginalized voices.

In a production produced, directed, and delivered by women, *Testament* offers us the life of Jesus from the point of view of the aging Virgin Mary – the archetype of suffering motherhood. The story may be familiar, but the version we are told is not the officially sanctioned version. For Mary, the saving of humanity is no salve against the death of her only son. *Testament* thus subverts the public narrative, offering us a personal history of grief instead.

If the direct subject matter of *Testament* places itself within the realm of Western religious tradition, Tóibín's allusive script makes it both universal in its reach and particular to Ireland at the same time. Director Garry Hynes, working with long-time collaborators Marie Mullen and designer Francis O'Connor, enhances this cultural significance by enforcing a clear Irish idiom in the performance and visual register of the work. Mullen's mournful performance builds into a moment of tragic keening that recalls the final lament of Maurya in *Riders to the Sea*, a character that Mullen played to tremendous effect in the 2005 DruidSynge production. The muted tones of O'Connor's set and costume, meanwhile, evoke O'Connor's earlier design for the DruidSynge project too: a bare earth floor, rough clayish walls, and a natural palette of rough linen clothing. In *Testament* there is also an elaborate digital cloud-screeding sky; unmistakeably Irish in temperament, it adds an epic feel.

However, it is the characterization of Mary where *Testament's* more wide-reaching narrative finds particular resonance with twentieth-century Irish culture. Inspired by the Catholic model of Christian purity the 1937 Constitution defined Irish women within the limited boundaries of her role as mother. Thrusting upon her the status of guardian of the nation and moral arbiter of the state, the Catholic contradictions of the virgin-mother and the relegation of the role of women to mere plaster saints ascribed symbolic power to Irish women while limiting her role to the domestic sphere and denying her actual agency. *Testament's* re-contextualization of Christ's death through the eyes of his suffering mother may not engage directly with Irish culture, but it certainly gained added potency in the context of its premiere in Ireland.

Grace Dyas' play *Heroin* dispenses entirely with myth and history in favour of a gritty post-dramatic presentation, which invents itself as it unfolds. *Heroin* draws from a residency that the director spent with Rialto Drug Team exploring the world of drugs and addiction in contemporary Dublin. Instead of a play text Dyas created a theatrical text in which repetition, inaction, and confusion replace development, drama and illumination. Three actors inhabit the theatre space without apparent regard for the audience. Their mundane monologues are mumbled rather than delivered, although Dyas integrates several performative interludes in which the actors deliver a rhythmic state of the nation address through microphones. The set too deliberately strips itself of self-conscious theatrical effect. A raw wooden frame suggests a domestic interior, which is made and struck, dressed with props and destroyed, several times throughout the ninety-minute show. Despite the production's title, however, there is little direct reference to drugs, while the word heroin is significant only for its absence in the impressionistic script. Yet the total absence of concrete reference in the body of Dyas' production is important; it mirrors what she sees as the total absence of the addiction narrative in contemporary Irish political culture.

Selina Cartmell's site-specific performance text *The Lulu House* takes a similarly experimental approach to providing a voice to the voiceless, albeit one which heightens rather than eschews theatricality. Inspired by George Pabst's silent film *Pandora's Box, The Lulu House* re-enacted key moments from *Pandora's Box*, but in the live contemporary context she gives 'Lulu' (and the actress Louise Brooks who plays her) an opportunity to speak, and Lulu and her lover rehearse scenes from the film in front of a screen on which Pabst's film is being played out. This layered visual effect throws the role-playing involved in sexual relationships into relief. Although Cartmell stays within the narrative framework established by the film (Lulu is murdered by her lover), it is Lulu who has the last word; she becomes the pursuant, haunting her murderer through his madness.

Ultimately, neither Cartmell nor Dyas' work was entirely successful in its execution. If Dyas' work relied on stripping away everything for the audience, leaving it with little substance from which to intellectually or emotionally engage with its subject matter, Cartmell's production suffered from its density; drawing on textual references to Wedekind's 19th century 'Lulu' plays, Louise Brooks's other films, and John Ford's film of the James Joyce story '*The Dead*', the production lacked focus and was confusing for those who did not have access to its wide range of influences. Both productions, however, displayed a willingness by the female directors to take bold risks with both material and production style, breaking new ground, even if the result was not entirely successful.

Indeed it was in the more conventional mode of theatre-making that gave the festival one of its more disappointing productions. Marina Carr's work is synonymous with feminist politics in Ireland; in plays like *By the Bog of Cats* and *Portia Coughlan*, she has deconstructed the woman-mother binary that lies at the heart of Irish culture. While Carr's work has always played with realist modes of representation – manipulating time frames, creating fluid expressionistic stage spaces – she has remained faithful to text and the boundaries of the theatre space throughout her oeuvre. In *16 Possible Glimpses,* with the help of director Wayne Jordan, Carr rendered a complex experimental reading of the life of Russian playwright Anton Chekov.

The style of both the play and the production was thoroughly unChekovian, relying on juxtaposition rather than organic atmospheric development for its effect. The scenes of the play follow no ordered temporal logic, live action is layered against filmed scenes, while in the production an onstage camera was used to show close-ups of the actors' faces; the camera providing shorthand emotional engagement. But it was the focus on a particular kind of male literary genius, exemplified in a scene between Chekov and his friend and mentor Leo Tolstoy that was most surprising and problematic. While Carr also gives voice to the women in Chekov's life in the play, she remains uncritical of the gender politics of the late nineteenth century Russian milieu, embracing stereotype instead in her characterization of Chekov's self-sacrificing sister, parasitic mother, and lusty needy lover.

Other new writing by women in the Dublin Theatre Festival this year included Amy Conroy's *I ♥ Alice ♥ I*, which offered a unique take on the documentary theatre genre and a stirring portrayal of a female same-sex relationship. However, what the 2011 festival really showcased was the rise of the role of the director – male or female; and this year, especially female – in Irish theatre. From established names like Garry Hynes and Lynne Parker – who offered a new version of Ibsen's *Peer Gynt* – to emergent talent like Lowe, Dyas and Cartmell, the wealth of talent on show bodes well for a vital theatrical future.

2 | Eating Tiny Cakes in the Dark: Maeve Higgins and the Politics of Self-Deprecation

Susanne Colleary

Maeve Higgins was born in 1981 in Cobh, Co Cork. After studying photography in Colaiste Dhulaigh, she began her stand-up career in 2004 by performing 'once on a bus outside a hotel in Cork and once in a room over a pub in Dublin.' Higgins came to recognition through the very popular series of *Naked Camera*, a hidden camera style of entertainment programming broadcast on RTÉ for three years until 2007. Higgins performs regularly on the Irish comedy and festival circuit as well as performing internationally including *The Edinburgh Fringe Festival, The Melbourne International Festival, The Adelaide Fringe Festival, The Kilkenny Comedy Festival*, and *The New Zealand International Festival*. She has a regular slot on the *Ray D'Arcy* show on Today FM entitled 'What would Maeve do?' where Maeve gives advice to listener's questions. In 2009, Higgins's RTÉ One television series *Fancy Vittles*, which she wrote and performed with her sister Lilly was very well received and enjoyed healthy ratings. Her stand-up comedy shows include *Ha Ha Yum* with her sister Lilly (2006-2007), *Slightly Amazing* (2007), *My News* (2007), *Kitten Brides* (2008-2009), *I Can't Sleep* (2009) *Blabbing Away* (2010), and *Personal Best* (2010). Maeve Higgins currently lives in and works from her base in Dublin, Ireland.

Introduction

Maeve Higgins loves telling stories. Her stand-up has been described as a 'great relief from the big loud boys, [winning] many people over with her quietly charming quality of comedy'.[6] Higgins has been winning people over with her personal storytelling style of stand-up for six years as a professional comic, and has created a comic persona which is deceptively charming. Her comic material is centrally concerned with the detailed minutiae of Higgins's everyday life, involving stories of family, of childhood, of female body image, of sexual politics and intrapersonal relationships. Higgins's style of telling stories has been variously described as effortless, uncontrived, natural, quirky and of course charming. However, Higgins's comic persona is a meticulously crafted construct, on the one hand sweet, awkward and delightful, full of stories about her cat or baking cakes or getting locked out of her apartment. On the other hand, Higgins consistently undercuts the surface of her whimsical persona with darker stories and material. Those stories operate as a series of critiques, making social commentary on cultural assumptions and stereotypes that perpetuate gendered inequalities in contemporary society.

Through the prism of her comic persona, Higgins self-reflexively plays with the boundaries of what has conservatively and historically been conceived of as self-deprecatory comedy traditionally allied to descriptions of female stand-up. While Higgins does employ the tactics of self-deprecation in her comedy, her stories also operate as a series of critical, satirical and subversive observations that work to undermine the inadequacies and the inequalities that, for her, frame the experience of being a woman in the twenty first century. In this article I will look at two comic narratives which encapsulate some of the central concerns and themes in Higgins's stand-up comedy. The first section of this article will address Higgins's neuroses and stories of personal anxiety around her body weight and body image. I will examine how Higgins subverts her constructed narratives of personal failure toward a critical commentary on the forces of cultural production that continue to define the parameters of what constitutes female physical beauty. The second section of this article will examine Higgins's incisive treatment of segregated notions which have more conventionally defined male and female subject matter in the stand-up comic form. I will look at the ways in which Higgins critiques outmoded traditions and gendered assumptions on what constitutes female stand-up comedy. In doing so, I wish to examine how Higgins, by controlling the discourse in performance, subverts and exposes gendered politics in stand-up comedy itself, while also undermining broader cultural stereotypes

---

[6] Dee Custance, 'Profile of a Serial Kidder', *The Skinny* 8 September 2007,

which both historically and formally have surrounded conceptions of the female comic.

If you're fat, just like *be* fat and shut up. And if you're thin – fuck you![7]

The comic narratives that constitute Higgins's performance material are constructions which are deeply connected to and drawn from her experiences of daily life. In interview with this author, Higgins defined her brand of personal storytelling as stand-up comedy. She described her comic style as:

Definitely low key, observational ... and as truthful as I can make it ... like this current show it's stuff that's happened to me in the last few months and trying to see the funny side ... it's just part of being, of trying to be honest ... this show is like from the fifteenth of December on, stuff that happened to me and I started doing it on the seventh of January, so you can imagine the seventh of January show was not that great, (*laughs*) Yea Yea, (*laughs again*) poor old Waterford.[8]

Themes of honesty and of Higgins's stories reflecting recent events in her life are evident in the scenarios under discussion in these pages. One such element of the personal that has a strong focus both in Higgins's live performances and on television appearances centres on anxieties about her body image. These are issues that feature prominently in Higgins's 2009 TV programme *Fancy Vittles*, which Higgins has described as 'stand-up to camera' (Higgins, 2010) and which has received some very good critical feedback. *The Tribune* extolled the virtues of the show stating:

Maeve Higgins rocks. And RTÉ has a new, genuinely original, very funny observational comedy programme in which [Higgins] and her sister Lilly makes dinner for a bunch of their lady friends. Actually Lilly makes the dinner; Maeve mainly waffles away to the camera.[9]

Higgins, over the course of this series, speaks directly to camera on her neuroses, obsessions and anxieties about the modern world. She talks about body image, about sex, boyfriends, girlfriends, dead pets and family and how she would like to know what 'normal' might

---

[7] Roseanne Barr, cited in Philip Auslander 'Brought to you by Fem-Rage', *Acting Out: Feminist Performances* ed. Lynda Hart & Peggy Phelan (Ann Arbor: University of Michigan Press, 1993): 315.

[8] Susanne Colleary, unpublished interview with Maeve Higgins, 25 March 2010. Subsequent references are cited in the text as (Higgins, 2010).

[9] Patrick Freyne, 'Freyne's World', *Sunday Tribune* 20 September 2009.

actually be. All the while Lilly is silently directing operations and cooking up a (quiet) storm in the background. The show is also punctuated with a selection of footage from the RTÉ archives, scenes from perhaps the nineteen-forties to the nineteen-seventies, which continually punctuate the programme with reminders of the way Irish cultural life used to be. *Fancy Vittles* has been described as a 'whimsical and quirky look at relationships and social behaviour,'[10] set against a backdrop of nostalgic footage which brilliantly illustrates the comedy and somehow suggests that Higgins is just not ready for the modern world. In the first episode of the series Higgins returns to the subject of the female body and speaks about what she conceives as current obsessions with a sexualized body image:

> I find in these modern times (*laughs*) I have a problem with this ... that everything has to be sexy all the time now. I think...like call me old fashioned ... that the most amount of people I would want to have sex with me at one time is one person. I don't want everybody thinking that I'm sexy. That's creepy (2009: 00.00-00.40).

She goes on to tell the story of turning up to a Halloween party where everybody was dressed in sexy costumes. Not surprisingly Higgins talks in irritated tones about this fact, as she herself had turned up as a 'medley of winter vegetables.'

The first scenario under discussion here, entitled *Thin Means Good Person*, was filmed by the author in Vicar Street, Dublin, Ireland in April 2010. In this scenario, Higgins again takes as her theme current preoccupations and anxieties relating to body size. This scenario is based on Higgins's (presumed) experience of attending a Weight Watchers meeting. This story addresses ideas surrounding Higgins's body image and her ongoing attempts to conform to current cultural perceptions of acceptable standards of physical beauty.

Thin Means Good Person

And I mean – I did go to
I've been to ... I joined weight watchers three times you know
Most people you talk to have been to more than one weight watchers
meeting
It's cause we're so sneaky
We just go to the other one and say

---

[10] John Boland, 'The Gong for the Worst Show Goes To...' *Irish Independent* 19 September 2009.

'Oh what's this?'

'Oh points, is it?' (*Pointing at imaginary information*)

'Oh that's interesting'

'Hee Hee Hee'

'Got my points chart six months ago bitch'

And when you go to weight watchers you get a leader

Which is quite sinister in itself isn't it?

And my last leader

She was a thin woman

Means good person in weight watchers (*sustained laughter*)

And...but some of my friends

They said that their leaders

Are like quite actually fat actually

So but they said it's too awkward to bring it up (laughter)

You know

'Cause I'd imagine it is

It's the woman's job and everything

But...ahem... I do think she's got it all sewn up

Because she's just like

'Don't eat that, give it to me' (*leader eating food*)

But I didn't like the vibe in weight watchers

Because everyone is very quiet and mortified because they're fat you know (*sustained laughter*)

So everyone's like (*makes sad fat face...looks at ground and sighs*)

Then you can understand the expression bovine

Everyone has big eyes looking at the ground

And then someone needs to stand over there

To herd us over to the weighing scales

They'd bang into each other and doesn't say excuse me and stuff

So that would drive me mad

So I would always try and be like a human

And answer questions and talk and stuff you know?

Our leader would always ask us questions

And everybody would just be like (*mortified fat face expression*)

I would always try and answer you know?

That's how I found out I was bad at weight watchers

Because one day our leader was like

'Ok ladies were gonna talk about the seven deadly c's'

'What would they be for us girls?' (*Dublin accent*)

'And I was like '(hand goes up)

'Pss Pss'

'Crime ... Car- Jacking?'
And she was like
'No No Crisps Chocolate'... I don't remember the other ones
Pretty sure cakes totally fine
Cause they're tiny
You eat them in the dark. (*Laughter and applause*).[11]

In the *Thin Means Good Person* routine, Higgins takes the audience into the duplicitous world of Weight Watchers as she describes herself (after presumably falling off the wagon), returning to a meeting under the pretence of being a first timer. She warns the audience of the ominous notion of having a leader which is the practice in Weight Watchers, and of the ethos which states that thin naturally means a good person, which results in sustained laughter from the crowd. The idea that the leader may often be as fat as those attending, but that it's simply too awkward to bring the subject up, also has the intended comic effect. Her personifications of the leader who eats everyone's food and of the herd-like class of embarrassed and ashamed pupils also feed into the audience's enjoyment of this story. Higgins reveals to the audience that she is bad at Weight Watchers, by attempting to be a human and not stare at the floor in shame. By answering the leader's questions incorrectly, Higgins points up her failure. The last two lines of the story attest to her guilty enjoyment of eating tiny cakes in the dark and this observation brings another round of sustained laughter and applause from the audience. Throughout the scenario, Higgins's pace and tone remain conversational and her personifications do yield big laughs. Her illustrations of the phenomena of weight loss programs and her personal failure would seem to create a direct connection and rapport with the audience. On one level the strength of the story would seem to lie in part with the recognition of the truths of her observations. The audience would seem to identify and empathize with Higgins's story of personal anxiety around her body image and her failure to conform to current societal standards of physical beauty.

The sense of the personal that informs this scenario and which constitutes a large part of Higgins's stand-up comedy is mirrored in the work of several successful female stand-up comics. In interview with Alison Oddey in 1999, the Perrier award winning British comic Jenny Éclair describes the personal in terms of gender. She asserts, 'I think

---

[11] Maeve Higgins, 'Live at Vicar Street' filmed by Susanne Colleary, 5 April 2010: 8.08-10.32 minutes. Subsequent references cited in the text as (2010a: counter)

that when comediennes do write and perform from the heart, they have a sort of consciousness of their lines, whereas men tend to be much more surreal or physical, and not so personal'.[12]   The high profile British comic Jo Brand responded in interview to Oddey's observation that several famous male comics (Jack Dee, Lee Evans and Harry Hill) tend toward the surreal rather than the personal as comic material. Brand stated:

> Yes. Well I think that's men and women all over. I think women are very talented at knowing what they need and expressing their emotions, whereas men are absolutely hopeless at it. I think just because there are more male comics you do get more variety of comedy, but none of it is particularly emotionally expressive. It tends to be played sort of far away from the person really (Oddey: 115).

Higgins too in discussion states that her response to some male stand-up comedy is 'I think, just say something about yourself, it doesn't have to be too deep or anything, just say what you think about something, not just like some corny ... like my girlfriend said this to me' (Higgins, 2010). This attitude is hardly surprising as Higgins's brand of personal story stand-up comedy, (*leaving out the boring bits as she readily admits*), is a closely constructed and honed performance drawn from her personal experiences.

Ideas surrounding female stand-up comedy and the personal lead the discussion toward the notion of female stand-up comedy as humour of self-deprecation. The tactic of self-deprecation is by no means limited to female stand-up comedy, however, as Danielle Russell states in her study on female stand-up comics,

> the variety of comedic approaches are as varied as the comedians themselves, [however] one form of humour continues to be identified with women in particular: self-deprecation.[13]

In this scenario Higgins would seem at times to take on the quality of self-deprecation as she deals with issues of her body image to produce comic material. A little earlier in the evening, Higgins refers to herself as a *chubster*, she apologizes to the thin people in the audience because they're like 'what's the problem... apple'(*at this point Higgins mimes eating an apple and then shakes her fist at all the thin people who enjoy fruit more than cakes*). At another point in the performance she tells the audience that 'when you are trying to lose weight you really will

---

[12] Alison Oddey, *Performing Women* (London: Macmillan Press, 1999): 22.
[13] Danielle Russell, 'Self-Deprecatory Humour and the Female Comic' *Third Space* 2.1, 2002, <www.thirdspace.ca/articles/druss.html>

do anything else, so before Christmas I was buying shelves, most important thing, need to get shelves or I won't lose weight' (Higgins, 2010a). There is a definite sense that the whole set is punctuated and peppered with Higgins's comic disapproval of her body size. Similarly comedian Jenny Éclair comments that she too can be self-deprecatory in the material, 'I admit to things I'm not good at, I admit to being a bit desperate – aging stuff: the make-up and the hair' (Oddey, 22). Jo Brand too talks about her comedy as at times self-deprecating, and she observes:

> I might as well get it all out, say it before someone else says it and say it worse than someone else would say it, so that gets it all out of the way. What point is there in someone abusing you when you have already abused yourself? If someone heckles you with 'Fuck off you fat cow,' I just say, I think we've covered that already, have you not been listening? (Oddey, 111)

In this sense Philip Auslander's discussion of female American stand-up and situation comedy becomes relevant. Auslander argues that in America, traditional female comics of the 1950s and the 1960s:

> tended to work within self-imposed restrictions that reflected the social stigma attached to aggressively funny women. The traditional female comic's chief strategy was to render herself apparently unthreatening to male dominance by making herself the object of her own comic derision in what is usually referred to as self-deprecatory comedy (Auslander, 326).

In order to attain and maintain success in a traditional and patriarchal culture industry, female comics such as Joan Rivers and Phyllis Diller deployed the comedy of self-deprecation. Their comic material was marked by a style of looking

> inward onto the female subject herself, rather than outward onto the social conditions that make it necessary for Diller and Rivers to personify themselves in this way (Auslander, 327).

Lisa Merrill discusses women and comedy by defining feminist humour as that which speaks *to* the value of female experience, which does not underpin or normalize a male perspective. What Merrill terms as a 'strong rebellious humour' is that in which women *self-critically* examine gendered stereotypes and the degrees to which as Merrill argues 'we have been led to perpetuate this objectification'.[14] If the humour traditionally associated with American comics such as Phyllis

---

[14] Lisa Merrill, 'Feminist Humour' *Last Laughs* ed. Regina Barreca (New York: Gordon & Breach, 1988): 279,

Diller and Joan Rivers has been named as self-deprecatory, thereby perpetuating the objectification which Merrill speaks of, the American comic Lily Tomlin's work is indicative of 'celebratory women's humour' (Merrill, 277). Tomlin's one woman show entitled *The Search for Intelligent Life in the Universe* (1986), involves Tomlin becoming twelve different characters, from prostitutes to middle class housewives. Merrill (277) argues that all Tomlin's characters 'display integrity and insight, which allows them to be self-critical without being self-deprecating.' This is a point worth pursuing when looking at Higgins's personal stories. Her set is layered with anxiety around her weight, and the fact that she tells a story constructed around those issues registers that sense of self-disapproval. However, I would argue that there are also clear signatures of self-critical examination at work in the *Thin Means Good Person* scenario. Higgins's story would seem to be suspended in tension between the desire to be thin, and the rejection of social conventions which insist on demonizing those who are not. Her conflicting emotions centre on her desire to conform to social perceptions of physical attractiveness and her own recognition of the absurdity of a belief system which reduces people to mortification and shame because they have failed those standards. The inference is that as she fails at Weight Watchers she succeeds at being a human being, and for a moment she escapes the conventional forces which place her within that system. However on the final lines Higgins turns her energies back onto herself and she again uses her sense of being physically unattractive as the source of her comedy. The imagery of Higgins sitting in the dark and eating tiny cakes would seem to place her back behind those conventional bars.

Higgins's *Thin Means Good Person* scenario reflects current critical arguments on the phenomena of slimming programmes in Ireland. Jacqueline O'Toole's essay on group slimming classes is relevant here. O'Toole frames her discussion by arguing that weight loss programmes are in the main targeted at women.[15] She cites the work of Chris Shilling, who argues that where societies of late modernity may no longer believe in political or religious grand narratives, the body would

---

[15] J. O'Toole, 'A Danger to Yourself? Motivational Talks in Group Slimming Classes' *Ireland of the Illusions* ed. M. Corcoran & P. Share (Dublin: IPA, 2010): 254. The research took place over a year's observation of slimming classes in Ireland. In footnote three, O'Toole notes that 'It is mainly women that are targeted by the diet industries and it is mainly women that participate in weight management and dieting on a regular basis in both public and private settings. Only two men attended the group slimming classes in the whole year that I spent in observation.'

seem to constitute a firm foundation through which to construct a dependable sense of self-identity. Shilling goes on to state that 'it is the exterior territories or surfaces of the body that symbolize the self at a time when unprecedented value is placed on the youthful, trim and sensual body' (Chris Shilling cited in O'Toole, 258). Presently, social discourse surrounding the body is in part framed by current public health concerns in Ireland. Contemporary lifestyles have become much more sedentary, resulting in health service concerns about body weight and obesity. As such medically sanctioned definitions of correct body weight have come to constitute the standard which defines a healthy body. And as O'Toole points out, a healthy body is also part of the active discourse with contemporary society's obsessions with health, beauty, youth and the pursuit of an ideal body. In this way, motivational talks in slimming classes are embedded in messaging two dominant storylines, as O'Toole argues:

> ... to achieve such a body, much emphasis is directed toward the responsible citizen, invoking notions of self-control, self-discipline and competency in the production and presentation of the self in everyday life ... overweight people are profoundly 'othered' in this context and depicted as irresponsible, unfocused and out of control. But they are encouraged to learn from the habits of (code=slim) people. A blame storyline permeates the control narrative with the clear invocation of the need to be responsible (O'Toole, 258-261).

O'Toole acknowledges that analysis of people's participation in weight loss programmes is complex. Her work centres on the performance power of motivational talks in slimming classes which 'articulates a narrative of individualism and agency where self-control and personal transformation are central features ... in order to improve ... individual bodies' minds and selves' (O'Toole, 268). However O'Toole also argues that motivational talks in slimming programmes have a strong focus on placing overweight women within simplistic narratives of blame. Those talks do not in any real way take into account what links there may be between social, psychological or material conditions and issues surrounding body weight. Historically, women have been viewed by nature as insatiable and out of control, as emotional and illogical. The contemporary manifestation of seeing women in this way can be understood through women's appetites, which must be kept under surveillance so that women do not lose control of themselves through under or over-eating (O'Toole, 261). As I have already noted, narratives of blame are directed primarily at a target audience of women, both as the narrators and the receivers of the blame storyline.

Insatiable desires for food and overeating represents women within a narrative which defines them as out of control and irresponsible. Further, those narratives are deeply layered with moralistic overtones. Food and eating behaviour are discussed in terms of 'good food' and 'bad food' and members are encouraged to recount their eating 'sins' for the weekly class. And as O'Toole notes, there is a definite sense of this moral discourse around eating behaviour as gendered, 'women must try very hard to be good when it comes to food and avoid temptation and being a temptress' (O'Toole, 265). In this way the narratives offer the potential for self-transformation; however, they also perpetuate gendered narratives which depict overweight women as irresponsible, uncontrolled and even dangerous.

Higgins begins her story on Weight Watchers by returning to the programme (albeit in a deceitful fashion) which signals her belief in the potential for self-transformation narratives that weight loss programmes offer. Nonetheless it is clear that by staging her personal experiences and failures at weight loss programmes, Higgins points up her frustrations and even anger at social expectations of physical beauty which are imposed upon women, and of viewing those who fail or refuse to conform as being deviant in some way. I would argue that Higgins's constructed comic persona is couched in self-deprecatory comedy in that she consistently pinpoints her failure at losing weight. However the story is also heavily laced with self-critical commentary which exposes and ridicules weight loss programmes. Her comic persona accommodates her desire to believe in narratives of transformation through dieting. However Higgins also resists, by ridiculing social standards of attractiveness perpetuated by slimming groups, which continue to define models of physical beauty and by implication, which shape and influence women's personal narratives of identity in contemporary society. In this way I would argue that Higgins's Weight Watchers routine could as easily mean *Thin Equals Good Person*. In attending slimming classes women are caught in a double bind. Currently, overweight people are deemed as irresponsible citizens, and women as the chief targets of slimming class narratives are not only labelled irresponsible citizens, but are also caught in a gendered blame narrative which perpetuates negative historical and contemporary stereotypes about women's identity. In my view, women, either willingly or otherwise, continue to be caught up in a web of discourses which seek to police the ongoing reductive and culturally conditioned borders of what it means to be 'good' woman. It must be said, however, that Higgins's style and delivery of the story is ambivalent, she does not inflect the work with any particular editorial comment and in the end it is really in the hands of the audience to decide for themselves. In the empathic impulse they may laugh with Higgins as she describes her situation of personal failure. As importantly, the audience may laugh in recognition at Higgins's subversive ridicule of a cultural coda which works hard to connect ideas of a 'responsible and in control' gendered self with personal and professional success in life, through attainment of a perfected and idealized body size. A cultural coda which also has the power to relegate those profoundly 'othered' overweight and 'out of control' women into a position which constitutes an element of risk to a community, where women are conceived as dangerous to themselves, their families and to a society for refusing or failing to 'act' like a responsible woman.

What's so Funny?

If Higgins actively plays with the boundaries of self-deprecation, self-criticism and social critique in order to subversively challenge the female body politic in contemporary culture, the next scenario under discussion works within a similar dynamic. In the *Male Periods* scenario (again filmed by the author at Vicar Street in April 2010), Higgins's constructed comic persona expertly deploys her particular brand of self-deprecatory comedy in order to interrogate ideas surrounding traditional segregated notions on what constitutes male and female humour. Throughout this scenario, Higgins deconstructs pervasive cultural assumptions which have until the very recent past sought to pigeonhole the subject matter and performance style of female stand-up comedy. In so doing Higgins exposes the gendered politics embedded in the performance form of stand-up, and undercuts normalized comic stereotypes grafted onto conventional conceptions of the female comic.

Male Periods
But first I wanna say
I'm a female comedian
I'm wearing this to prove it
And I don't think it's a very big deal
I don't even think about it actually
But then sometimes journalists say to me
What's it like being a female comedian
And I always say to them
'Sometimes I'm hungry other times then I'm tired' (*Laughter*)

I don't know what it's like for the men
I've never been actually one of the men ones...so
I don't know...and they'd be raging
And then I wouldn't bring it up but
Three different people have asked me
'What's it like for the men when you do a joke about periods?'
'Does that isolate the men?'
And I always think like actually
I beg your pardon
First of all I don't actually do any period jokes
And if you'd caught my set you'd know that
We call it set
Caught I mean like seen actually
Actually if you caught my set
And second of all I don't think it would be that bad
If I did a period joke
You know the men in the audience would be like (*Upset and distressed*)
'Hang on a minute'
'What's she actually saying?'
'Ooooh give me that candle' (*mock attack on her own body*)
'Oh my God ... Give me a knife'
Wsssshhh (*Slits stomach*)
I think you'd be like probably totally cool about it
So then to check
I was trying to think of a joke about periods
But I couldn't think of one
And then I was thinking
Oh my God you are an ok comedian
Why can't you think of a joke about periods?
I can think of a joke about nearly everything else
And why is it?
Is it because I'm mortified
I hope not
'Cause I shouldn't be
Ahem... but I know I am a bit
'Cause I still get embarrassed if someone sees the tampons near me
I'm just like
'Oh no that... I don't know'
'That's my dickey bow'
'Oh ho ho ho' (*operatic voice*)

'Casual Formal' (*moves tampon to and away from her neck*)
'Casual formal'
I'll pretend it's anything else
'Oh you found my bomb'
'That's my bomb'
'I'm a bomber'
'There you go'
'And what of it?'
'To each his own'
'I bomb – you sew'
Actually I'm not the only one because a lot...
There was a whole marketing campaign
A few years ago
That made tampons look like sweets
Yea and like so like if
Your boyfriend was like
'Oh can I have a sweet?'
You'd be like – 'no give that to me'
Gulp (*swallows tampon*)
Drink of water
Oooooooh (*Stomach explosion*)
Women all dressed up
And their stomach explodes
You know they've had a tampon
I feel like... I'm not sure
But I feel like that the men
You'd be more cool about it
You wouldn't be so embarrassed
You'd be like (*in a shop*)
'The purple ones there and the paper'
And be just walking down the road (*tampons in hand*)
La La La La La (*carefree male lilt*)
Which is your song
And hopefully you'd be able to have more crack with it than women
Do you know?
Like if you're in the pub and you want to make your friends laugh
You could just be like
'Watch this Watch this'
'Here Michael' (throws tampon)
Michael would be like
'Oh ya got me boy'

'You got me' (*wiping face*)
'I'll get you back in two weeks' time I will' (*laughter and applause*)
Sorry I hope that wasn't too gross
But remember it's just an idea (Higgins 2010a, 44.26-48.02).

This story is focused on Higgins's treatment of what can be considered as somewhat hackneyed and formulaic ideas surrounding the territory of female stand-up comedy. Notions of the binaries that have formed and continue to inform discourse on the nature of male and female stand-up comedy have been centred on the idea of the male as paramount. As previously discussed, the tradition of male dominance in the cultural realm of stand-up is allied to the notion that the form of stand-up comedy itself has, certainly from an historical point of view, centred on the male. Issues of phallic authority with observations such as 'holding a microphone is like holding a penis'[16] and the comic Jerry Seinfeld's assertions that 'to laugh is to be dominated'[17] make for strong arguments on the historical and formal power of the male stand-up comic. So much so that Auslander has contended that, 'women comics who choose to remain within the conventional form and performance contexts of stand-up comedy are essentially appropriating a cultural form traditionally associated with and still dominated by, male practitioners' (Auslander, 319). In this reading the historical and formal constraints inherent in live comedy clubs would seem self-evident. However within the live performance context both male and female comics maintain at least a measure of licence and control over their material, which may be lost when disseminated through mass cultural media, acting as a powerful tool to neutralize the female comic (Auslander, 324). Any discussion then of situating female comics within the patriarchal arena (within live and mass media formats) must in Auslander's view 'remain open-ended, for comedy's potential for empowering women is always accompanied by the potential for patriarchal recuperation; both can take place simultaneously, in fact' (Auslander, 324-325).

While it is vital to acknowledge the historical and formal frame of stand-up comedy as a male form of discourse, it is also important to recognize that perspectives on female stand-up comedy are continuing to change. Again Danielle Russell's study of self-deprecation in female stand-up comedy is useful here. While Russell also acknowledges the

---

[16] D. Collier & K. Beckett, *Spare Ribs: Women in the Humor Biz* (New York: St. Martin's Press, 1980): 99.
[17] B. Borns, *Comic Lives* (New Ork: Simon and Schuster, 1987): 20.

problematic nature of stand-up comedy and male dominance she also asserts that female comics are in general moving away from a more traditional and overtly negative, self-deprecatory style of performance. Russell states that 'all women in comedy challenge the validity of separate spheres based upon gender – male space is public, female space is private ... by seizing what has traditionally been male territory, women in comedy are staking a claim to the power that accompanies that realm' (Russell, online). Russell goes on to acknowledge that issues of who assumes power are complicated in a performance invested with aspects of self-deprecation (both male and female). However she also asserts that while it may seem that a female comic is ceding control to the audience in a series of self-putdowns, in fact the real authority always remains with the comic as 'the comic retains the microphone ... and centre stage. The surrender of power is an illusion' (Russell, online). While this argument can be extended to both male and female deployment of the tactic of self-deprecation, the assumption of the power dynamic in female stand-up comedy is significant. Female comics do have the power to exert control over live and media formats (for instance, Higgins controlled the editing process on her TV show *Fancy Vittles*), and that control can be invested with the power to identify what is in fact funny. Frances Gray puts it very well when she suggests that 'to define a joke, to be the class that decides what is funny ... is to make a massive assumption of power ... that of defining and thus controlling the immediate area of discourse' (Russell, online). Controlling the discourse is vital and as Russell states 'power dynamics are interwoven in comedy, by pursuing their personal agendas female comics expose the politics behind definitions of who and what is funny'(Russell, online).

These historicized and contemporary arguments on the current nature of female stand-up comedy within a traditionally male form of discourse become important when discussing Higgins's *Male Periods* story. Higgins begins this scenario by pointing to her own frustrations at being asked questions about being a female comic, and she makes this clear by mocking the offending journalists. Higgins initially frames the scenario by stating that normally she does not do period jokes, which positions her rejection of what could be conceived as stereotypical female comic material. She tells the audience that she wouldn't do it at all, save that she keeps being asked about how period jokes affect the men in the audience. Her depiction of male mutilation in the audience at the mention of periods is not only intensely funny but openly criticizes the notion that some men cannot handle the subject matter. There is also an underplayed critique of tampon manufacturers who mask the product to look like sweets. Higgins's portrayal of tampons as dickie bows, bombs and sweets is very funny and also attests to a sort of conspiracy of silence by manufacturers and Higgins, despite her better judgement, serves to perpetuate that silence. In what can be described as a deftly manipulated and incongruous comic turn of events Higgins then positions the story firmly back into the male sphere. Rather than isolate the men in the audience, Higgins suggests that men (with perhaps a generous pinch of ego flattery) might be far cooler about the whole period thing. Her descriptions of men not being embarrassed to go out and buy tampons *and* openly carry them down the street, as well as the graphic images of throwing period products around the pub is intensely funny. Higgins succeeds in making the scenario work without any sense of offending or isolating any section of the audience.

Higgins's tactic of suggesting that men could handle having periods better than women is on one level indicative of the tried and tested formula of self-deprecation. By assuming to cede authority to a section or sections of the audience, and by inhabiting a persona which seems to express her own inadequacies and insecurities around the topic, Higgins skilfully manipulates the audience into a position where they remain receptive to the story. This in a way is why ideas of self-deprecation in comedy are complex. Higgins's comic persona would seem to be in the act of disclosure about her failings. However, drawing upon Higgins's personal feelings on the subject I would argue that this act of self-disclosure is an illusion of sorts. Higgins may couch her messages in stories of personal failure, in that comedy of self-deprecation, however it is a mastered technique which packs a powerful and subversive message. Higgins sets up this scenario within a binary about male and female comics and the implied gendered differences in comic material. Her non-confrontational style and handling of the subject matter allows this story to travel without offence or rejection by any section of the audience. Higgins's performance of the *Male Periods* routine is multi-layered. There is of course comic ambivalence at work here, however, in my view Higgins deploys the tactic of self-deprecation by admitting her own personal discomfort at talking about periods in a public sphere. In framing the work in this way, I am arguing that Higgins exposes historicized and contemporary stereotypes grafted onto perceptions of the female body. Whereas in the *Thin Means Good Person* (woman) routine, the dominant storyline for women was couched in a gendered narrative of blame, here a conservative and hegemonic storyline is embedded in a gendered narrative of shame. By locating the comic discourse squarely in the story of her own body, Higgins exposes ossified cultural and social assumptions, embarrassment and even disgust about the functions of the female body. Higgins, by citing her own menstrual mortification and will to secrecy as comic material in a public sphere, points up the lingering and stubbornly persistent historicized, patriarchal and moral discourses surrounding sexual difference and cultural gender bias which in the past has insisted that 'the female body's moisture, secretions, and productions [constituted] shameful tokens of uncontrol'.[18] Such ossified assumptions surrounding the female body do continue to manifest themselves within the stand-up comic form itself. The presence of a female comic on the traditionally male dominated stand-up stage can be read as an aggressive act. To assume the power available in that formal aggressive space disconcerts persistent cultural definitions of 'femininity'. Danielle Russell argues that 'conventional definitions of 'femininity' and 'lady-like' behaviour render the stance of superiority inherent in stand-up comedy 'inappropriate' for women.' She cites Beth Littleford, who states that 'Society gyps women', because comedy is seen as boys' territory ... Women have to undo society's 'lady-izing' (Russell, online). In my view, by telling the story of her own body, Higgins exposes the personal, social and cultural embarrassments around menstruation. In doing so, Higgins reveals something of the story of the *communal* female body which has been so tightly held within a stranglehold of customary discourses. And although attitudes are changing, those discourses prove to be difficult to rout. Higgins's comic persona discloses her own discomfort and shame about her periods in the performance space. That 'act' of disclosure highlights broader societal complicity, which insists on locating cultural views of women's identity onto outmoded and redundant moral, and gender biased notions of sexual difference. Higgins insightfully points up the absurdity of those teetering, internalized and socialized narratives which continue, lichen like, to graft themselves onto contemporary conceptions and expectations of women's identity.

While Higgins certainly does point up culturally conditioned gender bias with women's bodies, the *Male Periods* routine is also layered with a critical commentary on gendered notions of male and female humour. Higgins chooses a subject which has been traditionally conceived of as

---

[18] Gail Kern Paster, cited in A. Stott, *Comedy: The New Critical Idiom* (Oxon: Routledge, 2005): 100

appealing primarily to a female sense of humour. She usurps that notion and by controlling the discourse makes a significant claim to the power of the performance space. That assumption of power allows Higgins to transform a subject matter customarily perceived as engaging only to a female sense of humour, into hallmark comic material with broad audience appeal. In this way I argue that Higgins very effectively points up the absurdity of the notion that the subject matter of menstruation will not be found to be funny by men, or that jokes on menstruation belong to particular formats of what has been perceived conventionally as more aggressive female comedy. Higgins challenges increasingly outmoded cultural and formal assumptions on what men will reject as the subject of humour. She criticizes the media who continue to differentiate the female comic from the male, placing emphasis on female gender over and above comic material. She subverts the hackneyed idea of the period joke, typically associated with female humour in order to critique conservative notions of difference between male and female humour. In this way Higgins subversively works to dismantle ghettoized notions of what constitutes female stand-up within the comic performance form itself. Politically, comic women's voices must do battle to be heard above the cacophony of male comics and that imbalance can at times result in reductive value assumptions and stereotypical attitudes toward female comic material. By subverting perceived notions of female comic material, Higgins subtly mocks those who relegate women's comedy as speaking primarily to their own sex and without the power that male comics possess, that of mainstream appeal. Additionally, from a broader perspective Higgins's use of this material is timely, as it taps into shifting cultural attitudes which are beginning to move away from making value assumptions about comic material based solely on the gender of the comic. That being said, there still exists an imbalance between the sexes in the stand-up performance form, historically, formally and in terms of numbers, men still significantly outweigh women comics. In this sense the claim to power of the performance space still reflects the influential male voice. However, Higgins by taking control of the discourse and defining what is and what is not funny, is making her own claim to the power of that stand-up space, a space which is increasingly becoming more attractive and open to women wishing to pursue a comic career. In this way, stand-up comedy continues to move away from the idea of the male as paramount and the growing presence of the female comic will in her turn continue to alter and influence the power structures of a traditionally male dominated form.

Conclusion

Maeve Higgins's position as one of the few highly successful female stand-up comics in Ireland is culturally significant. However, she is standing on the shoulders of those who came before her and who have shaped and influenced the female comic tradition in Ireland. Female performers trained in Irish Music Hall and Variety were eventually subsumed into media formats by the 1960s – I am thinking here of the comic talents of Maureen Potter and Rosaleen Linehan. Later on, cabaret acts such as Maxi, Dick and Twink (among others) continued in that vein of comic Variety. As a most recent precursor, Deirdre O'Kane is one of the few female stand-up comics who have carved out an international profile, and the fact that O'Kane is a well-known actress certainly helped that profile. And with the exception of jobbing female comics including Eleanor Tiernan, Sonya Kelly, Sarah Millican, Carol Tobin and Katherine Lynch (whose work is more tuned to cabaret than stand-up), Maeve Higgins is ploughing something of a lonely furrow. Although this is a much potted history of Irish female performers (I am excluding a discussion of Irish theatre actresses), it does point to the currently small number of female stand-up comics in Ireland, and certainly to those with the ability to draw a large audience base. Higgins has placed herself within a performance genre where, (at least in Ireland) she has few female peers and few precursors, and one in which male comics still outweigh their female counterparts.

Higgins's comic persona is constructed in a way which accommodates her subversive discourse and her stories of social satire. In this way Higgins manipulates the more traditional format of the comedy of self-deprecation; however, that manipulation comes not from any sense of self-loathing but from an assured self-confidence. The power of Higgins's personal storytelling lies in her manipulation of the strategy of female comedy as self-deprecation, which speaks to her control over the performance form. It also speaks to Higgins's stories as a discursive power in the comic space which works to expose and satirize contemporary cultural assumptions and structures that facilitate the perpetuation of social, political or cultural stereotyping of women's identity. In addition, Higgins's comedy, certainly in the performance discussed within these pages, works to expose the gendered politics inherent in stand-up comedy and to undercut broader traditional and cultural assumptions on what constitutes female stand-up comedy. Higgins has been a professional comic for the relatively short period of six years. She achieved popularity and success early on in her professional career through her exposure on *Naked Camera*, the hidden camera comedy show as previously mentioned. There is a clear sense that Higgins is still to a certain degree an evolving voice, that she is still actively finding her comedic range of attitude as Tony Allen would have it.[19] Perhaps gaining early success professionally mediated her constructed comic style as a means of negotiating her position as a successful mainstream comic both nationally and internationally. Higgins's self-reflexive style of story-telling can be read at times by some as benign comedy but her stories more often than not employ a scorpion sting in the tail. Higgins's comic persona may have been constructed as a means through which to navigate early success, the imbalance between male and female comics in stand-up and of certain expectations and assumptions around the value and role of female stand-up comedy itself. Perhaps it was necessary. Perhaps not. It is beyond the remit of this author to say for certain. What is certain is that Maeve Higgins has very skilfully negotiated the situation of being one of the very few female stand-up comics in Ireland, and has achieved national and international success as a stand-up comic. The fact that Higgins is successful both on the national and international stage, key those personal stories to a far broader and more widespread audience. In this way Higgins's subversive stories can be understood to operate as a series of questions, examinations, re-examinations, contestations and rejections of socially gendered constructions of women's identity in Western society. Maeve Higgins does describe herself as a stand-up comic who really wants to be 'the princess blabbing away' (Higgins, 2010). On the other hand she has a steely determination that 'everyone listens to her' (Higgins, 2010). Now everybody knows that for a fairy story to end happily, the princess is always granted her heart's desire. It seems that Maeve Higgins is no different.

Bibliography

Allen, T., *Attitude: Wanna make something of it? The Secret of Stand up Comedy* (Glastonbury: Gothic Image Publications, 2002).

Auslander, P., 'Brought to you by Fem-Rage: Stand Up Comedy and the Politics of Gender', in *Acting Out: Feminist Performances*, ed. Lynda Hart and Peggy Phelan (Ann Arbor: University of Michigan Press, 1993): 315-36.

---

[19] Tony Allen, *Attitude: Wanna Make Something Of It? The Secret of Stand Up Comedy* (Glastonbury: Gothic Image Publications, 2002): 39. Allen describes a stand-up comic's range of attitude as 'How we recognise and then express these sides of our personality, how we assemble an individual palette of available emotional states, how we learn to switch seamlessly from one to another, and how we laugh at ourselves and the world around us, is the stuff of discovering our own unique range of Attitude.'

Boland, J., 'The gong for worst show goes to …', *Irish Independent*, 19 September 2009, <http://www.independent.ie/entertainment/tv-radio.html> [Accessed 12 December 2009].

Borns, B., *Comic Lives: inside the World of American Stand up Comedy*, (New York: Simon and Schuster, 1987).

Collier, D. and Beckett, K. *Spare Ribs: Women in the Humor Biz* (New York: St. Martin's Press, 1980).

Custance, D., 'Profile of a Serial Kidder', *The Skinny*, 8 September 2007, <http://www.the skinny.co.uk/40232-profile-of-a-serial-kidder> [Accessed 7 June 2010].

Freyne, P., 'Freyne's World', *Tribune*, 20 September 2009, <http://www.tribune.ie/arts/article/2009/sep/20/freynes-world/> [Accessed 11 December 2009].

Higgins, M., Unpublished Interview with the Author, (25 March 2010)

---, 'Girlfriends Coming for Dinner!' *Fancy Vittles*, RTE 2009. <http://www.youtube.com/watch?v=c55IjFnp8CY&feature=related> [Accessed 12 September 2010].

Merrill, L., 'Feminist humor: rebellious and self-affirming', in *Last Laughs: Perspectives on Women and Comedy*, ed. Regina Barreca (New York: Gordon and Breach, 1988): 271-280.

Oddey, A., *Performing Women* (London: Macmillan Press, 1999).

O'Toole, J., "A Danger to Yourself?" Motivational Talks in Group Slimming Classes', in *Ireland of the Illusions: A Sociological Chronicle 2007-2008*, ed. Mary P. Corcoran & Perry Share (Dublin: IPA, 2010): 253-270.

Russell, D., 'Self- Deprecatory Humour and the Female Comic: Self-Destruction or Comedic Construction', Third Space: A journal of feminist theory and culture, 2:1, 2002 <http://www.thirdspace.ca/articles/druss.html> [Accessed 12 January 2011].

Stott, A., *Comedy: The New Critical Idiom*, (Oxon: Routledge, 2005).

3 | Marina Carr – Writing as a Feminist Act

Brenda Donohue

Introduction

As the Women's Movement enters its fifth decade, women in Ireland can look around at a landscape of changed societal, cultural and personal values. Once tied to domesticity, women have now entered professional and artistic fields previously inaccessible to them. The theatre has long been a male dominated industry - no role more so than that of the nationally revered playwright. Victoria White has stated that in Ireland playwrights are 'the shamans of the tribe'[1], they are the mythmakers of our collective cultural imaginations and, as such, are privileged in this role. Seen in this light, the absence of women from the rank of canonical playwrights is a significant one and makes the presence of any professional female playwright all the more momentous. This article investigates the work of Marina Carr, a woman born in 1964 and part of the first generation of women to grow up after the Women's Liberation Movement, who has claimed the title of professional playwright and presented her plays on the Irish National Stage. It suggests that Marina Carr performs feminism in two ways; firstly, that the very act of working as a professional female playwright in Ireland today can be considered a meaningful feminist act and, secondly, that her body of work, in narrating new realities and imagining new possibilities, plays a vital role in enabling Irish women to conceive of themselves and one another differently.

---

[1] Victoria White, 'Women Writers Finally Take Centre Stage', *The Irish Times* 15 October 1998: 16, *ProQuest Historical Newspapers*, 25 July 2012.

Working as a professional female playwright as a feminist act

The Irish theatrical canon is notoriously male dominated, as a number of papers in this collection contend, and in 2011 theatre continues to be a male preserve. Of the four new plays presented on the Abbey Stage in 2009, only one – Marina Carr's *Marble* – was written by a woman; the others were Tom Murphy's *The Last Days of a Reluctant Tyrant*, Sebastian Barry's *Tales of Ballycumber* and Sam Shepard's *Ages of the Moon*. Carr, through her plays, stakes a place for women playwrights in the Irish National Theatre. Her work brings women's art and self-expression to a forum that has been largely dominated by male perspectives almost since its inception. Her plays attract national and international critical attention. Carr, of all the contemporary female playwrights, seems most likely to achieve canonicity, though as Jill Dolan and other commentators have ably pointed out, the road to canonicity is a fraught and uncertain one. If Carr does attain canonicity she will provide future generations of Irish women with a model to work off or, indeed, against.

New Ways of Seeing Women

Marina Carr performs feminism through playwriting. While her presence in the Abbey, and other leading theatres, represents women and provides female models, her feminist act does not end at simply making up the numbers. This study also asserts that Carr's work, which presents new female models of experience and behaviour, allows women to conceive of themselves and other women differently. Her female characters disrupt the idea of woman as outlined by Catholic social theory and tropes previously found in canonical male works, portraying instead complex, profound, thinking women. It argues that in bringing new female figures to the stage, Carr is allowing Irish women and men to imagine 'woman' in new and sometimes difficult ways. There has been an ongoing debate on the nature of Carr's feminism for some time now. It should be noted that many of the analyses doubting Carr's feminist potential were written in the wake of her three plays *The Mai* (1994), *Portia Coughlan* (1996) and *By the Bog of Cats* (1998), each of which ended in the protagonist's death. I believe study of her most recent plays, especially *Marble* (2009), will allow a reconsideration of the argument.

Writing as a Feminist Act: A History of Women in Ireland

The history of women in Ireland is a varied, painful and, until recently, an often hidden story. It has been marked by slow progress in the attainment of basic rights accompanied by the rising of expectations, only to find that few of these have been met. After the founding of the new Free State, there had been hope that with a new republic women's circumstances would improve. But after playing a vital role in the achievement of independence from Britain, Irish women's hopes of improved social positioning were not fulfilled. The Irish State then went on to willingly subordinate itself to the Catholic Church, identifying and characterizing the Irish state 'as a Catholic nation' in de Valera's words and inscribing in law the Catholic Church's concept of female roles in the 1937 Constitution. The 1937 Constitution prescribed the role of women as that of wife and mother incorporating the 'assertion in article 44 that by her life in the home a woman made a contribution to the state without which it could not prosper'[2]. In Yvonne Scannell's view, the constitution was 'rooted in a patronizing and stereotyped view of womanhood'[3] specifically Article 41.2, where 'woman' was conflated with 'mother', reflecting de Valera's own vision for Irish women 'that of a full-time wife and mother in an indissoluble marriage, having a preference for 'home duties' and 'natural duties' as a mother' (Hayes & Urquhart 2004: 72). Ferriter points out that in facing restrictive legislation in the areas of employment and contraception, Irish women were not unique but rather shared the experience in common with women in Europe and the United States (Ferriter 2005: 420). State authorized discrimination continued up until the 1960s when women's groups effected legislative change in the areas of employment and property rights, reproduction and marriage. Perhaps what was unusual about the Irish situation was not so much the conflation of woman and mother in the 1930s, but the translation of such ideas into law and the persistence of these laws long after they had been removed from the statute books of our European neighbours.

With the election of Mary Robinson in 1990, many Irish women gained a new hope in the possibility of achieving true equality. This led to the growth of a belief in the 1990s that 'the task of liberating women had been completed' (Ferriter 2005: 725), some commentators like John Waters have gone so far as to suggest that the balance is tipping the other way and that women's gains necessarily mean losses for men.

---

[2] Diarmaid Ferriter, *The Transformation of Ireland* (New York: Overlook Press, 2010): 370.

[3] Yvonne Scannell, 'The Constitution and the Role of Women', *Irish Women's History*, eds Alan Hayes, and Diane Urquhart (Dublin: Irish Academic Press, 2004): 77.

During the Celtic Tiger years, a period of laissez-faire attitudes, this impression seems to have grown exponentially. Perhaps it was part of the overriding cultural ideology of success that saturated Ireland in the boom period, but it is not representative of the true situation. In reality, the progress in attaining full equality and other women's rights stalled and, in some cases, regressed during the economic boom. Today, women continue to be grossly under represented in many areas of Irish life, they continue to be almost absent in areas such as politics and the higher echelons of management. The issue of abortion is another women's issue that successive governments have failed to legislate for and one that currently remains unresolved. Thus, while there have been many improvements in women's rights and consequentially their material circumstances on the road to equality, it seems clear that there are still many issues that need to be addressed. In the aftermath of the economic crash, many women seem to be waking up to the reality that Irish equality may not be equal at all.

Carr and Feminism

Marina Carr was born in 1964, just 6 years before the First Commission for the Status of Women was convened. At that time, Carr's mother, a married woman, had no right to her property on the death of her husband, no right to use contraception to control the size of her family, her earnings (if she was allowed to continue in her post) were taxed at a higher rate than those of her husband. It's hard to know to what extent the young Carr was aware of the inequalities faced by her mother and women like her. The feminist campaign for women's rights took place as Carr was growing into a teenager and then a woman. The country she grew up in guaranteed far more rights and freedoms than her mother's generation could ever have expected. In this climate of restricted and oppressive past and a sense of potential and promising present, Carr became a professional playwright, something that few women had done in the history of the state. Many women had written for the theatre, but achieving professional production was often a stumbling block. This dual sense of past restriction and present/future liberty has created a unique imaginative and intellectual space for women of Carr's generation, who grew up taking the promises of feminism for granted, but who may recently have come to a reassessment of the actual situation. Writers such as Camille Paglia and Katie Roiphe supported and propagated the notion in the 1990s that power was available to women for the taking, it just needed to be grabbed with both hands. However, the continuing poor material situation of many women in

2010 prompted Kat Banyard to write *The Equality Illusion*, a book that clearly outlines the extent of ongoing inequality and discrimination against women. Many women of Carr's generation have in recent years come to realize that, despite the hype, the feminist project has not reached all its stated aims and that equality has not (yet) been achieved. Carr's work seems to open up an imaginative space to explore this reality and its concomitant disappointment.

Female Playwrights - Barriers and Obstacles

Writing for the theatre, as Gayle Austin notes, is a more challenging form for a woman to write in as it 'requires mastering to some degree a male-dominated, public production machinery'.[4] In short, it requires stepping out of the private sphere and into the public sphere of theatre - it is something that only notably few women have been able to achieve in theatre history. There are four important stages necessary for any writer's work to secure long-term recognition and acceptance. Plays must be written, they must then be produced, revived and finally, they must enter the canon. Women playwrights have mastered the first of these steps and, to some extent, the second. However, the revival and potential entry of their work into the canon continue to prove a challenge.

Studies such as that of Joanna Russ's *How to Suppress Women's Writing* (1984) have established that women have long written in all forms, including for the theatre. Feminist studies have recuperated the work of female playwrights like Hrotsvit von Gandersheim and Aphra Behn. Women writing for theatre is not a new phenomenon, then, but the professional production of their plays is somewhat more of a novelty. Female playwrights receive increasingly more critical and public attention. But while women writers gradually gain more acceptance, recent statistics show that there is still a long way for female playwrights to go. In a study of off-Broadway productions in the USA between 2001 and 2002, it was found that only 16% of dramas produced were written by women and a marginally better 17% of shows were directed by women.[5] This situation continues today. Commenting on the prestigious Tony Awards for theatre, Jill Dolan notes:

---

4 Gayle Austin, 'Feminist Theories: Paying Attention to Women', *The Routledge Reader in Gender and Performance,* eds Lizbeth Goodman, and Jane de Gay (London: Routledge, 1998): 136.

5 Janelle Reinelt, 'Navigating Postfeminism: Writing Out of the Box', *Feminist Futures:Theatre, Performance, Theory,* eds Elaine Aston, and Geraldine Harris, (Basingstoke and New York: Palgrave Macmillan, 2006): 17-29.

Since 2000, of the 48 titles nominated for Best Play, only six have been written by women, and only one has won – *God of Carnage*, by Yasmina Reza, in 2009. In other words, no American woman playwright has won Best Play since the turn of the 21st century and only 12% of those nominated have been written by women.[6]

The evidence supports the view that while many women write for the theatre, the industry often fails to produce their work. This would point to an institutional failure to appreciate and promote women's writing for the theatre. One could speculate on the reasons for the low production rate of plays by female playwrights being linked to the underrepresentation of women in theatres generally and the lack of female artistic directors, but perhaps of more significance are the standards set out by critics and academics alike in assessing the value (or otherwise) of a piece of work, as Headrick and Countryman argue in their essay in this collection. The canon outlines a set of criteria to be satisfied in order for a work of art to be considered enduring and worthy. These standards are applied retrospectively, but also inform critics' reception of contemporary work. As Jill Dolan has pointed out in *The Feminist Spectator as Critic* (1991), they are tailored to the ideal male spectator and so do not take other experiences and perspectives into account. Kim McMullan underlines how the failure of anthology compilers to 'take adequate account of gender as a constitutive element of cultural construction'[7] mirrors the tendency of the culturally dominant group, historically, to exclude narratives that aren't seen as 'representative'. Thus, ideas, experiences and even literary styles that do not fit those of the dominant group, such as those of women, cannot possibly satisfy critics who do not know how to interpret them. However, as the work of feminist criticism takes effect and more women enter the halls of academia and the field of theatre criticism, it might be reasonable to expect that the critical criteria could show some change. The standards, which for so long were fashioned to suit a male audience, may now widen to include other perspectives. This idea is part of a much wider argument which the constraints of this article do not allow me to consider in depth. Whatever the reasons, it is clear that

---

[6] Jill Dolan, 'The Tony Awards', *The Feminist Spectator Blog*, 18 August 2011, <http://feministspectator.blogspot.com/search/label/Tony%20Awards%3B%2 0David%20Lindsay-Abaire%3B%20Frances%20McDormand%3B%20Julie%20Taymor%3B%20 Kathryn%20Bigelow>

[7] Kim McMullan, 'Decolonizing Rosaleen: Some Feminist, Nationalist, and Postcolonialist Discourses in Irish Studies', *The Journal of the Midwest Modern Language Association*, 29.1 (Spring 1996), *JSTOR*, 25 July 2012, <http://www.jstor.org/stable/10.2307/1315256>

women struggle to get their plays produced even today.

Looking at the canon, then, we see that, for the most part, women continue to be excluded from its ranks. The Irish canon is poor in models of canonical female writers and even poorer when it comes to female playwrights. Canonical models are vital in the professional growth of writers. Sue Ellen Case argues that in the case of Hrotsvit von Gandersheim, she was denied the chance to set that all-important precedent which could have established a standard of comparison within the theatrical canon for future women playwrights.[8] This absence of female models leads each generation of women writers to believe 'itself to be faced with the burden of doing everything for the first time'.[9] Were Carr to enter the canon, her presence as a professional female playwright would provide a model for young women from which to work. There are some indications of potential entry into the canon; her work has achieved institutional acceptance, with all of her plays since *The Mai* (1994) premiering in Ireland's National Theatre or prominent theatres in Ireland and the UK ; her plays have often been revived since their premieres by professional, semi-professional and amateur groups both in Ireland and abroad and her work has attracted considerable academic attention in the form of edited collections and monographs. However, the problem of women's qualification for the canon is incredibly complex and in this context Carr's entry is by no means guaranteed.

In the Irish context, the absence of professional female playwrights is more significant than it may appear at first glance. Given the heavy emphasis in Irish theatre on the written word, the role of the playwright is paramount. A theatre that privileges the text above all other elements elevates the position of playwright to one of primary importance. Despite the many obstacles that continue to face female playwrights, Carr continues to write plays and have them produced professionally in high-profile and prestigious theatres. Women have historically been seen as a symbol for the nation, as Cathy Leeney puts it 'woman has been the icon, and not the iconmaker'.[10] Carr, through her writing, seeks to change that status for women and sets about the daring work of

---

[8] Sue Ellen Case, 'Re-Viewing Hrotsvit', *Theatre Journal* 35. 4 Ideology & Theatre (December 1983) *JSTOR, 26 July 2012*
<http://www.jstor.org/stable/3207334>
[9] Joanna Russ, *How to Suppress Women's Writing* (London: The Women's Press, 1994) 93.
[10] Cathy Leeney, 'Ireland's "Exiled" Women Playwrights: Teresa Deevy and Marina Carr', *The Cambridge Companion to Twentieth-Century Irish Drama*, ed Shaun Richards (Cambridge: CUP, 2004): 162.

making icons for the nation. This is a feminist act.

Complex Women

Given the lack of professional female playwrights, writing as a professional playwright can be considered a feminist act. But Carr's approach, in its presentation and treatment of complex and problematic female characters, can also be read as feminist. Rhona Trench notes that Carr's early experimental plays resisted 'the theatrical traditions of Irish theatre such as the rural, the land, the Catholic Church and the cottage kitchen',[11] but she was also immediately interested in resisting and dissecting the traditions of the ideal woman as characterized in Irish society and theatre. Her characters are women who battle with the demands of society, who are often dissatisfied with their lot and are in constant negotiation with a hostile world. They are modern women for whom the family can be a heavy burden and who seek out life experiences more meaningful than the humdrum of the domestic quotidian. Carr has been criticized in the past for her depiction of women and there is a palpable sense of disappointment from some feminist critics who seem to believe that Carr's oeuvre comes up short when viewed from a feminist perspective (see Wallace, McMullan, Murphy). It is my contention that her work can be seen as feminist in her determination to present new forms of womanhood on the stage. I also propose that her later work, in particular her 2009 play, *Marble*, is more overtly feminist than her earlier work. Carr refuses to draw her female characters in the mould of well-worn types, moving beyond the many simple portrayals of women that we have found thus far. Instead, she writes complicated women whose choices often aren't wise (*The Mai* 1994), talented women who sometimes choose the easier path in life to their own detriment (*Woman and Scarecrow* 2006), women whose actions are in conflict with their stated desires (*On Raftery's Hill* 2000; *The Cordelia Dream* 2008) and women who choose to change their lives in the hope of a more meaningful existence (*Marble* 2009). Underlying all these characterizations is an ongoing and courageous battle with an unfriendly world - one which at times proves stronger than the female characters. This redrawing of the female opens new imaginative spaces in which the idea of woman can be explored and reconfigured.

---

[11] Rhona Trench, *Bloody Living; the Loss of Selfhood in the Plays of Marina Carr* (Oxford: Peter Lang, 2010): 29.

The Ideal Woman

The Catholic Church had fixed ideas on women and their role in society. The unique position afforded to the Catholic Church by the Free State and later governments in Ireland meant that the particular identity the Church constructed for women had a material effect on their lives. Catholic and State discourse situated women firmly in the private sphere of the home in what they perceived as her supreme role as mother. Further to this, the characteristics of the ideal woman, according to Catholic social policy, were in Fr. D. Barry's words; 'the passive virtues of humility, patience, meekness, forbearance and self-repression'.[12] Women were thus tied to domesticity with no public role, and the characteristics of passivity, sexual purity and maternal instincts were prescribed.[13]

Underlying these affirmations on the nature of women are many assumptions about female behaviour; that women should submit to male authority, that they should remain passive, that their sexuality should be controlled by the institution of marriage and that all of their activities should be strictly limited to the private realm of the home, the 'public arena wherein political and economic power resided was no place for women' (Valiulis 153). In the context of this study, it is significant that the theatre resides firmly in the public realm and therefore has traditionally been beyond the bounds of acceptable female behaviour.

Woman as Trope

Catholic social policy and state legislation have led to a number of enduring tropes regarding women in the national imagination, tropes that have been propagated by theatrical representation. These motifs have been created, for the most part, by male writers and signified through the female body and voice. Woman has come to be associated with fixed and inflexible concepts of space, place, time and identity. Carr's work, coming as it does from a female perspective, disrupts these associations creating new possibilities for women in the national

---

[12] Rosemary Cullen Owens, *A Social History of Women in Ireland 1870-1970* (Dublin: Gill & Macmillan, 2005): 99.

[13] Maryann Valiulis, 'Neither Feminist Nor Flapper: The Ecclesiastical Construction of the Ideal Irish Mother', *Irish Women's History*, eds Alan Hayes and Diane Urquhart (Dublin: Irish Academic Press, 2004): 152-158.

cultural imagination,[14] disrupting meta-narratives,[15] challenging the traditional conflation of woman and maternity[16] and allowing for the reimagining of women's place and identity[17]. As Carr's women move out of the space afforded to them by traditional motifs, themes and notions, they emerge into a new arena where fresh possibilities can be explored.

Marble

Marble, produced in 2009 on the Abbey stage, marked a departure in Carr's presentation of women and showed a development in the representation of women on the Irish stage. Carr, throughout her body of work, has examined the key areas of motherhood and heterosexual relationships. *Marble* takes up the threads of these themes spun in Carr's previous plays and weaves them into a more explicitly feminist statement.

In Jeremy Herrin's production, the world of *Marble* was a shiny, grey cold metallic realm, broken up only by the uncanny movement of a sofa and dominated from on high by a towering column of cream *Marble*. There is a pervading sense of dissatisfaction in the personal lives of all the characters, and Robert Innes Hopkins' set reflected this in the greys of an unforgiving urban landscape. This shiny urbanity was not what one would generally have expected from a Carr play and, along with the change in location and society came a shift in Carr's representation of women. The play is about an awakening. Protagonist Catherine comes to a deeper knowledge of herself and an understanding of the dynamics of her life through a series of dreams. She shares a number of mutual dreams with her husband's best friend, Art, in which they make love in a *Marble* room. Both find the experience intoxicating and as the play progresses their waking lives are utterly transformed by the dream. The themes of heterosexual

---

[14] Enrica Cerquoni, 'One Bog, Many Bogs: Theatrical Space, Visual Image, and Meaning in Some Productions of Marina Carr's *By the Bog of Cats...*', *The Theatre of Marina Carr: 'before rules was made'*, eds Cathy Leeney and Anna McMullan (Dublin: Carysfort Press, 2004): 172-99.

[15] Lisa Fitzpatrick, 'Disrupting Metanarratives: Anne Devlin, Christina Reid, Marina Carr and the Irish Dramatic Repertory', *Irish University Review*, 35.2 (Autumn-Winter 2005), *JSTOR*, 25 July 2012, <http://www.jstor.org/stable/i25517260>

[16] Melissa Sihra, 'Playing the Body: Marina Carr's Comedy of (Bad) Manners', *The Power of Laughter: Comedy and Contemporary Irish Theatre*, ed Eric Weitz (Dublin: Carysfort Press, 2004): 157-72.

[17] Anna McMullan, 'Unhomely Stages: Women Taking (a) Place in Irish Theatre', *Druids, Dudes and Beauty Queens: the Changing Face of Irish Theatre*, ed Dermot Bolger (Dublin: New Island, 2001): 73-90.

relationships, of submission, self-sacrifice and of maternity, explored and deconstructed in the earlier plays, are now elaborated on.

Maternity

If we consider Melissa Sihra's assertion that '[t]heatre is an ideal forum within which to re-imagine conservative notions of corporeality, sexuality and gendered identity' (Sihra 2004 162), we see that Carr uses it to challenge one of the most ingrained cultural tropes relating to Irish women, the idea 'that 'woman' and 'mother' are innately linked.' (Sihra 2004: 168). Countering the idealized image of woman as loving and self-sacrificing mother, Carr's mothers are absent and longed for (*By the Bog of Cats...*), ill-equipped for the role (*Ariel*), detached, distant, and fall short of the task of loving their children (*Portia Coughlan, The Mai*), they are the destroyers of their children emotionally and physically (*Ariel, By the Bog of Cats...*), they measure motherhood according to quantity not quality (*Low in the Dark, Woman and Scarecrow*) and they ultimately query the myth that mothering alone can be enough to sustain a woman in life (*Marble*). The machinations, processes and emotions of motherhood are examined, exposed and deconstructed.

Low in the Dark (1989) begins a line of inquiry into maternity with a light-hearted exposure of the facade of Irish motherhood that would prove to be a continual presence throughout Carr's work. It is a satirical analysis of 'Irish motherhood as measured by quantity' as advocated by the Catholic Church.[18] The mother figure in the play, Bender, churns out baby after baby, unconcerned about its sex, name or character. The Church's policies against contraception meant many pregnancies for Irish women and large families, with children into double figures, were not unusual. This focus on the quantity of children, to the neglect of attention on the quality of parenting, was a feature of Irish life for many decades. Woman in *Woman and Scarecrow* lived out this policy, with children that span in age from Michael, who's climbing Everest, to her youngest, Hal, who isn't long in school and 'can't even read yet'.[19] Scarecrow links her obsession with pregnancy and motherhood to a desire for accumulation and possession.

> Numbers. You just wanted numbers. You just wanted to look and say this one is mine and this one and this and him and her and

---

[18] Bernadette Sweeney, *Performing the Body in Irish Theatre* (Basingstoke: Palgrave Macmillan, 2008): 192.
[19] Marina Carr, *Woman and Scarecrow* (Oldcastle, Co. Meath: Gallery Press, 2006): 13.

those and that pair up there in the oak tree. Mine. All mine. That's what you wanted. Greedy for numbers. Insatiable for the head count. The leg count. I own sixteen pairs of legs and the two that didn't make it and eight noses and sixteen eyes and the two that didn't make it and sixteen ears and eighty fingers and eighty toes and reciting their names and ages to knock yourself out after another exhausting day of counting and coveting and even still wondering if you could squeeze another one in as you slide into your grave. (Carr 2006:16)

Carr questions the value of such a form of motherhood, by placing it within an economy of possession. Woman has sacrificed her potential to a mediocre husband and her eight children. On her own admission she has used her children as a shield to hide behind, an escape route to avoid the difficult choices in life, an excuse to stay in a loveless and resentful marriage 'if it wasn't for the children I'd have walked years ago' (Carr 2006:39). There is a resounding criticism of this approach from Scarecrow who concludes that the children were her 'shield to beat the world away' (Carr 2006:66). Motherhood, instead of the selfless act it has long been perceived to be, is portrayed by Carr instead as self-serving.

Though Carr's early plays often depict women whose children are secondary to their own personal and sexual needs (*The Mai*, *Portia Coughlan*), her later plays (*Woman and Scarecrow* and *Marble*) explore the consequences of placing your children's needs before your own. Carr focuses in on the power dynamic within the mother-child relationship. Historically, a mother's rights have been considered secondary to those of the child, both in formal legislative terms and informally in society. Commenting on the privileging of the child in the mother-child relationship, Carr criticizes the tendency to elevate 'the child at the expense of the mother. It's like your life is not valid except in fulfilling this child's needs'.[20]

In *Marble*, Carr examines this interplay of mother and child's needs. Catherine is a housewife and stay at home mother, who ostensibly embodies the lifestyle so revered by tradition. Like Woman in *Woman Scarecrow*, Catherine seems to have had numerous children.[21] Instead of a picture of domestic bliss, however, we are presented with a troubled and restless wife and mother. Catherine, along with Art's wife Anne, is clearly disillusioned with the responsibilities, the lifestyle and

[20] Marina Carr, 'Interview', *Rage and Reason: Women Playwrights on Playwriting*, eds Heidi Stephenson, and Natasha Langridge (London: Methuen, 1997): 150.
[21] Marina Carr, *Marble* (Oldcastle, Co. Meath: Gallery Press, 2009): 29.

the rewards that her status as housewife, mother and wife brings. She is a caring mother who loves her children, showing no trace of the indifference, distance or fear evident in The Mai's or Portia Coughlan's relationships with their children. Nonetheless, Catherine echoes Portia's boredom and sense of defeat in the face of unrelenting motherhood '[a]fter seventeen years of crying children you get pretty immune' (Carr 2009:29). It is clear that her suffering stems from the subjugation of herself to her children. A terrible sense of a life of routine and endless monotony emerges from the first scene between Ben and Catherine; he repeats the same line he says every night when he comes home, she can predict what he had for dinner (Carr 2009: 15). Anne, Art's wife, also seems to be fossilized into the normative role of mother and housewife, finding it so unsatisfying that it has become no more than a lengthy wait for death. She is '[j]ust waiting for it all to end like everyone else' (Carr 2009: 26). In contrast to the traditional utopian ideal of domestic life and motherhood, for Carr's women it is instead a life of confinement and boredom edging on despair. Ben believes that they must rear their 'young until they can survive without us. And that's it' (Carr 2009: 57). This is simply not enough for Catherine. She rejects the renunciation of her hopes, desires and identity for her children. Instead, she leaves the family home, and her role as mother, in order to pursue her own personal desires. The needs of the mother are this time privileged.

Carr's depiction of mothers is complex, broad and varying. She explores through her characters a range of (un)motherly behaviours and examines their consequences. It would be difficult to describe her work as a celebration of motherhood; it is rather a dissection of the emotions, positions and sacrifices that can be concomitant to motherhood. Carr investigates the ambivalence women, as mothers, can feel towards their children and the process of motherhood. On the spectrum of emotions that accompany mothering, she notes that '[w]e mostly only acknowledge the good ones. If we were allowed to talk about the other ones, maybe it would alleviate them in some way.' (Carr 1997:150/1). Carr's representations address these 'other ones' on the national stage and thus begins an introduction of these diverging representations into the Irish cultural imagination.

Heterosexual Relationships

Carr explores women's attachment to and reliance on men, even where it is problematic. The traditional model of male-female relationships was that of the authoritative male, and the submissive, passive and self-sacrificing female. Carr resists this model. The incompatibility of men and women was a preoccupation articulated very early on in Carr's writing, in plays such as *Low in the Dark* (1989) and *Ullaloo* (1991). Examining this theme, many studies have noted how Carr's female characters are often attached to, and dependent on, unsuitable male partners or figures. Her women tend to search for meaning and identity through poorly equipped men, often ignoring the dire reality of their relationship. The Mai insists on welcoming Robert back with open arms, even though all the signs point to his faithlessness and disinterest; Frances in *Ariel* stays with Fermoy despite the lack of love and his propensity to violence. There is a definite sense that these women cannot bear to be without the men in their lives, that they do not know how to be alone. Throughout her *oeuvre*, Carr's women continue to choose unsuitable men, but the results of this unwise choice gradually become less dramatic as the years pass. Whereas rejection by Robert and Carthage led The Mai and Hester respectively to suicide and murder, Woman (*Woman and Scarecrow*) just loses all desire to live, having reached a point of bitter resignation. In the early plays the female characters' attachment to their men is intense and destructive. In the later plays, especially *Marble*, the power of the bond wanes, allowing the female character to see beyond the male partner and facilitating a more significant search for identity and meaning.

In *Marble*, Catherine does not hold fast to her unsuitable man. Unlike the protagonists of *The Mai* and *By the Bog of Cats...* who, in their ferocious attachment to the men in their lives fight tooth and nail to keep them, Catherine decides to leave her husband Ben. Provoked by the passion of her dream, she sets about unpicking and examining the threads of her relationship with him. When she finds it lacking, she detaches herself from it. Catherine throws off the trope of the passive and submissive woman and becomes authoritative in her evaluation of their marriage, assessing it as merely a product of social convention. Their incompatibility becomes manifest as Catherine begins to question the institutions and social norms that keep them together. She sees them as senseless and confining; Ben, however, regards them as necessary and reassuring – something that protects them from the anarchy of the world, 'I know the wilderness is out there, and that we are safe inside seems to me a great miracle' (Carr 2009:60). Ben's insistence on the importance of structure and order alienates Catherine, who instead feels compelled to deconstruct the façade of normality and ask the big existential questions of life: 'What are these senseless rules we live by? Who decided them and why?' (Carr 2009:32)

Whereas women like The Mai and Hester, and indeed Anne in *Marble*, wilfully ignore signs of incompatibility with their men, Catherine instead recognizes and accepts them, leading her to take up a position of agency in ending her marriage.

The historic authority of the male in heterosexual relationships is explored in Carr's plays. Dependence on men and women's concomitant self-sacrifice is shown to have negative consequences for the personal development and expression of females. The women that populate Carr's plays are rich and interesting individuals who possess talents and capacities. These talents are not always developed to the full, however. They are neglected or underdeveloped and suppressed for the gratification of the men in their lives. Historically, self-sacrifice was a quality expected of women; they sacrificed themselves for the greater good of the family in reproductive, material and emotional terms. This was an important factor in the promotion of male authority in the home. In her work, Carr questions this tradition. The Mai is an excellent cello player, better than Robert, but hasn't played in years because her brilliance bothered him. Similarly, Woman (*Woman and Scarecrow*) played the piano better than her husband, Him, a 'barbarian' who murders Chopin (Carr 2006:28) and admits that 'I suppose he never liked me to do anything better than him' (Carr 2006:28). Woman (*The Cordelia Dream*), sacrifices more than a hobby, when she brings a halt to her successful composing career to allow her father regain his status as a composer. This willingness to suppress the self comes to an end with Catherine, who refuses the path of self-sacrifice.

The moment in which Catherine leaves Ben has significant echoes in the representation of women in Irish theatre history. Echoing Nora's departure in *In the Shadow of the Glen* (1903) by J.M. Synge, Catherine leaves her husband behind in the private realm of the family home to face an uncertain, but independent, future. In contrast to Synge's Nora, who leaves her home and husband to walk the road with the Tramp – thus tying her future destiny to another man – Carr's protagonist leaves alone. Although, initially she saw a union with Art as a viable alternative – a simple substitution of one man for another – Art's refusal to go with her helps Catherine realize that her future existence cannot rely on any man. While Carr's previous female characters feared being alone, Catherine realizes that she does not need a male companion to continue. Art was, in her words 'just a signal, a beacon, not important in himself but a sign' that has brought her to a different place. Though she initially mistook him for 'the great magic thing that has been missing' (Carr 2009:58), Catherine comes to recognize that it is not Art that has been lacking, but rather her own identity. No man will provide her with wholeness and fulfilment, she must be her own salvation – she must look to herself.

In her examination of heterosexual relationships, Carr uncovers and exposes the weaknesses and confusion that women have in regard to men. She presents women who find it a challenge to conceive of themselves without a male companion and women who sacrifice themselves for the gratification of those men. In *Marble*, however, Carr presents a woman who critically scrutinizes the value of such roles and rejects them. Through Catherine, the figure of 'woman' moves from the traditional representation of the dependent and self-sacrificing wife (or lover) to one who strikes out on her own in a bid for independence and self-knowledge. Woman becomes the agent and decider of her own destiny.

Identity

Under the weight of the standards set out by Catholic Church and State, women's identities were for many years subsumed, repressed and hidden. Marina Carr chips away at and eventually throws off the heavy mantle of the 'ideal women' in an effort to find Catherine's true identity. *Marble* can be interpreted as one woman's search for identity through the casting off of the weight of traditional gender expectations and roles. Catherine seeks to uncover and understand an identity and a life that has been buried for many years under the demands of social convention. By stripping away the labels of wife and mother, Catherine attempts to come face to face with herself.

Bored with the monotony of her life, Catherine believes 'the life not lived is what kills' (Carr 2009: 17). Her dreaming life provides her with a sense of truth and meaning, until eventually her 'waking life is just pretence' (Carr 2009: 39). The dreams provoke in her an exploration for her identity. They allow her to imagine herself and her experience differently. In the dreams, Catherine is not a wife or mother, but a lover. When, in waking moments, she considers herself with the roles of mother and wife stripped away, she cannot articulate what is left. She has been undone by the dreaming and in her undoing she has discovered not a central identity, but a void. 'Feel I've been peeled like an onion. I'm down to the core and there's nothing there' (Carr 2009: 50) 'the mind, the heart, the soul, whatever there is that's me is just not there' (Carr 2009: 51). Caught up in social convention, the institution of marriage and the roles of mother and housewife status she has neglected herself. Without the assigned roles of wife or mother, she does not know what or who she is. This is a profound realization.

The decision to abandon her children is a momentous and significant event in Irish theatre history, marked in the text and in Jeremy Herrin's 2009 Abbey production by a lengthy and loud silence. In those 30 seconds without words, a spectrum of emotions swept across actress Aisling O'Sullivan's face, making Catherine's internal dilemma and anguish manifest. This was by no means an easy or unconsidered decision. Thwarting the trope of the dedicated and selfless Irish mother, Catherine's deliberation leads her to the decision that she needs to leave her children and her husband in order to find herself. There is a sense that the decision is agonizing, but ultimately she refuses to place their welfare over her own. The privileging of the child over the mother is inverted.

Catherine walks out of her house a woman liberated from the labels and roles of wife and of mother. She does not know what remains when these things are taken away, but is determined to discover and explore that which is left. Through Catherine, Carr demonstrates how prescribed societal and cultural roles can obscure a person's identity. By challenging and stripping away prescribed roles for women, Carr invites an exploration of women's identities that are not overlaid by stratums of social convention.

Conclusion

Carr's playwriting can be considered a feminist act. In the context of historical suppression of female writers and current lack of professional female playwrights, Carr is truly an exception to the rule. After well over one hundred years of an Irish National theatre that carried, with few exceptions, the symbolism, voices and representations of male writers, the female perspective has been brought to the National stage in Carr's plays. She has, through her writing, fearlessly put 'the emotional reality at the heart of so many women's existence on stage'[22] and opened up the National stage, which was 'a symbolic space which had no place for the symbolism of women' (White 1998) to the contemplation of a female perspective. Carr's feminism is not a politically aggressive feminism that seeks to forward the feminist agenda through the work of art. It is rather a theatre that seeks to explore issues from the perspective of a female writer. Her writing inscribes the female

---

[22] Victoria White, 'Twin Speak', *The Irish Times* 19 March 1996: 10, *ProQuest Historical Newspapers*, 25 July 2012.

experience, voice and symbolism into contemporary theatre, perhaps the canon and the national imagination. It is not representative of all women, but is a step.

Carr presents complicated and profoundly flawed characters who engage in a sustained negotiation with the machinations of patriarchy on an individual basis. Often, they are defeated by it. In this sense, their situation could be seen to resemble the condition of women under post-feminism, lacking in political awareness and organization, but filled with a sense of their own rights and self-worth. Carr's recent plays, especially *Marble*, investigate and interrogate tropes, offering new insights into areas such as motherhood, heterosexual relationships and identity. Carr's women are not open and shut cases that can be easily interpreted, defined and categorized. They are fallible, they are weak and strong, they often choose unwisely in their battle for survival under patriarchy. By providing the audience with such complex characters, Carr moves away from simplistic and reductive characterization of women and provides us with characters that reflect the true heterogeneity of female identity.

Bibliography

Austin, Gayle, 'Feminist Theories: Paying Attention to Women', *The Routledge Reader in Gender and Performance,* eds Lizbeth Goodman, and Jane de Gay (London: Routledge, 1998): 136-142.
Banyard, Kat, *The Equality Illusion: the Truth About Women and Men Today* (London: Faber and Faber, 2010).
Carr, Marina, *Marble* (Oldcastle, Co. Meath: Gallery Press, 2009).
---, *The Cordelia Dream* (Oldcastle, Co. Meath: Gallery Press, 2008).
---, *Woman and Scarecrow* (Oldcastle, Co. Meath: Gallery Press, 2006).
---, *Ariel* (Oldcastle, Co. Meath: Gallery Press, 2002).
---, *On Raftery's Hill* (Oldcastle, Co. Meath: Gallery Press, 2000).
---, *Marina Carr: Plays 1* (London: Faber & Faber, 1999).
---, 'Interview', *Rage and Reason: Women Playwrights on Playwriting*, eds Heidi Stephenson, and Natasha Langridge (London: Methuen, 1997): 147-155.
Case, Sue Ellen, 'Re-Viewing Hrotsvit', *Theatre Journal* 35. 4 Ideology & Theatre (December 1983) *JSTOR, 26 July 2012* http://www.jstor.org/stable/3207334
Cerquoni, Enrica, 'One Bog, Many Bogs: Theatrical Space, Visual Image, and Meaning in Some Productions of Marina Carr's *By the Bog of Cats...*', *The Theatre of Marina Carr: 'before rules was made'*, eds Cathy Leeney and Anna McMullan (Dublin: Carysfort Press, 2004): 172-199.
Cullen Owens, Rosemary, *A Social History of Women in Ireland 1870-1970* (Dublin: Gill & Macmillan, 2005).
Dolan, Jill, *The Feminist Spectator as Critic* (Ann Arbor: University of Michigan Press, 1991).
---, 'The Tony Awards', *The Feminist Spectator Blog*, 18 August 2011, <http://feministspectator.blogspot.com >

Ferriter, Diarmaid, *The Transformation of Ireland, 1900-2000* (New York: Overlook Press, 2005).

Fitzpatrick, Lisa, 'Disrupting Metanarratives: Anne Devlin, Christina Reid, Marina Carr and the Irish Dramatic Repertory', *Irish University Review*, 35.2 (Autumn-Winter 2005), *JSTOR*, 25 July 2012, <http://www.jstor.org/stable/i25517260>

Leeney, Cathy, 'Ireland's "Exiled" Women Playwrights: Teresa Deevy and Marina Carr', *The Cambridge Companion to Twentieth-Century Irish Drama*, ed Shaun Richards (Cambridge: CUP, 2004): 150-163.

McMullan, Anna, 'Unhomely Stages: Women Taking (a) Place in Irish Theatre', *Druids, Dudes and Beauty Queens: the Changing Face of Irish Theatre*, ed Dermot Bolger (Dublin: New Island, 2001): 73-90.

McMullan, Kim, 'Decolonizing Rosaleen: Some Feminist, Nationalist, and Postcolonialist Discourses in Irish Studies', *The Journal of the Midwest Modern Language Association*, 29.1 (Spring 1996), *JSTOR*, 25 July 2012, <http://www.jstor.org/stable/10.2307/1315256>

Murphy, Paula, 'Staging Histories in Marina Carr's Midlands Plays', *Irish University Review*, 36.2 (Autumn-Winter 2006), *JSTOR*, 25 July 2012, <http://www.jstor.org/stable/25517319>

O'Toole, Fintan, *Enough is Enough: How to Build a New Republic* (London: Faber & Faber, 2010).

Reinelt, Janelle, 'Navigating Postfeminism: Writing Out of the Box', *Feminist Futures:Theatre, Performance, Theory*, eds Elaine Aston, and Geraldine Harris (Basingstoke and New York: Palgrave Macmillan, 2006): 17-29.

Russ, Joanna. *How to Suppress Women's Writing* (London: The Women's Press, 1994).

Scannell, Yvonne, 'The Constitution and the Role of Women', *Irish Women's History*, eds Alan Hayes and Diane Urquhart (Dublin: Irish Academic Press, 2004): 71-78.

Sihra, Melissa ed. *Women in Irish Drama: a Century of Authorship and Representation* (Basingstoke: Palgrave Macmillan, 2007).

---, 'Playing the Body: Marina Car's Comedy of (Bad) Manners', *The Power of Laughter: Comedy and Contemporary Irish Theatre*, ed Eric Weitz (Dublin: Carysfort Press, 2004): 157-72.

Sweeney, Bernadette, *Performing the Body in Irish Theatre* (Basingstoke: Palgrave Macmillan, 2008).

Trench, Rhona, *Bloody Living; the Loss of Selfhood in the Plays of Marina Carr* (Oxford: Peter Lang, 2010).

Valiulis, Maryann, 'Neither Feminist Nor Flapper: The Ecclesiastical Construction of the Ideal Irish Mother', *Irish Women's History*, eds Alan Hayes and Diane Urquhart (Dublin: Irish Academic Press, 2004): 152-158.

Wallace, Clare, 'A Crossroads between Worlds: Marina Carr and the Use of Tragedy', *Litteraria Pragensia*, 10.20 (2000): 76-89.

---, 'Tragic Destiny and Abjection in Marina Carr's "The Mai", "Portia Coughlan" and "By the Bog of Cats ..." in *Irish University Review*, 31.2 (Autumn–Winter 2001), *JSTOR*, 25 July 2012 <http://www.jstor.org/stable/10.2307/25504887>

White, Victoria, 'Twin Speak', *The Irish Times* 19 March 1996: 10, *ProQuest Historical Newspapers*, 25 July 2012.

---, 'Women Writers Finally Take Centre Stage', *The Irish Times* 15 October 1998: 16, *ProQuest Historical Newspapers*, 25 July 2012.

4 | Damned if You Do; Damned if You Don't

Charlotte Headrick and John Countryman

While the last fifty years of Irish playwriting has been marked by an abundance of drama written by women, this phenomenon has not been matched by a similar abundance of productions and publications, or a rise in the public notoriety of the women responsible for generating these scripts. More recently, there has been a significant increase in the amount of critical attention devoted to the important works that women have written for the stage. This fact, however, has not resulted in the same degree of awareness about the contributions of Irish women to the development of drama on the part of audiences abroad. While a handful of women playwrights have enjoyed some well-deserved attention in Ireland itself, Anglophone audiences in London, Sydney, Toronto and New York among other cities have only rarely had an opportunity to attend productions of their plays in these major theatre capitals outside of Ireland. This essay will examine why plays by Irish women have not been produced, why there has been little critical attention paid to their work, and why there exists a lack of awareness of all the contributions Irish women dramatists have made and are continuing to make to the development of Irish theatre practice.

Those plays by women that have managed to attract the attention of the major establishment theatres abroad have only rarely become available in publications easily accessible to consumers outside of Ireland or appeared in major anthologies adopted by academics for the consumption of undergraduate and graduate students; many of these students will themselves become directors or teachers of drama and theatre in regional settings throughout English-speaking countries.

Even anthologies of scripts by Irish playwrights have, until very recently, overlooked the important work generated by women. The editors of the Field Day publications in Ireland itself had to be embarrassed into adding a later volume to their *Anthology* because they had virtually overlooked women. The second, updated, edition of John P. Harrington's anthology of *Modern and Contemporary Irish Drama* has been supplemented only by the addition of a single woman playwright beyond the obligatory attention devoted to Lady Gregory. The contents of the only other widely circulated anthology of Irish drama available to students in English and theatre classes outside of Ireland, Coilin Owen and Joan A. Radner's *Irish Drama: 1900-1980*, was almost exclusively the work of men and is now out of print. On very rare occasions plays by Irish women are produced on the stages of college and university theatres outside of Ireland (in favour of productions by Friel, Murphy, McGuinness, McPherson and McDonagh or the earlier plays of Synge, O'Casey, Behan, and Beckett) and almost never in professional productions in major theatre centres or well-known regional theatres.

Although plays by Irish women are certainly known by some professional and academic theatre practitioners, they are produced so infrequently as to have little or no chance of entering the consciousness of playgoers. Many of the plays by women that have been produced in Ireland and abroad have seen the light of day only because they have been brought to the public's attention by the same or other women who have, at great difficulty, created their own theatre companies and produced their own work or, less frequently, been produced by a handful of women producers or directors that have managed to insinuate themselves into the better known theatre establishments. Because the greater percentage of these plays have never been produced in the major theatre centres mentioned above, even avid theatre goers abroad are unaware of them.

Whenever women playwrights are acknowledged at all by working professionals and most theatre academics, it is the same handful of names that are introduced into the conversation and those conversations rarely translate into productions of plays by Irish women. Often theatre professionals and academics have to educate their colleagues about those and other women dramatists from Ireland and, more often than not, those doing the educating either are 1) drawn to Irish drama in general as a scholarly pursuit, 2) are Irish-Americans or transplanted Irish, or 3) are women themselves who became aware of the issue of Irish women dramatists as a consequence of an interest in women's studies and its ambition to recuperate the important contributions of women worldwide and to bring those contributions to the attention of a wider public. In approximately the last twenty-five years, articles, book chapters, and less frequently, entire volumes have been devoted to the work of women playwrights from Ireland. Some of these publications have been the work of other theatre professionals or the writers themselves, but the lion's share have been generated by theatre scholars or better known theatre commentators (primarily Irish themselves and many of them men). For the most part the same sort of appeals have been made by these writers on behalf of Irish women dramatists for the consumers of culture at home and abroad to pay more attention to these important writers. They argue that more of the culturally 'enlightened' (if not the wider population) ought to read these plays, ought to attend these plays, ought to educate themselves about the very different preoccupations of women dramatists and the alternative dramaturgical and theatrical 'aesthetics' they have adopted or created. (This is addressed in greater detail below.) At the same time, many of the publications mentioned above rehearse the same litany of reasons why women dramatists have not received the attention they deserve. Among the reasons (both spurious and genuine) given to explain why women have been marginalized, neglected, overlooked, or ignored are the following:

1. Women in Ireland create collective, collaborative or devised pieces that are not the typical scripts generated by a single author. Although this has been the case (most notably on the part of the now disbanded Charabanc – their most celebrated achievement, *Lay Up Your Ends*, took twenty-five years to get in print), most women still subscribe to the single-author, publishable text approach to play development.

2. Most theatre owners, producers, directors, and reviewers are men and consciously or unconsciously favor the work of male playwrights. These men argue (if they bother to engage in the debate at all) that women's plays often address parochial themes, do not embrace traditional forms, and use dramatic and theatrical means that are not mainstream and consequently will not have broad popular appeal. Anna McMullan has asked, 'What place is allotted to women's cultural production in the public spaces of print, media and the stage? The exclusion of most female writers from any place in the Irish theatre canon [has provoked commentators like herself to select for critical examination] female authored plays

that have received relatively little critical attention'[1]

3. Women playwrights are assumed to address topics that are only of interest to other women and fail to draw heterogeneous audiences, and in fact have created what many believe to be the 'theatrical equivalent of 'chick flicks'[2]

4. Women who claim to be 'feminist' are ghettoized. In many cases, women playwrights, whether are not they are avowed feminists, are assumed to be, and feminism 'turns off' many audience members, both men and women, and is considered likely to fail at the box office.

In 1997, Christopher Murray wrote, 'The general rule in the Republic is that plays by women may be heard, i.e., given a reading, but not staged.' This continues to be the case, with the exception of Marina Carr, despite the 2001 volume, edited by Cathy Leeney, titled *Seen and Heard*, and arguably none of the women playwrights in Leeney's anthology would be recognizable to more than a handful of American, English, Canadian, or Australian audiences. We would venture to say that the majority of audiences in Ireland *itself* have never heard of them either. Patrick Lonergan argues that, 'The message conveyed by drama since 1990 might be that men talk, but women dance'.[3] Before 1990, many commentators have mentioned that women have been characterized in Irish plays as abstract representations of Ireland itself, as Madonnas, Magdalens, or Matriarchs (the terms, although not original to her by any means, are identified, for purposes of examining their origins, in *Contemporary Irish Drama and Cultural Identity* by Margaret Llewellyn Jones) or in submissive, primarily domestic roles, and not as empowered, autonomous subjects in their own right. This issue of the mythic representation of women is addressed further in the essay by Maguire and Upton, in this collection.

Most of the arguments outlined above are legitimate and important. What we will attempt to do in the discussion that follows, in addition to augmenting these key arguments, is to provide a more comprehensive rationale for the lack of attention that women dramatists from Ireland have received. Many of our claims are rarely, if ever, discussed in the media, in the classroom, in publications, or in the rehearsal hall. Most of the better-known commentators on the subject of drama and dramatists are not engaged in the practice of theatre. Therefore, we

---

[1] Anna McMullan, ' Unhomely Stages: Women Taking (a) Place in Irish Theatre' *Dudes, Druids and Beauty Queens* ed. Dermot Bolger (Dublin: New Island, 2001): 72.

[2] Mary Trotter, 'Translating Women into Irish Theatre History' *A Century of Irish Drama* ed. Stephen Watt, E. Morgan & S. Mustafa (Bloomington: Indiana University Press, 2000): 164-65.

[3] Patrick Lonergan, *Theatre and Globalization* (Basingstoke: Palgrave Macmillan, 2010): 166.

have combined our careers as college professors and scholars with our experience of rigorous 'hands-on' activity as actors and directors in both academic and professional theatre. Our experience affords us unique outlooks on the issues discussed in this paper.

One of the areas where there was discussion of these issues was at the 1999 conference at Indiana University: 'Nationalism and a National Theatre: 100 Years of Irish Drama.' The issues were further explored in the volume published from that conference: *A Century of Irish Drama: Widening the Stage.* Anyone who attended the conference, or has read from cover to cover the volume of essays selected for inclusion in the publication, would be compelled to agree that nearly all of them, whether they directly address the marginalization of women or not (and Mary Trotter's does) add to a much more comprehensive understanding of the factors that have contributed to the problem. Headrick presented a paper at the Indiana gathering, and also brought with her a production of Patricia Burke Brogan's *Eclipsed* that she had directed while serving as artist-in-residence for the Department of Theatre and Dance at Western Kentucky University. After consulting with the playwright and Headrick and undertaking dramaturgical analysis of his own, Countryman also directed the play (at Berry College in Georgia).

We are in agreement that the majority of the essays included in the book that emerged from the conference (edited by Stephen Watt, Eileen Morgan, and Shakir Mustafa for Indiana University Press) challenge a host of long held judgments about Irish drama and Ireland itself. But before we tackle a summary and evaluation of those challenges, we'd like to offer a number of observations, drawn from our shared experiences that, as noted, are rarely, if ever, discussed.

In some areas, theatre is perceived as an elitist activity, not by choice or design, but because of economic exigencies (productions are expensive, thus tickets are expensive) and there is a lack of theatrical knowledge on the part of most consumers in America, Britain, Canada, and Australia. Of the minority of those inclined to attend live theatre, a significant percentage only attend plays that provide escapist entertainment or 'spectaculars' (mostly musicals) that premier (and often enjoy long runs) in the West End or on Broadway before touring the 'provinces.' This portion of the audience is very vocal about their decision to avoid productions that challenge cherished assumptions, expectations about what 'good theatre should be,' or their reigning world view. Audiences are frequently aided and abetted by popular reviewers (not 'critics' in the true sense of the word) who have established themselves as arbiters of 'taste' and generally legislate what will succeed and what will not in the commercial theatre. Pulitzer-Prize-winning dramatist Paula Vogel speaks to this situation: 'So women need to be fearless about writing plays. Do I think that there's still a bias of perception? Yes, I do. However, I don't think women should be stopping because of it.[4] She continues, 'One thing that always astounds me is people saying, 'Oh, that's not a good play.' And I say, 'Wait a moment. It's not a good play if you have an Aristotelian definition. But if your definition of a play is anything that happens in front of an audience, it's a very exciting play.' (429)

Most commentators, including bona fide scholars, who respond to drama and dramatists, do not themselves practice theatre and are consequently deprived of a full and immediate understanding of the phenomenon.

Most of the academics who write about drama and dramatists are affiliated with English departments and are inclined to treat drama as *literature*, and apply *literary* standards of evaluation to the works they consider, as well as emphasizing what the scripts reveal about the dramatist (autobiographical questions or psychoanalytical readings) or the circumstances of the script's creation (the time and place associated with the generation of the script or its value as an historical or sociological artefact). Drama, like other literary forms, is analysed primarily as a *text*. Additionally, English departments, for the most part, teach very little drama (with the notable exception of Shakespeare) because it is perceived as a 'lesser' form. For the most part, the study of drama occurs in theatre departments that are in the awkward position of assigning scripts to discuss in class, which they argue are of world class calibre, and must be experienced in performance to be fully appreciated. They are then consigned to produce in their own educational theatre settings, plays that will attract the largest audiences in order to please the community, the college administration, the parents, and to justify their existence by breaking even at the box office. These students become members of the audiences described above.

With the exception of Yeats and Joyce, Irish literature, in most colleges and universities, is treated as a 'sub-field' in most English departments. Most survey courses may include one or two Irish selections, even the occasional drama, but that's about it. Colleges fortunate enough to offer a course in Irish drama generally confine it to

---

[4] Paula Vogel, 'Paula Vogel' *Women Who Write Plays: Interviews with American Dramatists* ed. Alexis Greene (Hanover: Smith and Kraus Inc., 2001): 427.

one semester and adopt texts (anthologies) that contain scripts by male authors. As mentioned, the second edition of John P. Harrington's *Modern and Contemporary Drama* added only one female playwright beyond the obligatory Lady Gregory. Coilin Owens's far more comprehensive anthology, *Irish Drama: 1900-1980* is out of print and, again, includes only Lady Gregory. A soon to be released volume, co-edited by Headrick for Syracuse Press, seeks to redress this deficiency.

In addition to the circumstances detailed above, most playgoers have a very limited understanding of Ireland and Irish culture and society (even, regrettably, many Irish-Americans). Despite all the changes that Ireland has undergone in the last fifty years, many playgoers have antiquated images of the country that refuse to die and that have been perpetuated by a number of stereotypical notions of the country and its people that have been disseminated by the Irish themselves. In the minds of audiences abroad, Irish plays, to be 'authentic,' should, despite the 'Celtic Tiger' and its demise and the increasingly multicultural makeup of the country, conform with most of the following: 1) Occur in a rural setting and make reference to the 'local colour' (read 'peasants'), preferably in a thatched cottage or at least in a 'modest' country kitchen in a more contemporary home. Despite efforts by many in Dublin and Belfast to develop an alternative to the 'rural aesthetic' that gained a stranglehold on the Abbey, and despite the proliferation of regional theatres in Ireland that has resulted from a more progressive government and population and increased funding for theatres other than The Abbey, The Gate, and The Lyric, theatre consumers are comfortable with, and consequently most likely to endorse, productions that adopt this template, whether by Synge, J.B. Keane, Friel, or Martin McDonagh.

2) Feature male protagonists or women whose lives are 'narrated' or 'interpreted' by male voices and memories. So as to not disrupt racial assumptions, many of these men should be the 'masters' of the house, prone to violence and alcoholism unless the objective is to advance an image of the 'noble savage' in a pastoral idyll. Audiences nursed on these images, when presented with plays that advance images of female subjectivity that are outside of their comfort zone, claim that they either 'don't get' what scripts are saying, or that they are disturbed by what they see because 'they have been trained to understand and appreciate male discourses' (Trotter 2000:164).

3) Not ignore that Irish women, despite successful referenda on divorce and birth control, two female presidents back to back, an active feminist movement, and the severely compromised position of the Catholic

Church in Ireland, are generally repressed, sexually naïve or (as DeValera and those who rioted during performances of *The Playboy of the Western World* and *The Plough and the Stars* would have it) the virtue of Irish women should never be endangered or besmirched).

Contemporary audiences in Ireland itself would find these expectations and assumptions ludicrous, yet Bórd Fáilte (Irish Tourist Board) continues to propagate this image of Ireland for the consumption of tourists. These assumptions, we would argue, have been fuelled by over a century of misrepresentation of Ireland by its male playwrights and they persist because, in a frankly opportunistic manner, playwrights like Martin McDonagh continue to exploit such stereotypes in the interests of professional success and notoriety.

In what remains, we will first summarize the manifold reasons that these stereotypes persist, with frequent references to the conclusions of the contributors to *A Century of Irish Drama*, and their challenges to the 'received' impression of Irish drama that is at the heart of the problem; and, second, review the accomplishments that women have made, especially in the last fifty years, to advance a counter-narrative and to educate audiences to the genuine state of Irish affairs and of the many aesthetic innovations that have marked the creation of drama by women (and some men) on the island, both South and North.

David Grant has remarked that, 'the list of recognized living Irish playwrights [even when] far from complete, [reflects] the common tendency to exclude women'.[5] In *Theatre and Globalization*, Patrick Lonergan admits that, 'Of all the Irish plays that have achieved success throughout the world, only a tiny minority were written by women' (29). With regard to the earlier comment that nearly all of the essays chronicled in *A Century of Irish Drama* reflect shifting views about women playwrights from Ireland, the theme is perhaps best reflected in Carla J. McDonough's statement that

> portraits of women that reflect the complexities of women's lives reveal that there are rich stories yet to be mined in the theatrical project of presenting a nation's history, struggles, and conflicts to and for itself (191).

Anna McMullan attributes this condition to the 'lack of public engagement with women's playwriting in the channels of public

---

[5] David Grant, 'Introduction' *The Crack in the Emerald* qtd. Anthony Roche, *Contemporary Irish Drama* 2nd Edition (Basingstoke: Palgrave Macmillan, 2009): 244.

discourse.'[6]. This is so in great measure because, as Caroline Williams argues, 'we are so used to men's images of men, and men's images of women on the stage, that a play written by a woman is regularly criticized or rejected for not complying with these norms'.[7] Lonergan concurs when he says, 'globalization causes audiences to expect that theatre will confirm their expectations. It is for this reason ... that we see an increase in plays that reproduce the apparently old-fashioned gendered tropes, whereby masculinity and eloquence, and femininity and embodiment, are strongly associated with each other' (170). Cathy Leeney explains the challenge women face: 'Traditionally woman has been the icon, and not the icon maker. When she becomes the creator of representations the woman playwright must negotiate the representational inheritance in relation to which she inevitably works.'[8] Additionally, as Watts' volume reinforces, audiences outside of Ireland have not changed their perceptions and expectations regarding Irish identity as represented in its drama, but

> nostalgic images blended with simplistic notions of identity, particularly those linked with the rural landscape ... are no longer representative of the new more urban Ireland, which according to Fintan O'Toole, is 'essentially the same kind of place in which the exile now lives'.[9]

This circumstance is evidenced in a question posed in a critical commentary about Marina Carr by Melissa Sihra: 'How does Carr's representation of Ireland interact with typically received, pastoral-kitsch commodifications of Irishness abroad?'[10] Christopher Murray has gone so far as to say that,

> The consciousness has mutated; it is probably only in metropolitan centres abroad (among the diaspora) that the metaphysical

---

[6] Anna McMullan, 'Gender, Authorship and Performance in Selected Plays by Contemporary Irish Women Playwrights' *Theatre Stuff* ed. Eamonn Jordan (Dublin: Carysfort Press, 2000): 36.

[7] Anna McMullan & Caroline Williams, 'contemporary Women Playwrights' *Field Day Anthology of Irish Writing Vol. V*, ed. Angela Bourke et al (Cork: Cork University Press, 2002): 6-7.

[8] Cathy Leeney, 'Ireland's "Exiled" Women Playwrights' *Twentieth Century Irish Drama* ed. Shaun Richards (Cambridge: Cambridge University Press, 2004): 162.

[9] Margaret Llewellyn-Jones, *Contemporary Irish Drama* (Bristol: Intellect, 2002): 138.

[10] Melissa Sihra, 'Reflections Across Water: New Stages of Performing Carr' *The Theatre of Marina Carr: Before Rules Was Made* eds C. Leeney & A. McMullan (Dublin: Carysfort Press, 2003): 94.

Ireland, the *patria* claiming urgent allegiance, has a claim now.[11]

These attitudes and prejudices are not only theoretical but have an impact on the theatre industry. An example of a theatre apparently rejecting an Irish play because it is not set in a kitchen and does not contain 'local color' happened in 2010-2011 here in the United States. It is a case of a theatre choosing notoriety and popularity rather than going for an excellent new play by a woman. Shattered Globe Theatre in Chicago was slated to present the American premiere of Elizabeth Kuti's award-winning play *The Sugar Wife*. In 2010, the theatre ran into difficulty; it reorganized and it opened its new season in January of 2011 with Martin McDonagh's *The Beauty Queen of Leenane*. Gone from its bill was Kuti's acclaimed play, the 2006 winner of the Susan Smith Blackburn Award for the best play in the English language by a woman. In its place was the violence and darkness of McDonagh's world set in a kitchen with a cantankerous mother and an eventually murderous daughter.

Further examples of the privileging of male writers can be seen in the treatment of Lady Gregory by literary and theatre scholars. Without Lady Gregory, there might never have been an Abbey Theatre. This fact is widely conceded, but it has the effect of positioning her as an administrator rather than as an artist. That is the crux of what has happened to Irish women dramatists from the time of Gregory. Scholar after scholar dismisses her work as slight, not important. How unjust. Gregory's plays are little jewels of style and theme. Her translation of Goldoni's *La Mirandolina* is a wonderful, lively piece of theatre which she fashioned to be done with Irish accents matching some of the other 'country' plays of the Abbey (*The Playboy of the Western World*, among them). This is the story that has prevailed until very recently. Many, many of the plays that have been written by Irish women since the time of Lady Gregory (whose work may well have been disregarded for other reasons, as well) have feminist leanings but, feminist or not, they are definitely woman-centred.

One definition of feminist theatre is theatre that 'works in some way to present positive images of women or to raise the status of women in the theatre.'[12] The plays explored in this essay most often present positive images of strong women.

Lay Up Your Ends, like Hartigan's *La Corbière*, reclaims women's

[11] Christopher Murray, *Twentieth Century Irish Drama: Mirror Up to Nation* (Manchester, Manchester University Press, 1997): 245-46.

[12] Lizbeth Goodman, qtd. Elaine Aston *An Introduction to Feminism and Theatre* (London: Routledge, 1995): 64.

history. Hartigan's piece recalls the deaths of a group of prostitutes discarded by the Nazis in war-occupied Jersey. From Headrick's conversations with Hartigan, it is clear that she would acknowledge the feminist slant of her play, but in the early days of Charabanc, the founding actresses shied away from using the term. Their goal was to be inclusive and they prided themselves at being able to play in all areas of Belfast and Northern Ireland. Labels can be limiting, so they distanced themselves from the term. *Lay Up Your Ends* speaks for itself with its message of female strength. Charabanc's work has been well-documented: how a group of struggling actresses banded together to create community-based work. Their first play, conceived with some assistance from Martin Lynch, was *Lay Up Your Ends*. In 1997, Headrick directed the American Premiere of this play at Oregon State University. One of the hallmarks of this early work is that the women played the men's roles: husbands and bosses. Although there is one male character, he had no lines (with the exception of one line at the carnival). This play is feminist, woman-centered. It reclaims women's history. The Charabanc actresses interviewed women, the 'grannies' who were involved in the 1912 strike in the linen mill. Although the strike was unsuccessful, the women were empowered to demand better working conditions in the mill.

Through a series of vignettes, we see their life stories and what they endure and strive to overcome. There is great humour in the play as we see these women bond in their fight against the rich mill owners. Belle is the leader of the group and in her central soliloquy of the play when she prepares to clean the body of a mill worker who has died of brown lung, she vents her anger at the rich mill owners living on the Malone Road who have big steak dinners compared to the women's meagre fare and her cry against the injustice rings out on the page and in the theatre.

Hélène Cixous has called on women to 'write themselves.'[13] This is exactly what the women of Charabanc did and continued to do throughout their existence. Not only did they write, they also performed. Their template of interviewing and work-shopping the stories became their normal way of developing scripts. With minimal properties and scenery, they toured all over the world.

Christina Reid's 1983 *Tea in a China Cup* relates the story of three generations of Belfast women. Beth is the central character and narrator of the play. Like *Heritage*, also a memory play by Nicola

---

[13] Hélène Cixous, 'The Laugh of the Medusa', trans. Keith & Paula Cohen. *Signs* 1:4 (Summer 1976): 875.

McCartney, the play is seen through Beth's eyes. Like *Heritage*, the characters in *Tea in a China Cup* transform themselves from pre-adolescent children into adults, and in one of the funniest scenes in contemporary writing, we see Beth and her childhood friend Theresa discussing what they know about sexuality. This scene can be compared to the one in Churchill's *Top Girls* but it has a vibrancy that the *Top Girls* scene lacks.[14]

Not only does Reid include the scene with Beth and Theresa, the scene between Beth and her mother as she tries to explain menstruation brings down the house. It is a little jewel of a 1950's time machine with the 'down there' talk between mothers and daughters. Wendy Wasserstein and Caryl Churchill have characters discuss menstrual blood, but neither of them achieves what Reid does in this play. Audiences howl in recognition of universal childhood ignorance about sex and bodily functions. The two scenes in Reid's play are clearly from the viewpoint of a woman. The world Reid creates is strikingly different from the more celebrated memory play, Brian Friel's *Dancing at Lughnasa*. In an earlier scene, we see Beth's mother go into labor as her own mother (Beth's grandmother) is frantically trying to organize her daughter to get her to the hospital. She advises her to 'hold your knees together.' These are pure moments of female recognition and humor. Because Friel is male and his memory voice is that of the male Michael the world of the women in *Lughnasa* is drastically different from the warm, humor-laden world of *Tea in a China Cup*. This is not to say that there is no tragedy in Reid's women's lives. Son Sammy dies at Dunkirk in World War II; Sarah, Beth's mother, is dying of cancer; Beth's marriage crumbles. Moments of genuine female experience, the 'sunshine and the shadow' are depicted on stage. Theresa has had a baby on her own and is bringing her up in London; and hers is a life of struggle, but it is a life she embraces and when Beth's marriage dissolves, Theresa has invited her to share her life.

Although there are a few male roles in *Tea in a China Cup*, they are secondary. In Morna Regan's *Midden,* there are no men, and just as in *Tea in a China Cup*, we meet three generations of women. And again the women struggle with all the complications of contemporary modern life, balancing home and family with career, and in this family one daughter has carved out a successful life in the USA.

Hannah Scolnicov in her book *Woman's Theatrical Space* quotes

---

[14] Headrick: I cannot tell you how shocked I was at a Kennedy Center/American College Theatre Festival to be watching a production of *Top Girls* and to see that the male director had omitted this scene.

William Blake who wrote that 'Time is Man, Woman is Space'. Scolnicov writes:

> As the idea took shape, I discovered that the analysis of the theatrical space reveals not only the general ideology of the play, but, more specifically, its attitude to the place of woman in society. It suddenly became evident that woman is so closely associated with space that almost any articulation of space on stage or in the play is directly expressive of her position, her life style, her personality. In other words, I did not start my investigation from a feminist position: that position was forced on me by the material.[15]

Midden is different from some of the other plays mentioned in this essay in that it occurs in a contained space. It is not free-ranging, with multiple locations like some of the other plays that also represent 'woman's space,' but *Midden* is like *Eclipsed* (with its laundry room and environs) in that it happens in another kind of woman's space, the kitchen.

Hannah in Kuti's *The Sugar Wife* wants a baby and she breaks the code to impregnate herself by Alfred. Sarah in Nicola McCartney's *Heritage* chooses her own path, ready to defy her family and her religion in order to be with Michael. In the play, she is the prime mover, pushing Michael to be as defiant as she is. Sister Virginia in *Eclipsed* questions the authority of the church; she is in contrast to Brigit who demands the keys and finally escapes from the involuntary servitude of the laundry. In the last scene of the play, we see that Sister Virginia has ultimately made the same break as Brigit.

If we judge these characters by the standard of second wave feminism, they would fall short, but by the 'tenets' of third wave feminism, they are individual women following their own paths. Wendy Wasserstein received criticism in some quarters because Heidi adopts a baby at the end of *The Heidi Chronicles*, but Wasserstein defended the character saying it was Heidi's story, the inference being that Wasserstein was not writing to suit someone else's agenda, that is, a strictly feminist one.

Even a character such as Kate in Teresa Deevy's *Wife to James Whelan,* written in 1942, states that she won't marry Whelan because she realizes they won't suit: 'If you and I were a bit different ...' (Act II)

Jennifer Johnston's one-woman play *Twinkletoes* tells the story of Karen who has married Declan, an imprisoned IRA terrorist. Inspired by her work in prisons, Johnston's play is clearly influenced by real life

---

[15] Hanna Scolnikov, *Women's Theatrical Space* (Cambridge: Cambridge University Press, 1994): xiii.

stories. There are no easy answers for Karen; she has taken her marriage vows seriously and yet she longs for another child. If she divorced Declan, she would be shunned by the community. If she has an affair, someone will tell Declan. Yet, Karen endures, trying to keep her life together.

Some scholars use the terms feminist and woman-centred interchangeably. Many of the dramatists we discuss below shy away from the term 'feminist,' but given the choice, many would embrace the term 'woman-centred.' Feminist critics, among them Elaine Aston and Dolores Ringer define women-centred drama as that which has women as central characters, telling their own stories; women's issues are centre stage. (Our thanks to Kryn Freehling-Burton of the Oregon State University Women's Studies program for her advice on this definition.)

Delores Ringer, especially, cites a number of dramaturgical and theatrical approaches by women playwrights that, arguably, comprise the alternative aesthetic referenced earlier. These include:

1) Plays that intervene 'in the patriarchal production of meanings.'[16] Often these plays do not follow an orderly, linear (read 'male') plot line. Many are circular, such as *Heritage*, or episodic such as *Tea in a China Cup* and *Eclipsed*; there is no traditional 'hero's journey' sense of closure. Many are open-ended.

2) Many plays that incorporate 'explicit or implicit messages about power in gender relations.' (299) In *Heritage*, Sarah continues to see Michael although her father has forbidden her to do so, even going so far as to beat her when she defies him.

3) Plays that frequently 'de-objectify female characters [whose] mental and physical struggles and growth are at the sense of [the] drama.' (300) Beth is the prime mover and central character in *Tea in a China Cup*; the play is her story. The same is true for Gemma O'Connor's *SigNora Joyce*; it is not Joyce's story, but Nora's that is told. In *Heritage*, Sarah faces the audience and says that she will tell us *her* story.

4) Plays that make the 'assertion that women's personal experience is not trivial, is at least as valuable as public experience [;] inner 'psychological' conflicts and outer 'social' conflicts walk together, and equally, on stage.' (301) Brogan reclaims lost women's history in her account of the conditions in the Magdalene Laundries. (Most of the journalistic and subsequent artistic treatments of the scandal may be traced to Brogan's play.)

5) Plays that 'use the trivial and ordinary details of women's lives as the material.' (302) Christina Reid's depiction in *Tea in a China*

---

[16] Dolores Ringer, 'Re-Visioning Scenography: A Feminist's Approach to Design for the Theatre' *Theatre and Feminist Aesthetics* eds Karen Laughlin and Cather Schuler (Madison, NJ: Fairleigh Dickinson University Press, 1995): 299.

Cup, of the lack of sex education and the myths that Teresa and Beth pass on to each other, full of misinformation, are celebrations of girlhood bonding.

6) Plays that 'eliminate altogether the artificial division between emotion and thought.' (302) Without using a graphic sex scene in *Heritage*, Nicola McCartney's Sarah poetically evokes her love making with Michael. The scene in which her father beats her must be done as a kind of dance in the staging. When Headrick directed this play, in consultation with the dramatist, McCartney agreed that the scene demanded stylization. In the 2006 production of the play at the University of Central Oklahoma, three reviewers all mentioned how powerful the scene was. While Sarah is being beaten, she shares her emotion with the audience. She is both inside the beating and outside of it.

7) Plays that create 'inclusive rather than exclusive community groups ... as representations on the stage, and in their relationship to the audience ... to eliminate the physical and psychic barriers between the actors and the audience.' (304) *Lay Up Your Ends*, *SigNora Joyce*, Kuti's *The Sugar Wife*, and *Tea in a China Cup* all employ direct address to the audience, forming an intimate bond between characters and audience. Belle in *Lay Up Your Ends* lets her rage about a mill worker unjustly dying of brown lung disease spill directly into the audience. Alone, on stage, she attacks how unfair life is for the mill workers in 1911 Belfast.

8) Dramatists who assert that 'a single point of focus might not always be necessary ... the focus might be shifting, multiple, or diffused.' (305) Although Brigit is the central character in *Eclipsed* (some might argue it is Sister Virginia's story), every one of the 'Maggies' shares her individual story from confused Mandy to abused Nellie-Nora.

9) Plays that exhibit 'the tendency to evoke fragmented lives and world ... and represent them like a patchwork.' (305) Certainly in *Tea in a China Cup*, Beth's story fits this description; each scene depicts another episode in her life and that of her family in a roughly chronological pattern but it is dependent on glimpses into Beth's life through her eyes. This pattern is also apparent in *Eclipsed*; each scene is named and each scene tells another piece of the story (each episode like a square in the quilt) of the Magdalens and by the end, that story is very nuanced.

10) Plays in which the characters 'rarely transcend their contexts; more frequently they grapple with and attempt to reorder the ordinary activities of everyday life.' (309) Sarah in *Heritage* struggles to make sense of her love for Michael as it breaks the boundaries of her heritage and religious background. The day-to-day activities of life in early 20th Century Canada for these Northern Irish settlers are glimpsed through Sarah's eyes. Sarah longs to leave this life behind and start over with Michael in Toronto, but in the end her dream is not fulfilled.

11) Plays that break 'down the boundaries between art and life [and utilize] mixtures of forms, styles and genres.' (310) *Tea in a*

China Cup and *Heritage* mix realism with high theatricality in the
direct address to the audience. The poetic interludes in language
add another element into the blend. As Old Magda in Kuti's
Treehouses remembers her past, it comes alive on the stage. In her
award-winning *The Sugar Wife*, Kuti's Hannah speaks her internal
thoughts out loud using the device of the Quaker meeting to
facilitate these words. Hartigan's *La Corbiere* is an abstract
composition, employing a rush of images and sounds to tell the
story. One production of the play was performed in a swimming
pool.

12) Plays in which 'meaning emerges from the collision of
characters, contexts, and images rather than the sustained
unraveling of a plot.' (310) In Jennifer Johnston's one-woman play
Twinkletoes, Karen's monologue introduces us to a variety of
people: husband, daughter, son-in-law, dancing partner, father,
mother and others. The chaos of her life as an IRA wife is slowly
exposed to us through her direct address to the audience.

13) Plays that have as their objective 'transformation rather than
self-recognition.' (311) At the conclusion of *Eclipsed*, Brigit wrests
away the key from Sister Virginia and escapes the Laundry.
Whether she finds her John-Joe or not, we don't know. The play is
book-ended by the aged Nellie-Nora speaking to the young woman
in search of her birth mother. The audience is transformed by
Brigit's escape and we cheer her transformation. She refuses to be
a victim; she becomes a woman of action. And Sister Virginia is
equally transformed, as she leaves the convent to reveal the story
of the Magdalenes (Burke Brogan's own story).

14) Plays that are 'indicative of those who have been socialized to
be the watcher and the watched at the same time.' (313) As Beth
tells her story to us, she both participates in the story and
transforms herself into her younger self, listening to the
admonitions of her mother, grandmother, and aunt. In the scenes
where she describes the time prior to her birth, she watches the
action as the scenes enacted on stage. She says that her head is full
of other people's memories. As the play closes, she whistles a tune
that suggests an abandonment of her old life and the beginning of
a new one.

15) Plays that 'envision the audience as female ... disregarding the
male audience.' (312) These dramas play to all audiences but the
stories are women's stories. The woman is central in every play.
Men may play important roles but the women are those with the
agency. Although the wildcat strike is thwarted in *Lay Up Your
Ends*, the women are empowered; at the ending of the play we see
them touching their hair, defying one of the mill rules for the first
time. They have taken a risk and are stronger for it. Like Brogan
with *Eclipsed*, Charabanc recovered another piece of 'lost' women's
history in their depiction of the strike. The same is true of
Hartigan's *La Corbière*, which takes a footnote from history and in
an abstract, poetic, rhythmic text embodies the story of the
drowned prostitutes.

Other examples of a women-centred aesthetic may be mentioned. One is the use of very simple settings. These are often non-realistic and very suggestive. Charabanc toured *Lay Up Your Ends* using a clutch of beer cases and a few placards. *Eclipsed* can be staged in an elaborate recreation of a Magdalene Laundry but Brogan prefers the use of fewer and more evocative scenic elements. Several plays range over many years and locations and eschew elaborate scenery and costumes.

Teresa Deevy's *Katie Roche* and *The King of Spain's Daughter* deal with women's stories that are, coincidentally, also men's stories. Jonathan Mandell quotes Sarah Schulman in a *New York Times* article,

> Ms. Schulman believes that the worst consequence of theater-as-marketing is that there are plenty of good, vibrant plays with authentic characters written by playwrights who are not in the mainstream but are being kept out by the commercial theater establishment. "In New York City, you can see a bad play by a white man every night of the week," she said. "Why are there so few plays by anybody else? It is a profoundly discriminatory system."[17]

It is a profoundly discriminatory system in the United States but also in Ireland, and although a great deal of progress has occurred in both countries, there remains a good deal more work to be done.

Women dramatists have not been given their due. A reviewer of plays in the 1980s for the Abbey commented that several plays came across her desk that she considered stage-worthy, well-written plays, only to have the men reject them, citing implausible characters. This statement returns us to the whore/Magdalene/homemaker representations. If a play doesn't take place in a kitchen or a pub and is not centred on a gathering of men, save for the one hard-working kitchen slave, it seems it has no place on the Irish stage.

And, because these plays have failed to be anthologized (Cathy Leeney's *Seen and Heard* being the one exception; at last count, it was in its third printing), directors and students don't know about them. Editors know about Brian Friel and *Dancing at Lughnasa*, but community theatres and universities should be producing Christina Reid's gem of a play, *Tea in a China Cup* rather than *Lughnasa*. However, the track record speaks for itself. *Lughnasa* premiered at the Abbey, made its way to London, then travelled to New York and international stages; it is anthologized, published, and every college and university theatre wants to do the play because of the number of women

---

[17] Jonathan Mandell, 'When She Wrote, the Dross of Her Life Became Gold' *New York Times* 20 January 2002.

in the cast.

Irish women do write plays and they write very good plays, but because so many theatres are administered by men, (or at least by many who have a dated and inadequate image of Irish women) these plays are often overlooked. The Abbey has a dismal record of producing plays by women on the main stage. The record in the Peacock is only marginally better. In a 2011 article in *The Irish Times*, critic Sara Keating notes that Irish female playwrights have 'traditionally been under represented' and points to the 1992 and 1993 Glasshouse Productions two-part festival staged at the Project Arts Centre titled, 'There are no Irish Women Playwrights'.[18] Keating notes that there were two objectives driving the decision to stage works by Lady Gregory and Teresa Deevy and to showcase emerging dramatists. Keating cites the program for the event which stated that there 'are women playwrights in Ireland, it is just that they get neither the critical attention nor their historical due.' She goes on to argue that the festival could just as easily be staged today because Irish women playwrights continue to be under-represented in Irish theatre. She charts some of the high points: in the 1990s plays by Emma Donoghue placed female sexuality on the Irish stage in a significant way, while Dolores Walshe refracted the gaze outside of Ireland with plays set in South Africa and California. Hilary Fannin's *Doldrum Bay* and Stella Feehily's *Duck*, both premiering in 2003, made a significant critical impact, while Elaine Murphy's *Little Gem* continues to tour internationally following its premiere at the Dublin Fringe Festival in 2008. There are dozens more names that could be added to the list.

However, the work of these writers, like the work of pioneers such as Gregory and Deevy before them, remains largely on the fringes of Irish theatrical discourse. Why? Is it because they provide a more individual, personal engagement with Ireland than the largely patriarchal canon, which is for the most part defined by its interrogation of the state? Or, as has been suggested, because the 'private' discourse of the novel is less intimidating for women than the 'public' space of the theatre is? There appears to be no easy answer, but the reality of their under-representation remains.

In the persistence of Irish women dramatists we see the truth in Peter Barnes's *Red Noses*. At one point in the play, a character dressed in women's clothing decides he is much better off as a woman because

---

[18] Sara Keating, 'Female Voices Finally Finding a Stage' *The Irish Times* 2 March 2011.

'Men break, we women endure.'[19] Although there are many Irish women dramatists who have endured, the two best known of contemporary dramatists are Marina Carr and Marie Jones. One would be hard pressed to describe Carr's work as feminist although they are often woman-centred and in many cases, women 'crumble' through suicide (*By the Bog of Cats* and *The Mai*) or violent attack (*On Raferty's Hill*). The fate of Hester and the Mai, both a consequence of rejection by a man in their lives, and the brutal rape at the end of Act I of *Raftery's Hill*, position Carr in the world of Martin McDonagh. Both Hester and the Mai ultimately determine their fate by their suicides but there is little light at the end of either play. Plays do not have to have a fairy-tale ending to celebrate women, and the harshness of Carr's heroines often repels, but there is no doubt that we are fascinated by Hester's ferocity and single-minded desire for revenge.

As for Marie Jones, her best-known work, *Stones in his Pockets*, has two male actor/protagonists who portray numerous roles (of both genders) and the presence of the smart Hollywood starlet could be seen as a feminist note within the play. Jones's early works with Charabanc are distinctly woman-centred, ranging from such plays as *Lay Up Your Ends*, *The Hamster Wheel* and *Somewhere Over the Balcony*. In *The Hamster Wheel*, Jones explores what happens to a working class family when the male bread-winner is injured. The women of the family rise to the occasion and carry on in Belfast, in a traditional culture ordinarily based around the working father and the homemaker mother. In this play, the 'normal' life of the family is up-ended and new ways of coping are found.

Edwin Wilson and Alvin Goldfarb in their theatre history text *Living Theatre* feature one of the 'debates in theatre history' which is 'Are Women's Contributions to Theatre History Overlooked?' They point out that feminist historians 'argue that significant female innovators in theatre history are frequently overlooked.'[20] They even question if their own writing of theatre history is unbalanced. We are not alone in our examination of the marginalization of Irish women dramatists.

So, despite the lack of productions and publications, despite the lack of critical attention, and despite the general lack of awareness about the contributions of Irish women to the development of drama, we are encouraged by the recent article in the *Irish Times* about the new work of women dramatists and the mention of some of their predecessors.

---

[19] Peter Barnes, *Red Noses* (London: Faber & Faber, 1985): 43.
[20] Edwin Wilson & Alvin Goldfarb, *Living Theatre* (Boston: McGraw-Hill, 2008): 402.

George Heslin and his First Irish Theatre Festival in New York have made a huge commitment to featuring work by Irish women dramatists. He and the staff he works with have for the past few years of the festival featured plays by women: Paula Meehan, Morna Regan, Teresa Deevy, and others. Jo Catell and Paula Nance with the Festival worked to feature even more Irish women dramatists in the 2011 event.

Attention must be paid to these plays and dramatists. These plays and many more tell the stories of several varieties of Irish women; the plays need to be anthologized so that they can reach a wider audience. The plays need to be produced. Whether the writers we have mentioned are first, second, or third wave feminist or belong to the category 'post-feminist,' their work demands that we read them, direct them, and experience their power.

Bibliography

Aston, Elaine, *An Introduction to Feminism and Theatre* (London: Routledge, 1995).

Barnes, Peter, *Red Noses* (London: Faber and Faber, 1985).

Bolger, Dermot, ed., *Druids, Dudes and Beauty Queens: The Changing Face of Irish Theatre* (Dublin: New Island, 2001).

Bradley, Anthony and Maryann Gialanella Valiulis, eds, *Gender and Sexuality in Modern Ireland* (Amherst: University of Massachusetts Press, 1997).

Cixous, Helene, 'The Laugh of the Medusa,' trans. Keith Cohen and Paula Cohen, *Signs*, 1, 4 (Summer 1976: 875-93).

Deevy, Teresa, 'Wife to James Whelan: A Play in Three Acts', *Irish University Review: A Journal of Irish Studies*, Vol 25, no. 1, Spring/Summer, 1995: 29-87.

Grant, David, 'Introduction', *The Crack in the Emerald: New Irish Plays* (London: Nick Hern Books, 1990).

Harrington, John, Ed. *Modern and Contemporary Irish Drama*. 2nd ed. (New York: W. W. Norton, 2009).

Jordan, Eamonn, *Theatre Stuff: Critical Essays on Contemporary Irish Theatre* (Dublin: Carysfort Press, 2000).

Keating, Sara, 'Female Voices finally finding a stage' *Irish Times* 2 March 2011 in IrishTimes.com, 14 March 2011.

Leeney, Cathy, 'Ireland's 'Exiled' Women Playwrights: Teresa Deevy and Marina Carr,' in Richards, Shaun, ed., *Twentieth Century Irish Drama* (Cambridge: Cambridge University Press, 2004).

---, ed., *Seen and Heard: Six New Plays by Irish Women* (Dublin: Carysfort Press, 2001).

Llewellyn-Jones, Margaret, *Contemporary Irish Drama* (Bristol: Intellect, Ltd., 2002).

Lonergan, Patrick, *Theatre and Globalization: Irish Drama in the Celtic Tiger Era* (Basingstoke,: Palgrave Macmillan, 2010).

Lynch, Martin and Charabanc Theatre Company, *Lay Up Your Ends* (Belfast: Lagan Press, 2008).

McDonough, Carla J., "I've Never Been Just Me': Rethinking Women's
    Positions in the Plays of Christina Reid,' *A Century of Irish Drama:
    Widening The Stage*, eds Stephen Watt et.al. (Bloomington: Indiana
    University Press, 2000).

McMullan, Anna and Caroline Williams, 'Contemporary Women Playwrights,'
    The Field Day Anthology of Irish Writing Vol. V: *Irish Women's Writing
    and Traditions*, ed. Angela Bourke et al. (Cork: Cork University Press,
    2002).

---, 'Gender, Authorship and Performance in Selected Plays by Contemporary
    Irish Women Playwrights: Mary Elizabeth Burke-Kennedy, Marie Jones,
    Marina Carr, Emma Donoghue' *Theatre Stuff: Critical Essays on
    Contemporary Irish Theatre*, ed. Eamonn Jordan (Dublin: Carysfort Press,
    2000).

Mandell, Jonathan, 'When She Wrote, the Dross of Her Life Became Gold', *New
    York Times,* 20 January 2002.

Murray, Christopher, *Twentieth-Century Irish Drama: Mirror Up To Nation*
    (Manchester: Manchester University Press, 1997).

Owen, Coilin and Joan S. Radner, eds *Irish Drama: 1900-1980* (Washington,
    D.D.: The Catholic University of American Press, 1990).

Richards, Shaun, ed., *Twentieth Century Irish Drama* (Cambridge: Cambridge
    University Press, 2004).

Ringer, Delores, 'Re-Visioning Scenography: A Feminist's Approach to Design
    for the Theatre' *Theatre and Feminist Aesthetics* ed. Karen Laughlin and
    Cather Schuler (Madison, NJ: Fairleigh Dickinson University Press, 1995):
    299-315.

Roche, Anthony, *Contemporary Irish Drama*. 2nd ed. (Basingstoke,: Palgrave
    Macmillan, 2009).

Scolnicov, Hanna, *Woman's Theatrical Space* (Cambridge: Cambridge
    University Press. 1994).

Singleton, Brian, *Masculinities and the Contemporary Irish Theatre*
    (Basingstoke: Palgrave Macmillan, 2011).

Trotter, Mary, 'Translating Women into Irish Theatre History,' *A Century of
    Irish Drama: Widening The Stage*, eds Stephen Watt et al. (Bloomington:
    Indiana University Press, 2000).

Vogel, Paula, in 'Paula Vogel' in *Women Who Write Plays: Interviews with
    American Dramatists*, ed. Alexis Greene (Hanover, NH: Smith and Kraus,
    Inc., 2001): 425-48.

Watt, Stephen, Eileen Morgan, and Shakir Mustafa, eds, *A Century of Irish
    Drama: Widening The Stage* (Bloomington: Indiana University Press,
    2000).

Wilson, Edwin and Alvin Goldfarb, *Living Theatre: History of the Theatre*
    (Boston: McGraw-Hill, 2008).

5 | Myth and Gender in Irish Drama

Tom Maguire and Carole-Anne Upton

Much of the critical discussion of the history of gender in Irish theatre has been engaged in a twin project of restoration and restitution: restoration of women's contribution to the history of the Irish stage; and relatedly, a restitution of agency to real women for the discrimination which had silenced their historical counterparts. Sihra's approach in summarizing her edited collection is typical: 'This book explores the rich legacy of Irish women playwrights over the course of the twentieth century, ultimately challenging the notion that Irish drama is primarily a site of male authorship and authority' (11). In this essay, we aim to examine the deployment of specific dramaturgical and performance strategies to renegotiate the representation of the female on the Irish stage. We focus on two productions in which Irish mythology, in this case stories from the Ulster cycle, were reworked to contest dominant discourses around gender: Big Telly's *The Pursuit of Diarmuid and Grainne* (1999) and Storytellers' Theatre production of Mary-Elizabeth Burke-Kennedy's *Women-in-Arms* (1988).

While noting that each of the plays was produced in a context in which women were the lead artists, our concern here is with staging strategies, as we question the extent to which formalist dramaturgical innovations on the stage might either disrupt spectatorial responses or challenge wider political discourses. The context for the present discussion consists of a pedagogic project in which students were invited to participate in a production by staff and students at the University of Ulster of *Women-in-Arms* at the Studio Theatre of the Millennium Forum in Derry in 2005. Although the work was explicitly embedded in the academic study of deconstructionist feminist theatre practices, our finding was that the students and indeed audiences repeatedly reconstructed the mythic narrative in accordance with dominant patriarchal principles. As we discuss below, this tendency to sublimate the feminist revisionist strategies was evident in rehearsal choices, in discussion, and in the reception of performance itself, where, at its simplest, a strong desire to recognize and celebrate the familiar 'traditional' versions of hegemonic myths seemed to lead to a general reluctance to engage with the deviant potential of a feminist reinscription.

Myth has two crucial functions in relation to groups or communities: to maintain and develop collective identity. According to Kearney, these two aspects may be considered to be in tension, which he characterizes in the contradictions between ideological and utopian myths:

> Ideology refers to that complex of myths and images which serve to maintain the status quo; utopia refers to the deployment of myths and images to challenge and transform the status quo. Utopia can accordingly be equated with that unconquered power of imagination, that surplus of symbolic desire which resists the closure of ideology. Utopia has to remain critical, lest it congeal into a new ideology subordinating the catalysing power of dream to the literal demands of propaganda (123).

Given this tension, myth would appear a fruitful area through which playwrights might seek to reimagine social relations by challenging dominant ideological constructions. Marvin Carlson, for example, has observed that:

> The three great grounding theoretical texts for the world's drama, both East and West – Bharata's *Natyasastra*, Aristotle's *Poetics*, and Zeami's writings on the Noh – [...] consider the superior and more significant drama to be that in which the material is already familiar to the audience, drawn from a shared body of historic, legendary, and mythic material treating heroes, kings and gods. (18).

He suggests that one reason for the superiority of pre-existing narratives is that the focus shifts in the audience from the remote subject of the narrative itself to the manner of its articulation in the here and now of performance. Kearney's formulation of utopian myth suggests a similar potential, since this form of myth

> alienates us from the inherited state of affairs and engages in the imagining of an alternative community, other ways of seeing and existing. This commitment to radical otherness sometimes produces an experience of 'uncanniness'. While mythology generally provides us with what is most familiar, utopian myth re-presents stories in an unfamiliar guise, with a twist in the tail, a shock of alterity at the heart of the habitual (123).

Such an attempt at a utopian use of myth is particularly apparent in the appropriation by Irish theatre makers of mythic narratives as a means to engage with contemporary reality, since the distance that they have from immediate circumstances should lend itself to a reassessment of both the immediate context and the source myths themselves (Maguire). This is apparent in the significant appropriation by Irish theatre makers of classical Greek mythology in recent decades, quite often as a tool to explore the Northern Irish conflict (McDonald and Walton), for example. While direct knowledge of Irish mythology may be scant within the population, particularly in Northern Ireland, its dominant forms of representation have reflected and reinforced specifically gendered structures of Irish identity. The identity of the island itself and thence its sovereignty has variously been represented mythologically as female. While this has its roots in a pre-colonial Gaelic tradition, as Mac Cana (1980) notes, the impact of colonialism and the response to it amplified this gendering of national identity in ways that have continued to resonate. According to Walter:

> In the nineteenth century ... the Irish were racialized in two distinct ways, each strongly gendered. Masculine images were of uncontrolled subhumans incapable of self-government. Feminine images were of weakness requiring protection. Both representations justified continued British rule whilst bolstering images of the ruling centre as the antithesis of these negative characteristics (81).

Of course, as Kearney (1985) noted, Irish nationalist discourses have been complicit in such gendering of national identity also insofar as Ireland has been figured variously as female: Mother Ireland, Cathleen Ní Houlihan, Róisín Dubh, or The Shan Van Vocht (Sean Bhean Bhocht), for example. Elsewhere, Kearney identifies how this depiction of Ireland as motherland was reinforced in the late nineteenth century by 'the counter-reformational cult of the Virgin Mary ... Indeed, it is interesting how elements in the Irish hierarchy - which offered women no real power - increasingly came to equate Ireland with a virginal motherland best served by safeguarding the native purity or 'faith and morals' against the threat of alien culture' (119). Discourses of gender and national identity can therefore be seen as having been intertwined historically (Dowler).

These discourses have continued to be operational in the ways in which the social and political roles of women on each side of the border are both circumscribed and contested. Mahon's 1996 essay, tracing the negative effects of the Catholic Church's role on women's rights in

Ireland, drew together ample evidence that women continued to be unfavourably treated in every aspect of Irish life at the end of the twentieth century. The *Gender Inequality in Northern Ireland* report for the Northern Ireland Assembly in 2002 was able to point to improvements in women's positions in the North, while identifying key areas where inequality persisted, including levels of economic activity, pay, positions of power and as victims of abuse and violence. Likewise, in the Republic, a report to the United Nations in 2004 identified where legal and policy initiatives had had a significant impact on reducing gender inequality in the previous ten years. It noted, nonetheless, a pay gap of 15% per hour and a highly segregated labour market; and the low rates of women in positions of political power, despite the election of two women successively to the office of President. In 2010, the European Court of Human Rights ruled that Ireland's constitutional ban on abortion continued to violate women's rights.

In addition to the gendering of Irish identity and Irish life, Irish nationalism has also drawn readily on Irish mythology for its foundational narratives in what Hanafin has characterized as 'an example of recourse to myth in order to compensate for colonial domination' (251). Despite the prominence of actual women within the revivalist movements, the source myths were sanitized rapidly so that they could be accommodated within very limited tropes of Irish womanhood that saw a woman's place within the home as the 'bearers and cultural reproducers of the ... nation' (Quinn 41). Much has already been written about the ways in which very specific versions of Irish womanhood were institutionalized in the new state following partition and subsequently within the 1937 constitution (Daly; Shannon).

The potential of such myths within artistic representation can be seen in their use by women in the vanguard of the nationalist revival exemplified in the tableaux vivants of Inghinidhe na hÉireann, Augusta Gregory's playscript *Grania* (1910) and Eva Gore-Booth's *The Buried Life of Deirdre*. However, Quinn (1997) is one of a number of scholars who have traced the tensions that such representations provoked, demonstrating, for example, how the split of the Inghinidhe from the Irish National Theatre Society over the staging of *In The Shadow of The Glen* illustrates a vigorous debate over the relationship between real women and the iconography of the stage. As Trotter notes, the limitations of the tropes of womanhood that emerged from the early use of such myths have exercised a dominance within Irish theatre that can be traced to the present day:

The nationalist dramatic tradition was founded on the premise that this tradition would seek to rid the theatre of the stage Irishman, but far less attention was paid to rewriting the long-suffering mother figure or the idealized Colleen. And from Yeats' and Gregory's *Kathleen ni Houlihan* (1902) to McDonagh's virgin/whore 'Girleen' in *The Lonesome West* (1997), Irish female characters have embodied the nation, the land, the desire or responsibilities of male characters, but rarely have they been authentic, complex, autonomous women. (Trotter 164)

This echoes the observations of Margaret Llewellyn Jones, in her study of contemporary Irish drama who noted, 'the persistence of cultural battles round the stereotypical Madonna, Magdalene and Matriarch, which conflate the ideals of Catholicism and Nationalism' (75). Rolston's taxonomy of female figures within novels concerned with the Northern Ireland conflict adds two further categories which can be seen on the stage too: 'unmotherly mothers' and the violent woman or 'woman as villain'. These further define the familiar tropes of unnatural women denying, or defying, definition according to biological function. 'Unmotherly mothers' operate as seductive influences drawing others into the violence: 'They are often older women, often grandmothers. Deprived now of what is supposedly their only real reason for existence they become cranky. Aged, asexual, unfeminine, they can become purveyors of violence against their previous natural instincts' (409). 'Violent women' reject the role of motherhood for an engagement with violence expressed as an emotional force. However, 'having abandoned their natural vocation of motherhood, they can never be real 'terrorists' like men. (411-12). Elsewhere, Maguire has added a further type to this typology of female characters, the Penelope-figures who 'remain behind loyally awaiting the return of their absent husbands, essentially passive victims, brides awaiting fulfilment through the love of the right man' (105).

Such a narrow typification of female stage figures, of course, is not a specifically Irish phenomenon. Throughout Western European theatre, dominant patriarchal discourses have produced a narrow range of character types within which many roles for women both onstage (and off) have been configured. Jane de Gay (2003) identifies two tropes of female representation in classical mythic drama, namely Victim and Villain, where a third category, that of Visionary (Cassandra), often combines the passive and fearsome aspects of the first two. So, often dramatic material with its origins elsewhere has merely reinforced the limited roles for and representations of women when it has been produced on the Irish stage.

So it is that while it is possible to demonstrate that the position of women in contemporary Irish society is considerably different to the conditions of women at the first part of the twentieth century (Coulter; Daly), Irish theatre-makers and critics remain concerned with the representation of women. This concern has been focused particularly on issues of form. For example, arguing in defence of realism as a performance strategy for Irish feminist theatre, Esther Beth Sullivan proposes a liberal model for the reinscription of women's (largely domestic) lived experience into Irish history, as an alternative to the once radical poetics of Brechtian alienation which had by that point come to occupy the centre-ground of feminist theatre practice. She identifies the absence of realism from the Irish dramatic tradition as having sidelined women's lived experience in favour of essentialist archetypes: '[B]oth myth and Modernity have formalized 'Woman' to such a degree that many Irish women desire to be seen in their 'quotidian' best" (Sullivan 224).

We turn now, then, to the two case studies, to examine how these concerns with form have played out in practice. Mary-Elizabeth Burke-Kennedy's *Women-in-Arms* was first commissioned by Cork Theatre Company in 1984 and a revised version was presented at the Dublin Theatre Festival in 1988 by Storytellers' Theatre Company. It was revived for a tour in 2002 in a joint production between Storytellers and Cork Opera House. The script was one of six plays by Irish women collected in 2001 as *Seen and Heard,* an anthology remarkable for its uniqueness in Ireland in publishing plays by women. It uses a non-naturalistic idiom to stage four myths from The Ulster Cycle, with just seven actors who play multiple roles and also represent both landscape and thematic motifs in the kind of Poor Theatre that relies heavily on the physicality of performance. The stories of the four women: Nessa, Macha, Deirdre and Maeve are retold in a deliberate attempt to refocus the narrative perspective of the myths towards that of the women.

Big Telly Theatre Company was founded in June 1987 by Zoe Seaton and Jill Holmes. While founded and run by women, the company has never espoused an overtly feminist perspective, with its ideological outlook extending only as far as 'the performance of non-racist, non-sexist work with a distinctly local emphasis' (Meany 34). However, it has produced three stage versions of Celtic myths, the second of which *The Pursuit of Diarmuid and Gráinne* toured nationally in 1999. The myth was staged using only four actors, augmented by the use of puppetry and masks. Debra Salem provided an electronic dance beat soundtrack and the stage was dominated by a geodesic dome climbing-frame that, serving for a wide range of fictional locales, ensured that the production eschewed any naturalistic idiom.

Both productions then exemplified the very turn to 'Brechtian' modes of performance against which Sullivan argues, as mentioned above. Both employed episodic structures; narration; direct audience address; multiple role-playing; and an ensemble style of performance. Burke-Kennedy notes in an afterword to the published script that, she 'looked for a fresh theatrical idiom in which to present them, free from the shackles of naturalism, poetic drama, or pageant' (47). Each production can be read as producing both a celebration and an expansion of the dimensions of femininity. While Macha in *Women-in-Arms* can be seen as a repetition of the traditional mythic role of mother, the curse that she unleashes on the men of Ulster for forcing her to race and then give birth before the assembled throng attests to a potency that resists ideas of passivity. Maeve and Nessa demonstrate the capacity to act as cunningly strategic and effective leaders, with Maeve's husband Ailill able to remain in the background due to her capacity to inspire and lead her army. Deirdre's position as the faithful lover might not be regarded as an extension of the mythic type, yet in Burke-Kennedy's realization of this role, she is much more than an embodied trope for the psychological projections of a masculine hero. She has already taken flight from Conchobar's fortress when she encounters Naoise, for example, demonstrating a degree of agency. Similarly, in *The Pursuit of Diarmuid and Gráinne*, Gráinne is more multi-dimensional and active than dominant mythic discourses of femininity allow for.

A crucial aspect of this is in the ways in which these female figures are spatially liberated. Massey, for example, has identified the ways in which the spatial confinement of women has been a hallmark of patriarchal discourses, such that women's agency and activities have been limited to the domestic sphere and the importance of that space has in turn been denigrated. In Ireland it was only in the 1970s, for example, that the legal ban on the employment of married women in the Civil Service (which applied on each side of the border) was removed. Massey notes that, 'Many women have had to leave home precisely in order to forge their own version of their identities' (11). It remains the case that a huge number of women seeking an abortion travel to the United Kingdom to avoid the constraints of both the Northern Irish and Republic's legal systems. The legal control exercised by the Republic's government over access to contraception and family planning persisted into the 1980s. Notably, the much freer availability of condoms on the northern side of the border allowed the contravention of the law for those mobile enough to access it. The action of feminists in May 1971 who travelled by train from Dublin to Belfast, returning laden with contraceptives highlighted the illogicality of the law. Cleary has noted too the ways in which the spatial restriction of women is articulated in and reinforced by dominant fictional forms. Masculine forms are action-orientated and 'assume 'open' spaces and dynamic heroes'; while feminine forms (family tragedy and domestic tragedy) 'operate within a more enclosed and immobilized environment where the characters tend to be acted upon' (Cleary 521). He demonstrates convincingly how pervasive these forms are throughout Irish drama dealing with the Troubles.

It is a crucial marker of each of the narratives represented here that the women are mobile and that through their movement undertake a journey of self-definition. Gráinne is defying the constraints of acting as a dutiful daughter in choosing the man that she will love. To be herself, she cannot exist under Fionn's roof and must flee. Likewise, Conchobar has kept Deirdre in seclusion, firstly as her guardian, then as he grooms her to be his woman. While the landscape of his kingdom is an open playground for her as a child, as a woman, she is to be corralled. Fleeing with Naoise is Deirdre's only option. Nessa is forced from the seclusion of her cloister by its destruction and it is through the hunt for the murderers of her tutors that she learns the art of soldiering and the strength and resolve to follow the logic of Cathbad's prophecy. When she returns to Fergus's court, it is she who manipulates the structures of power, deciding ultimately on the building of the fortress of Eamhain Macha and its three distinct houses. For Macha, in this version, her arrival at the house of Cruinnic is at the end of a journey the details of which are unrevealed. It is a journey, however, that she decides has ended in settling with Cruinnic and his sons. Maeve's sovereignty is defined by the decision to avenge the slight she has received when the owner of the Dun Bó Cuailinge refuses to sell the bull to her. This requires her to mount a campaign against Ulster, Fergus leading them astray until eventually they find and retrieve the bull, at a huge cost in human lives. Each of the female figures here refused to be subordinated and domesticated.

Such a reconfiguration is more than an inflection of, or contemporary gloss on, the mythic narratives. Instead, it is a restaging of the female as subject and agent within the drama. It is accompanied too by the deployment of deconstructive strategies in both the dramaturgy and the staging. As Case has argued:

 With the deconstruction of the forms of representation, and

dialogue and modes of perception characteristic of patriarchal culture, the stage can be prepared for the entrance of the female subject, whose voice, sexuality and image have yet to be dramatized within the dominant culture. (cited Goodman with de Gay 147)

One key strategy adopted in both productions is the foregrounding of identity more broadly, and gender specifically, as a construct. Rather than the actors disappearing behind the fiction of character, here characterization is seen as the putting on of roles. Within both performances, actors take on multiple roles, switching identity rapidly, sometimes through a change of voice or posture, at other points through the ways in which specific props or item of costume is deployed. Playing across gender also foregrounds the extent to which gender can be regarded as something that you do, rather than something that you are. In *The Pursuit of Diarmuid and Gráinne*, the use of puppets and masks, further emphasizes this plasticity of gender and identity. Sustaining this representation involves the actors in a kind of triple presence as actor, teller and character, marking the virtuosity of the performance. This can be a deep source of spectatorial pleasure through which the apparent disintegration and discontinuity of character is juxtaposed with the assured performance of the actors' rapidly alternating selves. This at least is the proposition of the theories which underpin such deconstructive strategies.

The susceptibility of the source myths to such potentially radical reconfigurations has, however, to be weighed against a number of factors which militate against any subversive power. At a narrative level, each of the myths sets the agency of the women as a source of threat to their own people. The threat that they present must, ultimately, be removed, through either their rehabilitation or death. These women must suffer, justly or unjustly, to redress the disruption that their agency has caused. While Nessa's eventual triumph is to secure the kingdom for her son and the palace for herself, she must first endure the slaughter of her tutors and destruction of her hall of study, a punishment for daring to be an intellectual. Macha is forced to race against the king's horses when her husband boasts of her speed, even though she is pregnant. Deirdre kills herself when she realizes that she is to be shared between Conchobar and Eoin, the man who assassinated her lover, Naoise. Maeve's lust for control sees her army decimated and defeated. As Llewellyn Jones comments, 'Although content and performance style embody feminist strategies, the power of masculine myth is not entirely broken since the fate of these women is not entirely positive' (87)

These restagings cannot either avoid the ways in which the myths position women in relation to the specifically masculine sphere of violence. Maeve demonstrates a kind of psychotic blood-lust when she takes up arms. In contrast to the characterization of the male heroes and their prowess in battle, she is configured as out of control, unwomanly, a villain. The contrast with, for example, Cuchulainn is telling. Likewise, Nessa's hunt for revenge earns her a name change from Essa to 'Nessa – the Tough One'. Yet this very toughness is abandoned for the use of her sexual allure to entrap Fergus, following the prophecy of Cathbad. This patriarchal unease at female violence reflects and has determined the actual experiences of women through the conflict in Northern Ireland, for example (Maguire 101 ff). Greenhalgh has argued that women can only ever be 'token terrorists', masochistic victims of this demon lover, who seduces them into an alien world' (161). It is ironic that feminist analyses which emphasize essential differences between men and women have coincided with the same kind of gender role fixing in Northern Ireland within which actual women activists have been marginalized through masculinist discourses. Even Derry Playhouse's recent Theatre of Witness production, *I Once Knew a Girl* (2010), in which verbatim accounts of the effects of involvement in the Troubles on individual women's lives, found it difficult to present openly the violence in which female members of paramilitary organizations were involved. The sense that each of the women had somehow both endured and thereby triumphed over adversity inflicted on them by others produced a distorting sensation of victimhood rather than agency.

As Maguire (2006) has argued casting was also an important factor in the promotion, performance and reception of *The Pursuit of Diarmuid and Gráinne*. The role of Gráinne was played by Briana Corrigan, who had returned to Northern Ireland having made her name as a singer with the band The Beautiful South. Cast as the most beautiful woman in Ireland, Corrigan was the focus of the company's pre-publicity posters and flyers and a recurrent story in newspaper previews. The effect was to put her 'sexually on display' (Kruger 50) despite attempts within the script to make her character a more feisty and active agent within the narrative than traditionally allowed for. Moreover, Corrigan played only Gráinne, such that the potential disruption suggested by actors playing multiple roles was replaced by an assertion of the persistent identity of the performer. In the University of Ulster production of *Women-in-Arms*, student performers displayed a similar insistence on their identity, untouched by the rhetorical strategies through which the characters were performed. Female students attended rehearsal wearing full personal make-up, for example, and this became a source of tension even during the performance period.

This issue of casting also brings into question the extent to which any deconstructive dramaturgical strategies will be understood as resistant or subversive by actual audience members. Kruger has noted, for example, that

> even those innovations whose initial purpose may have been to critique the social as well as theatrical status quo can become essentially a profitable trademark. We can see this in the practice, ubiquitous in British theatre with radical claims, of disrupting the naturalist imitation of life and indiscriminately calling these 'Brechtian'. Techniques such as *gestic* acting, direct address, songs or abrupt scene changes do not in themselves guarantee critical effect; on the contrary they have become so much part of the repertoire of advertising, let alone theatre, that they no longer offer a critique of convention (53).

One further reason for this may well be the proliferation of forms of performance through which audiences see the adoption of such approaches as merely a pragmatic response to the economics of performance which is read outside the signifying frame.

Further, Trotter has articulated a cultural resistance to overtly feminist performance on the part of both audiences and box-office minded theatre managements:

> Audiences, trained to understand and appreciate male discourses, are often reluctant to embrace feminist forms, or they regard dramas with female protagonists as the theatrical equivalent of 'chick flicks,' designed for a solely female clientele. Such an attitude can only change by increasing audiences' exposure to alternative, gynocentric forms, but most theatres are reluctant to risk productions that do not have an established audience base. [...] In Ireland, feminist playwrights find themselves on the margin of a theatre on the margins. (Trotter 165)

Likewise, Williams commented in 1993 that

> we are so used to men's images of men, and men's images of women on the stage, that a play written by a woman is regularly criticized or rejected for not complying with these norms' (7).

The question remains then, whether, in relation to gender, the use of myth in performance provides for 'a shock of alterity at the heart of the habitual' as proposed by Kearney. The deconstructive strategies deployed in these productions seek to place the spectator in a ludic role which 'turns performance into a kind of ideological experiment in which the outcome has no necessary consequence for the audience. Paradoxically, this is the first condition needed for performance efficacy' (Kershaw 24). This use of myth in performance as an 'ideological experiment' rests on the assumption that myths operate only as symbols: whatever resolution is proffered exists at only a symbolic level. After all, as Barthes identified, myth evacuates history from representation. According to Kearney: 'myths are concerned with wish fulfilment and reversal, with making possible at an imaginary level what is impossible in our real or empirical experience' (109). The use of myth functions to contain the performance twice: firstly as myth it is placed outside the realm of the historical; and secondly, it is contained within the rhetorical conventions of the drama, framing it off from the extra-theatrical world with which it seeks also to connect.

In this reading, it is difficult to see how pre-existing mythic narratives might provide role models for contemporary Irish women. Resistance to iconicity in the representation of women is arguably therefore a precondition of performance to a contemporary audience in anything other than 'heritage' drama. What then can Grainne, Maeve, Nessa, and their sisters offer to contemporary audiences? The goal of deconstructive feminist practices is to reveal identities already constructed and enshrined within cultural forms (myths) which are difficult to re-appropriate or to resist. Herein lies the double bind which is the familiar Catch 22 of postmodernist and indeed any deconstructive performance practices: the very act of presenting mythic subjects of pre-established narrative structures, even in a frame designed to subvert those representations, cannot avoid invoking the dominant patriarchal narrative in order to establish itself comparatively as a deliberately transgressive variant, or deformation of it. In so doing, it risks further legitimating the mythic narrative in an attempt to do precisely the opposite.

Bibliography

Burke-Kennedy, Mary Elizabeth, *Women in Arms*, in *Seen and Heard. Six New Plays by Irish Women*, ed. Cathy Leeney (Dublin: Carysfort press, 2001): 1-47.

Butler Cullingford, Elizabeth, 'Gender, Sexuality and Englishness in Modern Irish Drama and Film', *Gender and Sexuality in Modern Ireland*, eds Anthony Bradley and Maryann Gialanella Valiulis (Amherst: University of Massachusetts Press, 1997): 159-86.

Carlson, Marvin, *The Haunted Stage* (Ann Arbor: University of Michigan Press, 2001).

Cleary, Joe, 'Domestic Troubles: Tragedy and the Northern Ireland conflict', *South Atlantic Quarterly*, 98.3 (1999): 501-37.

Coulter, C., 'The Changing Face of Cathleen ní Houlihan: Women and Politics in Ireland, 1960-1996', *Gender and Sexuality in Modern Ireland*, eds Anthony Bradley and Maryann Gialanella Valiulis (Amherst: University of Massachusetts Press, 1997): 275-299.

Daly, Mary E., '"Oh, Kathleen Ni Houlihan, Your Way's a Thorny Way!": The Condition of Women in Twentieth-Century Ireland', *Gender and Sexuality in Modern Ireland*, eds Anthony Bradley and Maryann Gialanella Valiulis (Amherst: University of Massachusetts Press, 1997): 102-126.

De Gay, Jane and Lizbeth Goodman, *Languages of Theatre Shaped by Women*, (Bristol: Intellect, 2003).

Dowler, Lorraine, '"And They Think I'm just a Nice Old Lady" Women and War in Belfast, Northern Ireland', *Gender, Place and Culture*, 5.2 (1998): 159-76.

Hanafin, Patrick, 'Defying the Female: the Irish Constitutional Text as Phallocentric Manifesto', *Textual Practice*, 11.2 (1997): 249-73.

Kearney, Richard, 'Myth and Motherland', *Ireland's Field Day: Field Day Theatre Company*, eds Seamus Deane *et al.* (London: Hutchinson, 1985): 61-80.

---, *Postnationalist Ireland: Politics, Culture, Philosophy* (London: Routledge, 1997).

Kruger, Loren, 'The dis-play's the thing: gender and public sphere in contemporary British theatre', *Feminist Theatre and Theory*, ed. Helene Keyssar (Basingstoke Macmillan, 1996): 49-77.

Leeney, Cathy, ed., *Seen and Heard. Six New Plays by Irish Women* (Dublin: Carysfort press, 2001).

---, 'The Space Outside: Images of Women in Plays by Eva Gore-Booth and Dorothy Macardle', *Women in Irish Drama: A Century of Authorship and Representation*, ed. Melissa Sihra (Basingstoke: Palgrave Macmillan, 2007): 55-68.

Llewellyn-Jones, Margaret, *Contemporary Irish Drama and Cultural Identity* (Bristol: Intellect, 2002).

MacCana, Proinsias, 'Women in Irish Mythology', *The Crane Bag*, 4.1 (1980): 520-24.

Maguire, Tom, *Making Theatre in Northern Ireland: Through and Beyond the Troubles* (Exeter: University of Exeter Press, 2006).

Mahon, Evelyn, 'Women's Rights and Catholicism in Ireland', *Mapping the Women's Movement: feminist politics and social transformation in the North*, ed. Monica Threlfall (London: Verso, 1996): 184-215.

Massey, Doreen, *Space, Place and Gender* (Cambridge: Polity Press, 1994).

McDonald, Marianne and J. Michael Walton, *Amid Our Troubles: Irish Versions of Greek Tragedy* (London: Methuen, 2002).

National Report of Ireland to UN Questionnaire to Governments on Implementation of the Beijing Platform for Action (1995) and the Outcome of the Twenty-Third Special Session of the General Assembly (2000), June 2004 [online]. <http://www.un.org/womenwatch/daw/Review/responses/IRELAND-English.pdf>

Northern Ireland Assembly Library and Research Service, *Gender Inequality in Northern Ireland, Research Paper 28/02* (Belfast: Library and Research service, 2002).

Quinn, Antoinette, 'Cathleen ni Houlihan Writes Back: Maud Gonne and Irish
    National Theater', *Gender and Sexuality in Modern Ireland*, eds Anthony
    Bradley and Maryann Gialanella Valiulis (Amherst: University of
    Massachusetts Press, 1997): 39-59.
Sullivan, Esther Beth, 'What is "Left to a Woman of the House" when the Irish
    Situation is Staged?', *Staging Resistance: Essays in Political Theater*, eds
    Jeanne Colleran and Jenny S. Spencer (Ann Arbor: University of Michigan
    Press, 1998): 213-226.
Sihra, Melissa ed., *Women in Irish Drama: A Century of Authorship and
    Representation* (Basingstoke: Palgrave Macmillan, 2009).
Trotter, Mary, 'Translating women into Irish Theatre', *A Century of Irish
    Drama: Widening the Stage*, eds Stephen Watt *et al.* (Bloomington:
    Indiana University Press, 2000): 163-178.
Walter, Bronwen, 'Gendered Irishness in Britain: Changing Constructions',
    Ireland and Cultural Theory: The Mechanics of Authenticity, eds Colin
    Graham and Richard Kirkland (Basingstoke: MacMillan, 2000): 77-98.

6 | Gendering the Nation in Iconography and Historiography

S. E. Wilmer and Mary Caulfield

Historical monuments in a city landscape portray an impression of that city's and nation's cultural memory and values. However, monuments disguise as much as they reveal. As Peggy Phelan argues, 'representation always conveys more than it intends' (1992:.2). In this essay we will consider the role of monuments within the Dublin landscape and question the way in which one specific figure, Constance Markievicz, has been memorialized.

Throughout the world there are a variety of iconographic symbols to represent national identities. These became especially prominent during the Romantic nationalist movement in the nineteenth century. The most obvious symbols are national flags, the geographical contours of the nation, the national buildings or monuments, the heads of state and/or monarchs, and specific animals associated with the nation. Such symbols frequently appear in conjunction with one another in order to make the iconographic representation more identifiable. In addition, as Floya Anthias and Nira Yuval-Davis have shown, women frequently act as 'a focus and symbol in ideological discourses used in the construction, reproduction and transformation of ethnic/national categories' (1989: 7). In this sense, symbolic renderings and monuments serve as performative installations setting ideological expectations for women. Marina Warner suggests that the female form is an allegory for the Nation's plight and with that a 'symbolized female presence both gives and takes value' (1996: xx) for actual women whether as a literary or dramatic convention or through architectural representation.

The notion of personifying and gendering territory is not new of course. The concept of mother earth, for example, goes back to the ancient Greeks, with the goddess Gaia being worshipped as well as the goddess Demeter, who weeps for her daughter Persephone when she descends into Hades annually, providing the justification for the different seasons of the year. The Swiss nineteenth century anthropologist Johann Bachofen argued that matriarchy was the common pattern of society in pre-historical times, until patriarchy replaced it and coerced women into monogamous relationships so that the fathers of their children could be more easily determined. According to Bachofen (1992), the goddess Demeter was then displaced by an interim phase of worshipping the transsexual Dionysus, followed finally by the emergence of patriarchy through the worship of Apollo, the sun god.

While both the notions of motherland and fatherland have been used somewhat interchangeably, Hegel, for example, regarded women as providing young soldiers for the country. Their duty was to serve the *Volk* and fatherland. He saw women as a potential danger to the state. Referring to those who put their family before the nation, such as the eponymous hero of Sophocles' play *Antigone*, he called women 'the everlasting irony [in the life] of the community' (1977: 288). Nevertheless, the nation is frequently represented as a woman both in Germany and in other countries, but her characteristics vary considerably. Sometimes she appears as a goddess, sometimes as an ordinary citizen, sometimes chaste, sometimes sexualized, often representing a specific value in society such as law, justice, liberty or national awakening, sometimes as a protective figure or as a colossal mother leading her people into battle (such as the memorial at Stalingrad) or a mother mourning her dead children, sometimes as a military figure, and sometimes as a vulnerable victim of an oppressive foreign force.

One of the earliest prototypes for this kind of representation was Athena. As she was the patron goddess of the city-state of Athens, one can regard her as an early form of the personification of the state. Because she was not only the goddess of wisdom but also of war, she has often been depicted as sporting military attire, such as a customary shield and regal helmet as well as a spear. Often this helmet includes a facemask with eyeholes, which she wears on the top of her head, as opposed to covering her face. Contrasted with her military shield, helmet and spear, she normally wears a modest gown showing her figure but not revealing her body.

In the nineteenth century national personifications took on some of the characteristics of Athena. For example, we can see in the image of Britannia the helmet and shield reminiscent of Athena as well as the modest gown, and her weapon has been adapted from a spear into a trident, perhaps indicating the importance of the navy for Britain's protection. In France, rather than the regal looking Britannia, the commoner Marianne often represents the nation, reflecting the republic rather than the monarchy. In the well-known image depicted by Delacroix in 1830, showing Marianne leading the revolutionary struggle over the barricades in Paris, this national figure is much more active and sexualized, with the top of her dress falling down, and her strong physique depicted in aggressive movement. Instead of a sword or trident, she carries a more modern rifle with a fixed bayonet, and is identifiable by the French tricolor that she carries as well as her Phrygian cap (a symbol reminiscent of the Roman slave in revolt). Rather than a regal figure, her identification with the common people is emphasized by her lack of shoes, her state of undress, and her soiled garment. Interestingly, she towers over the male figures around her, including a youth brandishing two pistols, and she strides across dead bodies leading the way into battle.

Joan of Arc, as an historical figure, contrasts with Marianne, who is a mythical character. She is also a cross-cultural archetype who has been adopted by cultural nationalists in many countries engaged in their national liberation movements. Joan is portrayed as a virginal and, sometimes, holy or saintly figure. She is usually depicted in a suit of armour, but with her face visible rather than covered by a helmet. Like Athena and Britannia, she normally is visually and at times dramatically rendered as a chaste, androgynous, and military character. The most important feature of Joan of Arc, of course, is that she is a historical figure who has been romanticized and mythologized but is based on a real person.

By contrast 'Mother Ireland', the personification of Ireland-as-woman, is a symbolic figure that has been artistically rendered through a myriad of incarnations throughout Ireland's colonial history.[1]

---

[1] Earlier representations of 'Mother Ireland' can be found in James Clarence Mangan's work in the mid-nineteenth century. He translated from Irish and popularized the sixteenth-century ballad *My Dark Rosaleen* or *Róisín Dubh*. The *aisling* or vision poem was an eighteenth-century Gaelic *genre*, which 'envisages Ireland in a dream vision as a beautiful woman pleading for rescue from the invaders, or, less frequently, as a harlot collaborating with them'. (Quoted from C.L. Innes, *Woman and Nation in Irish Literature and Society 1880-1935* (Hertfordshire: Harvester Wheatsheaf, 1993): 19.

According to C.L. Innes she is: 'Hibernia, Eire, Erin, Mother Ireland, the Poor Old Woman, the *Shan Van Vocht*, Cathleen ní Houlihan, the Dark Rosaleen' (1993: 2). The general stereotype that has come down to us today is of a mother or maiden who is always dependent on men while other national renderings of female figures suggest a strong woman with agency and autonomy. Hibernia, in contrast to both Britannia and Marianne, is often dressed in modest yet flimsy peasant costume and is at times depicted as bound in chains. 'She' as a hyper-fetishized figure rests in a tentative position in which she is vulnerable to both sides of the colonial coin.

Despite Ireland being a land that has been named for a Mother Goddess, *Eire*, and which celebrates mythological figures such as Queen Maeve and legendary heroines such as the pirate leader Grace O'Malley, depictions of commanding and liberated women are scarce in Ireland's theatrical canon. Many of its plays suggest the symbolic meaning of the feminine, particularly the mother figure, to the nationalist enterprise. Cathleen, in W.B. Yeats's and Augusta Gregory's *Cathleen ní Houlihan* (1902), enforces the homologous relationship between woman and nation or *as* nation. Cathleen bears a resemblance with the Shan van Vocht, or Old Woman, who appears in literature as early as the twelfth century as the character Ériu 'literally as old as the hills yet endlessly restored to youth through union with her rightful mate' (Mac Cana, 1980: 7). She reappears in different forms as a highly sexualized character with many male lovers, such as The Hag of Beare, who takes many royal lovers and Queen Maeve, who dominated her husband and organized a legendary cattle raid (this figure would take her place in the performance of *The Bull* by Fabulous Beast Dance Theatre in 2007). By the Victorian era, their descendant Kathleen Ni Houlihan had become a chaste figure, and when W.B. Yeats and Augusta Gregory used her as the protagonist of their drama, she was not only chaste but also a woman rallying young men to fight for independence. Renderings of 'Mother Ireland' can be distilled into three distinct forms: mother, maiden, or crone – all of whom seem to be variously represented in Cathleen, seemingly restrained and submissive yet at times subversive and purposeful. As the early twentieth-century Irish stage at the start of Ireland's modern theatrical canon was to construct the nation's identity with *Cathleen* serving as a seminal figure, alternative representations of women would face an uphill battle.

In the first production of the play in 1902, a leading nationalist, Maud Gonne, played the part of Cathleen. Yeats, who co-wrote the play with Lady Gregory, set the play in the context of the 1798 rebellion led by Wolfe Tone, but he avoided the obvious strategy of characterizing the male leader. Instead he invoked a mythical figure of mother Ireland calling out her 'sons' to fight for their country. She is the spirit of a suppressed people longing for independence who speaks in metaphors to her audience on stage as well as the theatre's audience, urging them to fight for independence. She complains that there are 'too many strangers in the house' and that her 'four beautiful green fields' (1952: 81) (the four provinces of Ireland) have been taken from her. She inevitably persuades the young man of the house who is about to marry to go off with her to fight for the country as she warns, 'They that have red cheeks will have pale cheeks for my sake, and for all that, they will think they are well paid.... They shall be remembered for ever, They shall be alive for ever, They shall be speaking for ever, The people shall hear them for ever' (86). Within the play, there is an odd transformation in her character. After she leaves the house, the younger son Patrick enters and is asked if he has seen an old woman 'going down the path'. Patrick replies: 'I did not, but I saw a young girl, and she had the walk of a queen' (88).[2] Thus Yeats combines the images of old mother Ireland, the young maiden and the regal Cathleen into one. Moreover, Cathleen had taken on some of the qualities of a vampire, regaining her strength and youth through the blood sacrifice of young men. Maud Gonne's organization *Inghinide na hÉireann* (Daughters of Ireland) presented *Cathleen ni Houlihan*, which evoked a desire for Irish rebellion, and the play became a regular feature of the fledgling Abbey Theatre's repertory.

The scant efforts to represent women within the Nation's historical and literary canon permeate the Dublin cityscape today, where there is an obvious lack of memorialization of female activism. This lack is reflected by the presence of roughly twenty-seven statues of men representing 'real' moments in Irish history, in contrast to one bust and one statue of Constance Markievicz [See Figures 1 and 2]. Of course there are also the fetishized statues of Molly Malone in College Green and additionally, Anna Livia in the city centre on O'Connell Street, until she was displaced by the Dublin Spire in 2003. It is important to note that two of these four statues of women in the Dublin cityscape are mythical and male literary constructions, by contrast with the 'real'

---

[2] W.B. Yeats, *Cathleen ní Houlihan* in *Collected Plays of W.B. Yeats* (London: Macmillan, 1952): 88. This characterization bears a strong resemblance to that in an early nineteenth century poem "Kathleen-Ní-Houlihan" by James Clarence Mangan.

status of the commemorated men[3] and only one 'real' Irish woman Constance Markievicz is monumentalized. Moreover, it is interesting to examine the way that Constance Markievicz is represented. Her statue shows her, not in military uniform on a high plinth on a major street, but at street level in a side street, dressed in an ankle length domestic skirt and blouse, standing beside her dog 'Poppet'. This depiction contrasts strikingly with her career as a prominent nationalist and military figure, especially as the statue is placed near a public bathing facility, which bears her name. Markievicz created and enforced her own iconicity – an iconicity, which promoted active female agency and social change. It is as if her persona was too iconoclastic to gel with Irish notions of female modesty and subservience and could not be represented in a public monument. More recently a monument of Constance Markievicz was erected in 2003 in Rathcormack, County Sligo near her ancestral home that conveys a more activist character leading a group of downtrodden figures. These figures are of the poor, however, not of the St. Stephen's Green regiment, which she led into battle.

Markievicz, an often contested yet sometimes romanticized figure, is largely forgotten today, but she was a major figure in the nationalist, labour and suffragist movements in the early years of the twentieth century. She operated within a new social setting for women, who had become activists in Ireland through the Land League disputes following Charles Parnell's imprisonment at the end of the nineteenth century, and through the nationalist activities of Maud Gonne's Daughters of Erin, the suffragist movement, and the labour movement. Markievicz, like another Protestant aristocrat, Lady Gregory, maintained an independent lifestyle particularly after her husband Count Markievicz returned to Poland without her, shortly before the First World War. Constance Markievicz relished exposure. She addressed crowds and took important leadership positions in various organizations such as Sinn Féin and Cumann na mBan.

For Markievicz, Joan of Arc was a figure that personified all the essential qualities of a Nationalist and woman warrior. Joan of Arc remained a potent trope throughout Markievicz's theatrical, artistic, and journalistic renderings. Markievicz drew from and contributed to a tradition of female militancy and mobility to incite and inspire contemporaneous female action within the Nationalist movement and,

---

[3] Anna Livia is a character in James Joyce's *Finnegan's Wake* and the lyrics to Molly Malone have been attributed to James Yorkston.

Figure 1: Constance Markievicz and Poppet, Tara Street, Dublin

**Figure 2: Bust of Constance Markievicz in St Stephen's Green
Dublin**

for her, Joan of Arc epitomized the ideal female militant. Joan of Arc was physically superior, morally linear and a woman whose love of country helped lead France to freedom and thus served as the absolute example of patriotism for both Nationalist men and women. If divine intervention claimed Joan of Arc, the call of Cathleen ni Houlihan was answered by Markievicz, who with her 1909 lecture 'Women, Ideals and the Nation' revealed her departure away from non-violent political resistance to a military insurrection akin to a spiritually motivated crusade.

In 1908 she helped found and contributed to the all-woman's nationalist journal, called *Bean na hÉireann* (Woman of Ireland), which in 1909 printed her appeal for a Joan of Arc to save Ireland: 'May this aspiration towards life and freedom among the women of Ireland bring forth a Joan of Arc to free our nation!' (1:9: 8) She formed an Irish version of a boy scouts group which she called the *Fianna na hÉireann* (soldiers of Ireland) whom she taught to shoot and prepare for an Irish rebellion and with whom she staged plays. Her role in training the boys to fight for Irish independence echoed Cathleen Ni Houlihan's to whom she referred in her manifesto,

We have heard the imperious demand of Cathleen ni Houlihan, her call to those who would serve her, to give her all, to give her themselves. It will take the best and noblest of Ireland's children to win Freedom, for the price of Freedom is suffering and pain. It is to the young that a nation must look for help; for life itself. Ireland is calling you to join Fianna na hÉireann, the young army of Ireland, and help to place the crown of freedom on Her head (Van Voris, 1967: 67).

She also tried (unsuccessfully) to establish the troupe as a co-educational organization. In a suffragist pageant in 1914 she dressed in a suit of armour as Joan of Arc in a tableau vivant, offering a hand to an Irish suffragette on hunger strike, visually and historically linking her own representation of self with that of Joan of Arc's legacy. She became friends with political leaders like James Connolly and Patrick Pearse (who would both be executed by the British after their involvement in the Easter Rising of 1916), and was an active supporter of the workers in the Dublin strike and lock-out in 1913. In 1916 she was clearly determined to become a military leader in the insurrection against British rule. Rather than just inspiring others to fight like Cathleen Ni Houlihan, she was prepared to take an active role herself and, like Joan of Arc, risk becoming a martyr for the nationalist cause. She was appointed a lieutenant in the Irish Citizen's Army and would be one of the few women carrying a gun in the Easter Rising. In his

autobiography Sean O'Casey conjured up an illuminating portrait of
Markievicz marching with James Connolly a week before the Rising:

> Connolly determined to try to dam the stream of men flowing out
> of Ireland, and was seized with the idea that he could turn the sky
> green for all to see by hoisting a flag of the same colour over
> Liberty Hall ... The Citizen Army, numbering about one hundred
> and seventy men, paraded outside, and Connolly, followed a pace
> behind by Madame Markievicz, inspected them. Connolly wore his
> new dark-green uniform for the first time, and didn't look too well
> in it, for he had a rather awkward carriage; and bow-legs, partly
> ensnared in rich, red-brown, leather leggings, added to the waddle
> in his walk. He carried an automatic gun in his left hand, the barrel
> resting in the crook of his arm. Madame having dressed herself in
> man's attire to fight for liberty, was in full green uniform too, and
> carried a big automatic pistol on her thin hip. There was a dire
> sparkle of vanity lighting this little group of armed men: it
> sparkled from Connolly's waddle, from the uniformed men stiff to
> attention, and from the bunch of cock-feathers fluttering in the cap
> of the Countess. But it was a vanity that none could challenge, for
> it came from a group that was willing to sprinkle itself into
> oblivion that a change might be born in the long-settled thought of
> the people ... Here was the purple heart of Ireland (1945: 316-7).

After several days of fighting the rebellion was suppressed and the
leaders were executed. Being the only female officer, Markievicz's death
sentence was commuted to life imprisonment. She reputedly retorted, 'I
wish you lot had the decency to shoot me.'

While in jail, she allowed her name to go forward as a Sinn Fein
candidate for a Dublin constituency in the 1918 election. In February
1918 women (over the age of thirty) were granted the right to vote for
the first time in Britain. She was among seventeen women candidates in
the United Kingdom and was the only one to be elected, thereby
becoming the first woman ever elected to the British parliament. On her
release from jail in 1919, she refused to take up her seat and became
Minister of Labour in Eamon de Valera's illegal Irish government. For
the next few years she was often on the run from the British authorities.
According to Sheehy-Skeffington:

> Her acting gifts helped her with various disguises, necessary when
> she was on the run, a much-wanted Cabinet Minister. She often
> chose the role of an elderly and rather feeble old lady, with
> Victorian bonnet and cape. It was all right as long as she did not
> speak. But her voice instantly gave her away! During all the time
> that she was on the run, staying a night here and there with a
> friend, (we all had lists of friendly houses where, if pressed, we
> might pass the night) though Constance was well known to tram
> conductors, newsboys, basket-women, and all over Dublin, none of

them ever gave her away, or even pretended to recognize her as she passed. 'The Countess,' as Dublin called her, (accent on the second syllable) had the freedom of the city, literally (MS24189, NLI).

In 1922 following a protracted guerrilla war, the British government signed a treaty with representatives of the Irish Dail, which allowed for the Partition of the island and the establishment of the Free State under the British Crown. De Valera and others (including Markievicz) did not agree with this compromise of Irish sovereignty and a civil war ensued. Following the end of the civil war, Markievicz continued to fight for the ideal of an Irish Republic. In 1924 she started a new theatre group, the Republican Players, to keep alive her nationalistic ambitions. The Players produced plays that promoted the hope for a fully independent Ireland. When she died in 1927, the people of Dublin crowded into the streets for her funeral procession and she was buried with her military uniform.

Since her death, her role as a military leader in the Irish rebellion has been minimized and contested. While her arrest and death sentence following the Rising substantiated her nationalist efforts, her reprieve due to gender prevented her memorialization as an Irish Joan of Arc and re-enforced women's position as symbol, catalyzing male efforts. By contrast, male blood sacrifice served as a necessary agent in strengthening the popular appreciation of the uprising, a process of cultural mythification that devalued Markievicz's contribution. Sean O'Casey was notoriously suspicious of Markievicz's commitment to Ireland and undermined her self-sacrificing efforts with ironic comments:

> Now there were two Cathleen ni Houlihans running around Dublin: one, like the traditional, in green dress, shamrocks in her hair, a little brian-boru harp under her oxster, chanting her share of song ... the other Cathleen coarsely dressed, hair a little tousled, caught roughly together by a pin, barefooted, sometimes with a whiff of whiskey off her breath; brave and brawny; at ease in the smell of sweat and the sound of bad language, vital, and asurge with immortality. (1945: 266)

O'Casey's description of the 'tousled' *Cathleen ni Houlihan*, emphasizes the perception that public representations of women that were counter to the expectations of the symbolic nature of Cathleen ni Houlihan, were unnatural, at times vulgar and certainly 'unfeminine'.

Perceptions of Markievicz, incongruous and ever-changing, can be read partly as self-stylization of their own. Markievicz was very active in the Dublin theatre scene and contributed strongly to her own idiosyncratic self-image. Her husband, Casimir Markievicz, wrote and directed plays and formed the Independent Theatre Company. He set one of his plays, *The Memory of the Dead*, in the 1798 Irish rebellion and Constance played the heroine. This was performed in the Abbey Theatre in 1910 and revived several times and toured around the country. She also played Eleanor in a light-hearted satire of Irish society, *Eleanor's Enterprise* by George Birmingham at the Gaiety Theatre in 1911. Hannah Sheehy-Skeffington, one of the leaders of the Irish suffragist movement, wrote, 'As an actress her high-pitched voice and English accent, and her short sight which in later years entailed the wearing of glasses, were disabilities. But her temperament suited rebel and heroic parts, and these she shone in' (MS24189, NLI). George Birmingham (whose real name was James Owen Hannay) wrote of her unconventional attitudes towards female modesty,

> I was not at all sure that I wanted her to take the leading part in my play. There was a scene in which the heroine, the part which Madam Markievitch [sic] played herself, had to emerge from her bedroom in the middle of the night. I was anxious that my name should not be associated with anything *risqué* and I feared that Madam Markievitch [sic] would be inclined to wear as little as possible when making her appearance. I wrote her several letters urging the wearing of a dressing-gown, bedroom slippers and other similar garments. She wanted to reduce her clothing to a minimum. (1934: 170-1)

Markievicz's theatrical writings amount to three complete plays: *Blood Money* (1925) and *The Invincible Mother* (1925) are both one acts and her final play, written just before her death, *Broken Dreams* (1927), is a play in three acts. *Blood Money* is an unpublished and forgotten play by Markievicz. It was produced at the Abbey Theatre on 1 March 1925, when the country had become a Free State but while Markievicz was continuing to campaign for an Irish republic. It was staged as part of a triple bill on a Sunday night by Markievicz's Republican Players, along with *The Invincible Mother* (1925) and an additional play in Irish. Joseph Holloway, an inveterate theatregoer, recorded the evening in his diary. He inadvertently missed the performance of *Blood Money* but saw the other two and indicated that Markievicz's second play, *The Invincible Mother*, was better presented than the play in Irish. At the end of the evening, according to Holloway,

> Calls for author ... brought forth the Countess who addressed the crowded audience and told them that the members of the company were all ex-internees and that the proceeds of their performance went to those out of work. Many were writing new plays for them,

she wrote her 'two little pieces' in her leisure time to show up phases in the Irish struggle for freedom and she concluded quoting some of John Mitchell's words to the effect that Ireland would be a free country when the British Empire was a thing of the past (MS1892: 371).

The audience was evidently attracted to the performance by the nature of it being as much a political as a theatrical event. At the time, although the civil war had ended, there was still a strong ongoing debate in Dublin between the Free Staters and the Republicans, and the Free Staters were worried about being seen to attend a Republican event.

The press did not review the play and it is not recorded to have been produced again. Her plays have virtually disappeared from theatre history. There is no mention of *Blood Money* in the biographies of Markievicz and only the scantest identification of it in a book by an actress (Maire nic Shuibhlaigh) who may have acted in it and who took part in the Easter Rising. Nevertheless, it is a significant document, which reflects the feelings of one of the leading figures in Irish politics at the time. The play displays some uncanny similarities with Markievicz's own real-life situation, especially the role of the heroine in the play. It addresses the tradition of rebellion against British rule in Ireland and demonstrates the active role for women in trying to achieve independence. Set in a rebellion against British military authority, which could be one of the earlier rebellions such as in 1798 or 1803 but equally could be the one to come, she casts the British army officers as the enemy. An Irishman serving in the British army, who has revealed the hideout of the Irish rebels, is depicted as the main villain of the piece. He is tried by the rebels at the end of the play and sentenced to hang. In the final speech of the play one of the Irish rebels says, 'Take him and hang him, and leave him swinging there, a lesson to all Irishmen who wear England's livery' (MS22636: 4). This is a clear statement to the audience about the danger of informants who plagued earlier attempts at rebellion as well as a warning to anyone who might be like-minded in the future.

The heroine of the play, a young woman named Peggy, intercedes (rather like Antigone) for the body of Donal McCarthy, one of the rebels who has been captured and hanged by the British army. In so doing she discovers amongst the group of three drunken British soldiers (two of whom are Irish) that one of these (the informant) was a former friend. When he defends himself saying that he is one of 'His Majesty's soldiers', she replies, 'His Majesty's soldier you've named yourself, and what worse could I name you? You traitor ... you soldier ...' (4). By equating soldier with traitor, Markievicz, through the character of Peggy, was attacking the right of the British to recruit Irishmen for the British army, which was a major issue before 1922. During this scene, Peggy's pretense as an innocent pretty Irish girl is unmasked, and the sergeant becomes suspicious and threatens her. Surrounded by two Irish drunken soldiers who are asking her to sit and drink with them and the British sergeant who is raising questions about her motives, she hints at some form of bribery to the sergeant. He orders the other soldiers to march away, leaving them alone. Provocatively she says to him when the others have disappeared, 'Come here till I give you what you've earned ... You've earned it well ... and God will forgive me ...' (6) whereupon she shoots him dead.

The sudden murder of the sergeant is quite surprising. First, his murder is not plotted as being necessary. She does not seem to be in a life-threatening situation where she is forced to kill in self-defense. She might have talked her way out of the predicament she was in. Second, there is no apology for a woman doing the shooting, which could have been expected if the play had been written by a man. The act is clearly calculated and premeditated, and yet it is portrayed as a courageous act of defiance against an oppressor rather than as a savage murder. There is little evidence of remorse from Peggy other than, God rest his soul! He was a dirty villain, but maybe there's some poor soul praying that he may return to her safe' (6). In other words Peggy expresses sympathy for some female who might be waiting for him to return home, but none for the sergeant. The play also depicts the invisibility of women in guerrilla warfare, i.e. their ability to be part of the military movement while the enemy treats them as only feeble women. The fact that she shoots an officer shows that she is as formidable in the nationalist struggle as any of the men.

Markievicz's female protagonists in all three of her plays seditiously promote female agency by the means available to each woman, in contrast to the fallen male soldier. In *Blood Money*, Peggy's agency manifests in her ability to penetrate the enemy hideout and her assassination of the British captor. This ultimately renders Donal free from captivity, as Donal is not dead at all. Peggy's infiltration was in fact a rescue mission rendering her the true hero of the play. In *The Invincible Mother* Markievicz's heroine, Mrs Fagan, travels a great distance in the guise of the trusted trope of Mother/Crone, to ensure her captured son continues the family tradition of silence by not 'ratting' on his Fenian co-conspirators. In *Broken Dreams* Eileen O'Rourke, Markievicz's most developed character, attempts to shoot her traitor husband when it is revealed he has duped her and her republican colleagues into thinking he was an Irish rebel and war hero. The women in Markievicz's plays have agency; they drive the action of the dramas. This demonstrates Markievicz's opinion that the Nationalist movement was a collective effort, with both women and men playing an active part. Markievicz's characters wear the emblematic 'uniform' of 'Mother Ireland' as a strategy of war. Markievicz female characters are the unforeseen heroes of the play thus reversing the Irish nationalist narrative. Instead of Cathleen calling her 'sons' to fight, it is her daughter who has led the charge in the name of Irish freedom.

In real life, Markievicz, along with her representations of subversive women in her plays, contributed to a collective narrative that widens the spectrum of symbolic potential for the remarkable nationalist woman. However, Irish historical accounts and monuments often fail to convey such engagements. Her domesticated representation today in the Dublin monumental landscape, standing beside her dog and a swimming pool, along with the absence of female monumentalizing generally, contributes to the subconscious or deliberate marginalization of women from Dublin's cultural and political landscape, which subsequently results in an excess of representation and the privileging of the patriarchal foundations of history. Peggy Phelan alludes to such gaps in representation as a deficit in 'representational visibility' (1992: 1). Therefore, inherent in remembering is mis-remembering. Even though representation, according to Phelan, is never 'totalizing', if you remember anything at all, you are immediately and simultaneously forgetting that which you did not represent (1992: 2). According to Friedrich Nietzsche, cheerfulness and a confidence in the future depends 'in the case of the individual as of a nation, on the existence of a line dividing the bright and discernible from the unilluminable and dark; on one's being just as able to forget at the right time as to remember at the right time' (1997: 63). Careful analysis and integration of female efforts is essential for a complete and balanced historical narrative resulting in the Nietzschean prescription for the health of an individual and of a modern people and culture (62-3).

With the ideal female form often the fodder for most National symbols, the gap between actual women and their represented expectations has been set enormously wide. Joan of Arc, a figure depicted as everything from patriot to witch, was the essential counter-figure for Markievicz. They were two women united by principles, sex, fearlessness, and determination and together they would exceed 'foreign' boundaries and normative gender expectations. Nevertheless, their cultural memorialization differs considerably. The trivialization of Markievicz into a domestic figure accompanied by her dog indicates the inability of the civic fathers of Dublin to cope with her real persona.

An urban landscape is filled with monuments, which locate the past as well as define the present; and while the building of new structures on the sites of older memorials, or the complete lack of monumentalizing in general is often a conscious act to destroy memory, the ghosts of the past are not so easily defeated. Nuala Johnson suggests that the cityscape of Dublin was architecturally and spatially inscribed so that it acted as a key site for the nationalist struggle. Further, it served as a dynamic yet chaotic stage on which revolutionary women performed their activism. These performances were not limited to traditional theatrical presentations but included staged protests, riots, marches and speeches. This city, which was once both a playground and battlefield for women such as Constance Markievicz, now fails to reflect their integral engagement. Alternatively, Dublin now serves as a battleground to a semiotic war where the symbols representing women's engagement with cultural and political nationalism fail to serve as adequate artillery. This lack of representation now stands as a performance in itself, forever monumentalizing the binaries between male and female and the disparities in equal gender representation. Responses to this point of view bring up important issues in the ways in which people now think about men and women in history. Michael Shanks and Mike Pearson suggest that:

> Landscape has provided a basis for locating new communities of nationhood in a kind of collective cultural memory of belonging. Monuments and landforms have come to be seen to give history and shape to human communities, nations included (2001: 39).

In essence, nations use monuments and architecture, purporting to give a sense of an 'authentic' representation or affinity with its past. However, the Dublin case demonstrates that city fathers use monuments to create and misshape its cultural, social and political memory in favour of patriarchy.

Ireland, of course, is not an isolated case. During the more recent civil war in the Balkans, Julie Mertus complained that women were being depicted as powerless victims of the military struggle:

> As long as they exist, nations will continue to attempt to harness Woman in service of their national identities. By recognizing this trend, however, we will begin to strip it of its potency ... Yes, the war in the Balkans has created a large number of women victims,

all of whom deserve redress. However, these women stand to gain nothing from further exploitation. Rather all women – victims, activists, activist women – would benefit if we recognized the full breadth of their lived realities and allowed all women to voice their differing struggles. (1994: 23)

Like Markievicz, women throughout Ireland's history and throughout the world have engaged with nationalist struggles in varied and complex ways. However, as in many other countries, the majority of monumental and popular representations in contemporary Dublin have failed to reflect this engagement. Instead, there is a commemorative 'blind spot' in the memory of contemporary Dublin - an allegorical missing page in the history books. Women in Irish history have been depicted within a narrow range of cultural stereotypes, while women's roles within nationalism have been, and continue to be, diverse, multi-faceted and dynamic. The gap between the 'real' woman and established 'symbolic' expectations will narrow, with further analysis of representational visibility and iconography. Phelan suggests that what one can see is directly related to what one can say and therefore when we frame more and more images of the 'under-represented other', culture then finds a way to name or recognize the previously unmarked subject, especially when there is excess as a result of the over-privileging of the historicized over the not yet uncovered. If to avoid such is considered a valid aim, then let us not just celebrate cultures of modernity and women's integral place within them, but interrogate them, especially for those who have been left in the dark.

7 | 'Midwives to creativity': Irish women and public(ation), 1975-1996

Megan Buckley and Julia Walther

In her introduction to *Mondays at Gaj's: The Story of the Irish Women's Liberation Movement*, Anne Stopper claims: 'Sociologists have noted that a successful movement is the point of intersection between personal and social change' (2006: 5). Indeed, in the 1970s and 1980s, feminist acts were being performed by Irish women in both personal and public arenas – in courts of law, in public demonstrations on the streets and in private homes. They were also being performed within the many writing workshops and community writing initiatives that sprang up in Ireland in the late 1970s, 1980s and into the mid-1990s. If publishing can act as the public articulation – or public(ation) – of a movement, then these initiatives provided three vital stages of development for the women writers involved in them: individual encouragement, group facilitation, and, ultimately, through the feminist presses, publication.

Focusing on creative writing as one significant part of second-wave feminism in Ireland, we seek to explore the crucial catalysts that encouraged women writers to sit down at their private writing desks, and then to step onto the public stage represented by publication through a feminist or non-feminist press. By 'writing', we mean all forms of textual production: poetry, drama, fiction, and non-fiction. A significant part of the abundance of Irish women's writing from the last three decades of the twentieth century has been fostered by those 'midwives' who realized that a wealth of dormant creativity could be brought to life within a supportive network of other women. As a frame of reference we have chosen the most active period of feminist publishing in Ireland, from the foundation of the first women's press, Arlen House, in 1975, to the year 1996, when Attic Press, Ireland's most prolific feminist publishing house, ceased to exist.

In her study, *Twentieth-Century Fiction by Irish Women*, Heather Ingman (2007: 1) establishes a correlation between the emergence of

Irish feminist presses and the increase in women's fiction writing in the eighties and nineties. Arlen House, Women's Community Press and Attic Press had indeed been vital facilitators in this context from the mid-1970s to the mid-1990s. It would, however, be false to assume that there was no previous history of women's writing in Ireland, as Anne Colman points out:

> The period from 1800 to 1930 was a rich and fertile time in the history of Irish women writers, and there were in excess of 500 women publishing in all genres. This was not an era of specialization for writers, hence there was no feeling of limitation regarding genre. Writers were simply writers, and they wrote in whatever genre they deemed suitable to the subject, or their interests (1995: 129).

As Colman explains, the Irish publishing landscape of the nineteenth century was different, with publishers and printers based in various cities throughout the country apart from the major centres of Dublin and London. Some of the newspaper printers also provided publishing services to writers both male and female, and, according to the author, 'paying to have one's book published was another option for those with the financial means, and vanity publishing did not have the stigma it now carries' (131).

One of the reasons why women writers of the past have not been documented adequately – creating the impression that women had not been writing much at all until the advent of feminist publishing – lies in the fact that 'women writers published anonymously, and pseudonymously, under maiden names, married names, titles, in some cases under their name in religion, their initials and even under the initials of their pseudonyms' (Colman 130). Nonetheless, while women were indeed being published, there is no doubt that they were responsible for only a fraction of the literary output, a situation that did not change rapidly overnight with the appearance of feminist publishing as a major feature of second-wave feminism.

In 1983, for instance, the Irish branch of the organization Women in Publishing carried out a survey, which found that only 11% of Irish poetry published was by women poets and almost all of it (9%) had been published by Arlen House.[1] Referring to Virginia Woolf's *A Room of One's Own*, the editors of the 1984 publication *Irish Feminist Review '84* lay only half the blame on the lack of proper writing facilities for women; equally responsible in their eyes was the existing publishing system, which was dominated by men:

---

[1] The survey is referred to in: Hannon, DJ & N Means Wright, 'Irish women poets: breaking the silence' *Canadian Journal of Irish Studies* vol.6:2, 57-65. However, this article wrongly names Attic Press as the women's press responsible for providing an outlet for women poets. This should, of course, read Arlen House, since Attic Press was not founded until 1984.

It is not necessarily true that all male publishers have an innate prejudice against any manuscript bearing a woman's name, although some undoubtedly do, but for some reason women's writing has not been acceptable to the publishing world. There must be some connection between this fact and the fact that most publishers – although emphatically not most workers in publishing – are male. Women's writing simply doesn't speak to them. It is surely out of this situation that feminist publishing – the publication by women of women's writing – was born (170-171).

There is undoubtedly a direct connection between writer and publisher, where the written word is to enter the public sphere by becoming a published work. It would be too simplistic, however, to assume that feminist publishing was a logical consequence of an abundance of unpublished women's writing. Rather, the two sides correlate with each other: Irish women's presses, and those affiliated with them, fostered the work of women writers both individually and collectively, and in many cases the fruits of that support in turn strengthened the feminist publishing enterprises. This chapter aims to investigates both sides and, in particular, the intersection between them.

What does it mean to be a writer, as an individual, and what are some of the obstacles that the individual woman writer encounters? Eavan Boland, in her essay 'In defence of workshops' (1991), delves into the mystique surrounding the idea of what it means to be a writer, and especially a poet. 'The truth is that there is such a thing as a societal permission to be a poet', Boland asserts:

> Even the notion offends many literary sensibilities. The idea that a society issues subtle, strict and often ungenerously distributed permissions to exercise an innate gift upsets the contrary elite and romantic view that excellence will out. The poet in the garret. ... The sudden recognition of the irrefutable voice. These are the conventional, nineteenth-century views of poetic development. They are also male, white and middle-class. Langston Hughes could tell a different story, and does in his autobiography. As does Sylvia Plath in her memoirs and Adrienne Rich in her essays. ...
> Whether we like it or not, societal permissions do exist. They are, at least in part, the unseen element in bewildering statistics and disabling absences. And of course they are unequally distributed on the basis of gender, class, and colour (42).

The idea that true talent will triumph over all obstacles – personal, economic, gender-, race-, or class-based – is an idealistic one, Boland believes. In the words of American novelist and journalist Katherine Anne Porter, she continues,

> I have no patience [...] with the dreadful idea that whatever you have in you has to come out, that you can't suppress true talent. People can be destroyed: they can be bent, distorted, and

completely crippled. In spite of all the poetry, all the philosophy to the contrary, we are not really masters of our fate. We don't really direct our lives unaided and unobstructed. Our being is subject to all the chances of life (41).

An individual's writing life is certainly shaped by her circumstances. Yet an emerging woman writer's chances of success can take a significant turn for the better when if she makes a connection with an established writer. Poet Joan McBreen, now the author of four collections of poetry and the editor of two, frankly describes her first attempts at poetry: 'I was slowly and tentatively writing and hiding my first poems in kitchen drawers more often than sending them out for consideration', she confesses (1994: 12-13). Then she travelled from her home in Tuam, Co. Galway to Galway city for a reading by Eavan Boland. There, McBreen, a mother of six, had asked Boland, 'How can you be a mother and a poet?' (12). Months later, as she continued to write, she found that her insecurity began to diminish. 'Suddenly the journey made to Galway that February day to hear [Boland] read began to assume the significance I had subconsciously felt it would', writes McBreen. 'I attended a workshop she was giving in Dublin for the Women's Education Bureau (W.E.B.) in January of 1987, and under her fine direction, self-doubt began to give way to self-trust' (13). That self-trust quickly bore fruit: McBreen won a contest sponsored by an American publisher (Lendennie 10) with her first volume of poetry, *The Wind Beyond the Wall* (1990), less than three years after she attended Boland's workshop.

According to McBreen and others, some writers, both male and female, found living and working outside of Dublin a challenge to developing their careers. Since the majority of publishers and literary magazines were Dublin-based, the idea of 'breaking into' a literary world that was perceived as elitist and exclusionary could seem even more overwhelming for women writers, many of whom might have felt isolated from any writing community at all. Theo Dorgan, poet and then director of Poetry Ireland, the national organization for poetry in Ireland, describes the ways in which the presence of non-Dublin-based outlets for creative work encouraged both readers and writers:

> It is a particular source of pride to us all that Salmon, the most exciting of our publishing houses, is based outside of Dublin. This is important in many ways: important for perceptions of Ireland, important for poets – most of whom are non-Dublin, and important for readers, since it challenges the Dublin-centred ethos that disfigures and strains our sense of ourselves. That a venture like Salmon could take root and thrive outside the capital is one of the most telling arguments I know for the health and vigour of Irish poetry today (Dorgan in McBreen: 22).

Other enterprising women based outside of Dublin had also found ways to encourage the individual woman writer who wrote alone or who tended to conceal her creative work in desk drawers rather than submit it for publication. As early as 1975 Catherine Rose, who had previously worked for Irish publisher Mercier and subsequently relocated to Galway, decided to set up her own press in order to self-publish her manuscript *The Female Experience: The Story of the Woman* [sic] *Movement*. Arlen House, Ireland's first women's press, then moved to Dublin, where three co-directors, among them journalist Terry Prone, joined Rose and continued to publish two more non-fiction titles over the following two years.

In 1978, the four directors managed to secure commercial sponsorship for a short story competition from coffee producers Maxwell House. Some were mystified at what seemed like an unlikely alliance: a women's publishing house and a coffee manufacturer. A short entry in *The Irish Times* suggested that this was 'a little odd' at first glance, but quoted Paddy Maguire, managing director of Maxwell House on the issue:

> [h]e said that the link between coffee, writing, literature and reading seemed entirely proven. He also said, with beguiling frankness, that Maxwell House was interested in finding directions for sponsorship in which they could do some positive good by giving something a lift, or getting something started, not spend too much money and do themselves some good as well, and that this seemed to fit the bill on all counts ('An Irishman's diary' 15).

The competition was announced in Dublin on 12 October 1978, and all unpublished women writers were eligible. An *Irish Times* article from the following day ('Short Story Prizes for Women') quoted Prone, who claimed that there had been 'accusations "mainly from men" of discrimination because the competition is only open to women. But Arlen House was unashamedly a feminist company, she said, and the competition was being organized to encourage women to write [...]'. While *The Irish Times* thus announced the competition without any judgemental comments, the Irish publishers' trade magazine, *Books Ireland*, adopted a flippant, slightly condescending tone in their coverage of the same event:

> ... Terry Prone thanking Maxwell House the coffee people for sponsoring a short-story competition for Irish women (over 16 and without a novel or an anthology to their credit yet). Eavan Boland, Mary Lavin and David Marcus (the latter presumably in a wig) will be judges, and the ten best stories will make a book under the Arlen House imprint. Entries to Arlen House by 15 December please, girls ('Social Whirl Dept.').

Arlen's short story project was not the only such initiative which excluded men at the time; *The Irish Times*, for example, ran a similar competition open only to female playwrights, something that Cormac Ó Cuilleanáin (Ó Cuilleanáin: 118) would regard as 'insufferably matronizing' in the future.

Irrespective of such criticism, the judges received entries from 'more than 1,000 Irishwomen from all parts of the world' ('Reading the Writing on the Arlen Wall'). Arlen House subsequently organized two more rounds of the competition, 'publishing the results in ground-breaking anthologies which revealed the store of stifled imagination, wit and ability of women writing throughout the country' (Smyth 16). *The Wall Reader: And Other Stories*, published in 1979, was the first volume to evolve from this competition, followed by *A Dream Recurring* in 1980. The third volume, *The Adultery And Other Stories and Poems* was not published until 1982, shortly before Arlen launched their first original novel-length fiction title. Catherine Rose (Rose 2008) confirmed that the anthologies were 'a source of income and publicity and the books would have sold because of the publicity' generated through their co-operation with Maxwell House.

The precise amount of sponsorship contributed by Maxwell House remains unknown, but securing external funding was essential because it covered 'the prize money, the judges' fees and the promotion for the competition, while Arlen House would finance the publication of the book of winning entries and take care of the administration of the competition' (Rose 1982). Maxwell House withdrew their support after three years, which, according to Rose,

> left a gap for the unknown writers of this country, as well as for the sponsors who have subsequently found nothing to equal the amount of comment and even controversy this competition aroused. 'I think they could never see the kind of publicity they were getting, and they couldn't quite adapt to sponsoring the arts – they just weren't comfortable with the idea' (Rose in Leland 10).

While the project was certainly very effective in raising Arlen House's public profile, it also helped several women to launch their writing careers. The most successful of them was Mary Rose Callaghan, who was among the winners in the initial round of the competition; she subsequently published her first novel, *Mothers* (1982), with Arlen House and eventually became a regular author on the Attic Press teenage fiction series, Bright Sparks.

The concept of a competition can be regarded as a welcome catalyst for 'closet writers': that is, those women who were not professional writers, had no previous connections to editors or publishers, and who would never have approached a publisher 'cold' with a manuscript. Sending in a story on the basis of a competition, on the other hand, is a completely different matter. Cadman Chester & Pivot had highlighted the fact that the 'main reason which prevents women identifying themselves as "professionals" and therefore adopting the label of "writer" is the economic one. In our society you are identifiable as something when you earn money doing it' (Cadman Chester & Pivot 7). The opportunity presented by Arlen House was less visibly business-oriented, or financially 'serious', making it much less daunting for those women whose motivation to write was creatively or politically inspired rather than inspired by the desire for fame and fortune. Yet again, from the publisher's point of view, such a project would provide an opportunity to discover hitherto unknown and undiscovered writers who could become part of the publisher's list. Eavan Boland, as one of the judges on the panel, defended the rationale behind a women-only competition:

> Therefore, by the lights of this argument I see an instructive distinction between this competition and the anthology which has emerged from it. The first belongs to that legitimate ploy of encouragement which is due to any community in which one suspects an inverse proportion of energy to expression. It has been generously sponsored by Maxwell House and the size of the entry alone suggests a vitality that should be sustained by this fosterage.
> The anthology on the other hand is part of the more exacting search with which the future of good writing, not just good writing by women, is crucially involved. It is this search with which Arlen House, and all presses like it in Britain and America, has associated itself. It is motivated by the belief that there is an excellence of perception and expression latent in the community of women, and that as long as it lies dormant it is a wasting asset, to everyone, not just to one part of a society (Boland 1978, n.p.).

Significantly, this 'inverse proportion of energy to expression' was not (and, perhaps, is not) confined to Ireland: women writers' tendency to allow their work to 'lie dormant' seems to extend beyond national boundaries. Beth Joselow, former editor of the prestigious, though now-defunct, American literary magazine *Washington Review*, also encountered women's reluctance to submit work for publication, and noticed the same tendency in her attitude to her own work. 'It is surprising to me always how many more submissions from men than from women I get at the [Washington] Review,' she remarked in a letter to Jessie Lendennie. 'And even I see that I do all the work up to the point of sending things out, then hesitate longer than necessary before getting them into the mail. Sometimes I decide in advance that something won't go over, so I don't even try'. The reasons for this gendered difference remain unclear, but Joselow speculates: '[p]erhaps men depersonalize it more – make it really "business" more than women do. I don't know many male poets who are as apologetic as I am when asked what their professions are. Or perhaps their embarrassment just takes a more aggressive, defensive posture' (Joselow). Clearly, women writers' ambivalence about their own work is widespread.

Without doubt, the Maxwell House short story competitions served several purposes. They gave individual Irish women writers a goal towards which to aspire: moreover, simply but crucially, they brought women writers and the women's publishing house together. This helped to create and strengthen a support network essential to the women's movement in general, a network amongst the writers themselves on the one hand and between the writers and those with the means to put creative work out into the world on the other.

While encouraging and nourishing women writers individually was of vital importance, the collective needs of women writers also needed to be embraced. To be sure, writers of both genders needed – and continue to need – spaces in which they could share and criticize each other's work, freely discuss the difficulties that arise during the writing process and even engage in practice exercises within a communal setting. The Galway Writers Workshop, for example, sought to satisfy these needs during its regular meetings from its inception in 1981 until the late 1980s. The Workshop, which published the broadsheet that would quickly become the long-running *The Salmon* literary magazine (1981-1991), fostered a welcoming, creative atmosphere that appealed to writers of both genders. Poet Joan McBreen joined the Workshop in October 1986, and remembers it thus:

> We sat around a large mahogany table in ... [a] dusty room, upstairs over a noisy public house. It was filled with one family's memorabilia, usually heated in winter by a smoking open fire, set earlier on the evening of each Tuesday workshop by [proprietor] Mick Taylor. As we worked, read and discussed one another's poems and prose, I believe each person there felt strangely connected to the other. The magical elusive 'something' that is at the heart of a good poem was sought, sometimes found, and always respected. The environment, I believe, was the key to the now increasingly well-known Galway poets and writers (McBreen 14).

These needs might have been felt even more keenly by women, who might have suffered from isolation to a greater degree than their male counterparts: perhaps this is why it is often women writers, like McBreen, who enthusiastically articulate the ways in which a communal group setting benefits not only their own creative work, but also that of all group participants. *The Salmon*'s publisher Jessie Lendennie agrees wholeheartedly: 'Galway in those days; it was wonderful. With the whole new discovery of it. And all the women poets ... it was this enormous solidarity' (Lendennie 3).

Another significant Arlen House project, which might have developed out of the aforementioned short story competition, fits into this context. In October 1984, the women behind the Arlen publishing venture ran a weekend-long, all-women writing workshop in Dublin, which would include sessions on 'how to get fiction, poetry and drama published', as advertised in *Books Ireland* (Addis 147). [2] While the event was still listed as an Arlen House project, the official organizing body was probably WEB, The Women's Education Bureau, which 'had been

---

[2] This is the first documented workshop of this kind; however, similar training events might have been run by some other body previous to Arlen's event.

founded in 1984, directly out of Arlen House, as the national organization for women writers ... The aim was that new writers would be discovered in these workshops and that their work would be fed to Arlen House to be published (Hayes 145). While Hayes stresses the mutually beneficial aspect of the workshops for writers and publishers here, publisher Rose claims the motivation for setting up WEB had been 'the very concrete aim of sharing knowledge among women with a particular end in view – that of confident creative writing' (Leland). Indeed, sharing knowledge among women had become a crucial issue within local community groups such as the Kilbarrack Local Education for Adult Renewal (KLEAR), located in Dublin 5, and was to be central to the Women in Community Publishing training course set up by Irish Feminist Information in 1983.

Despite the fact that the services provided by KLEAR and others were geared towards general knowledge, such as Leaving Certificate courses in Basic English or Basic Maths, and could be useful to both genders, it was mainly women that took advantage of them. According to the official history of KLEAR, '[t]his can partly be explained by the different perceptions of men and women to the value of adult education, together with the fact that it is primarily women who are at home during the day'. KLEAR also made childcare a central component of its services, a revolutionary decision that acknowledged the tangible, day-to-day needs of the women it was trying to support. Importantly, it recognized that being unable to find time away from child-rearing – often for financial reasons, as many participants in KLEAR programmes were unemployed or low-income – constituted an obstacle to furthering education and personal growth, especially for women. All of KLEAR's courses offered childcare, funded by contributions from all members, whether or not they had children themselves. This 'no-crêche-no-classes' approach, as they called it, was remarkable for its commitment to working around and with the realities and responsibilities of child-rearing: motherhood and personal growth did not have to be mutually exclusive for women whose finances could not support the luxury of full-time childcare.

Both community initiatives that supported women in both practical and intellectual ways and dedicated women-only writers' workshops could give women the skills and self-confidence they needed to trust their own talent. Evelyn Conlon, whose work was later published by Attic Press, recalled that 'the real turning point was a national writers' workshop which ran over a number of weekend ... It's not that I learned how to write at this workshop, but it was the push I needed to make a go of it '('The Difference between Women and Men' 42).[3] Even though it is not certain that Conlon is referring specifically to the WEB workshop here, her comment does support the claim that workshops

---

[3] Other well-known participants in WEB's annual workshops included Roz Cowman, Éilis Ní Dhuibhne, and Ivy Bannister.

like these were important for the development of women's writing in Ireland.

Significantly, whether or not the writers who benefited from WEB's annual workshops would go on to publish extensively, these workshops became a safe place where – and from whence – women writers could take risks. Workshop participant Philomena Feighery wrote 'An Eyewitness Account of the Annual Workshop for Women Writers, 1986' for the Spring 1987 WEB newsletter. 'It's not easy to read aloud one's own writing to a group, especially when so many of them have such a track record [as writers] ...' she admits. But her fears were assuaged when

> [h]onest criticism and suggestions were generously offered and discussed at length. I felt so encouraged that I immediately resolved to put my pride in my pocket and submit work that I was having difficulty with. I got no end of help! Incidentally, one woman, having read out her work on the first day, had it accepted and printed by the Irish Press by the last day of the workshop ... Finally, and very importantly, I don't have the feeling anymore of being a writer in seclusion (Feighery n.p.).

Of course, the cheerful tone Feighery uses for her WEB newsletter audience may elide some of the realities that can potentially challenge the effectiveness of writing workshops regardless of gender, such as competitiveness; destructive, rather than constructive, criticism; or even the simple difficulty of reading, engaging with and suggesting revisions for poems over several hours at a time. However, there is no doubt that she genuinely views the WEB workshop as a possible solution to the isolation that can be suffered by the fledgling writer.

Clearly, Feighery was not alone. Demand for the first WEB workshop drastically exceeded supply: the organizers received two hundred applications for only twenty places. As a result, two more workshops were offered. Between 1987 and 1988, WEB even designed a twenty-week FÁS course on 'women into writing', coordinated and directed by Catherine Rose.[4]

> Unlike so many of the 'writers' workshop' groups, the course was strongly oriented towards the practicalities of marketing and presenting work to editors and publishers. The twenty-seven women students were chosen for their motivation to break into creative or feature writing, PR, editing or theatre work ... ('Women's Press Renaissance').

There are parallels between the broader approach taken here and publications by Arlen's imprint Turoe Press, such as *Write and Get Paid for It* (1979) or *Just a Few Words: How to Present Yourself in Public* (1984). Because of Rose's background in publishing, she was aware of the practical aspects of creative writing. By the time the FÁS

---

[4] FÁS is the Irish National Training and Employment Agency, formerly AnCo.

course took place, Attic Press had entered the scene, providing even more publishing opportunities for women. Thus, whether workshops focused on honing and revising creative work, or dealt with the 'practicalities of marketing' or other aspects of publishing, they were highly in demand. Workshops had certainly become valuable venues for women who were genuinely concerned with developing as writers. In Eavan Boland's words, 'I have met – who hasn't in this world? – arrogant and complacent poets. I have yet to meet an arrogant and complacent workshop' (Boland 1991: 48).

Workshops such as the ones hosted by WEB were certainly useful tools for women writers, but as many critics note, the term 'woman writer' is a broad one, and it can be difficult to determine which attributes are necessary for a writer to belong to this category, apart from her gender. Janet Madden-Simpson, editor of the anthology *Women's Part*, published by Arlen House in 1984, discusses the problem in her contribution to *Personally Speaking* (1985):

> The usefulness of any literary label is that it helps identification. By indicating what we may expect to find in a writer or a work, it may help our understanding. But a label can also be intrinsically reductive. Because we associate certain qualities with it, the connotations of the label may interfere with our reading to the extent that we see only what we expect to see. 'Woman writer' has not, in general, served writers well. It has always been an emotive label. We do not use, and have never used, the label 'man writer' precisely because we do not perceive the condition of being male and a writer to be in conflict – it is understood as a normal condition. 'Woman writer', on the other hand, is highly suggestive in that its very use encompasses our cultural attitudes towards women and art (Madden-Simpson 178).

These workshops and community initiatives whose activities we have discussed became integral sites where women's liberation was 'performed' via the written word and the altered way in which the written word made the crucial journey from private to public sphere. For some women, ultimately, writers' groups and writing workshops would function in a similar way to the consciousness-raising groups run by Irish, British and American feminists in the 1960s and 1970s (Stopper 3): the audiences for their creative work would be limited to group members and to themselves. For these women, the act of writing and participation in writing groups had therapeutic as well as creative value; it could be used as a space in which to achieve self-awareness and self-expression, without the goal of publishing their work. Other women writers and workshop participants, though, were keen to publish their work. Of course, using the written word to bring about social change was not a new concept. Anne Stopper describes this combination of writing and activism in the context of the Irish women's rights movement in the 1970s: 'For the IWLM [Irish Women's Liberation Movement] journalists, there was never any doubt between them that they should combine their journalism and their activism in their fight for women's equal rights', she declares. 'They would use every influence they could at their publications and through their colleagues in the broadcast media to get their message out to Irish women' (Stopper 2).

However, the majority of Irish women were (and are) neither journalists nor members of activist groups such as the IWLM. Many of them might have been, understandably, reluctant or unable to publicly 'fight' to effect social change. If such women were members of a writing workshop or writers group, though, publication of a workshop book or pamphlet could help bring their work – and thus the personal experiences and social concerns that were being written about and discussed within the group setting – into the public sphere, without having to engage visibly with radical politics or travelling through the daunting, male-dominated channels of traditional publishing. Once published, a creative or critical text is able to 'perform' on its own: moving into the public sphere, it takes on an almost independent power as it becomes part of a larger discourse, to be read, re-read, reviewed, criticized, theorized, praised, discarded, archived, and returned to. There, its very *presence* has the power to disrupt, to effect social change. One writer whose work has been 'returned to' time after time over the past two decades is the poet Rita Ann Higgins. First published in the early issues of *The Salmon* literary magazine, Higgins was a long-time member of the Galway Writers Workshop. The mother of two from a working-class background had only begun to write in her late twenties, after developing a love for literature while recovering from tuberculosis. Restrained, sarcastic and gritty, in Higgins's poems such as 'The Deserter' from her second collection, *Witch in the Bushes* (1992), the private voices and grievances of Irish women, and the reality of their daily lives, take central stage:

> He couldn't wait
> just up and died
> on me.
> …
> He couldn't wait,
> never,
> like the time
> before the All-Ireland
> we were going to Mass,
>
> he said he had to have a pint
> or he'd have the gawks, he said.
> that's the type he was,
> talk dirty in front of any woman.
>
> He's not giving
> out to me now

for using Jeyes Fluid
on the kitchen floor ...

The next time
I spend two hours
ironing shirts for him
he'll wear them
(Higgins 17-19).

Higgins is especially adept at binding the dissatisfaction of the private individual – that is, the narrator's own loutish husband who 'up and died' on her – to the public, social equivalent of that dissatisfaction: the narrator is aware that her 'listener' or reader is only too familiar with just the 'type' of man the speaker's husband was, talking 'dirty in front of any woman'. In her ability to bridge the private and the public spheres, Higgins's speaker – and the text she inhabits – performs a particularly powerful, and potentially disruptive, social critique in a way that, perhaps, a living person could not. Writing workshops and feminist publishing initiatives provided ways for texts such as Higgins's to be made public, making them vital conduits for social change. Once a text exists within the realm of published work, it achieves a kind of immortality: it can perform or articulate feminist acts each time it is encountered by a reader.

The presence of writing workshops and feminist publishers such as Arlen House were signs of a sea change within Ireland's larger social landscape. Eavan Boland was among those who sensed this change, and she noted it in her introduction to a 1984 collection of journalist and IWLM co-founder Nell McCafferty's articles, *The Best of Nell*, (McCafferty 10): 'What is much harder to measure, to quantify [than hard facts]', writes Boland,

> are shifts of perception. They are the slow, unseen rock-slides that begin in every generation without anyone being aware of the first slip, the first boulder loosening and scattering small pebbles. I have no doubt, and equally no proof, that there have been such shifts and changes in the climate of thought in this country in the last ten or fifteen years (Boland in McCafferty 10).

Jessie Lendennie, publisher of poetry press Salmon Poetry and former editor of *The Salmon*, believes she had become aware of a similar shift in perception as she began to publish collections of poetry by women in the 1980s. 'I mean, you just know these things', she says. 'Hey, the time was right, let's have some women['s voices] here' (Lendennie 3). In order for these women's voices to be heard, however, space had to be created for them: writing workshops and feminist publishers helped to create these spaces by encouraging their creativity as individual writers, providing them with networks of support and enabling many of them to becomes published authors. To paraphrase the poet Michael Hartnett, for Irish women in the 1970s, 1980s, and into the 1990s, the act of writing was a not only a rebel act: it was also a feminist act (Hartnett 145).

Bibliography

Addis, Jeremy, 'Uiliséas Anyone?', *Books Ireland* 86 (1984): 146-47.

Boland, Eavan, Preface, *The Best of Nell: A Selection of Writings Over Fourteen Years*, by Nell McCafferty (Dublin: Attic Press, 1984): 7-13.

---, Preface, *The Wall Reader* (Dublin: Arlen House, 1978).

---, 'In Defence of Workshops', *Poetry Ireland Review* 31 (1991): 40-48.

Cadman, Eileen, Gail Chester, and Agnes Pivot, *Rolling Our Own: Women as Printers, Publishers and Distributors* (London: Minority Press, 1981).

Colman, Anne, 'Nineteenth-Century Irish Women Writers: An Overview', *Women's Studies Centre Review* 3 (1995): 129-39.

Feighery, Philomena, 'Women's Education Bureau spring newsletter' (1987). University of Delaware: Archive of Salmon Publishing, Ltd. MS 438, Box 10, F220.

'The Difference between Women and Men', *Books Ireland* 211 1997: 41-42.

Hartnett, Michael, 'A Farewell to English', *Collected Poems* (Oldcastle, Co. Meath: Gallery Press, 2001): 141-45.

Hayes, Alan, 'Big Women, Little Women: Toward a History of Second Wave Commercial Feminist Publishing in Ireland', *Women's Studies Review* 6 (1999): 139-50.

Higgins, Rita Ann, *Witch in the Bushes* (Galway: Salmon Publishing, 1992).

Ingman, Heather, *Twentieth-Century Fiction by Irish Women: Nation and Gender* (Aldershot: Ashgate, 2007).

Irish Feminist Review' 84 (Dublin: Women's Community Press, 1984).

Joselow, Beth, Letter to Jessie Lendennie dated 30 July 1987. University of Delaware: Archive of Salmon Publishing, Ltd. MS 438, Box 10, F221.

Kilbarrack Local Education for Adult Renewal (KLEAR), Letter to Jessie Lendennie dated 16 June 1987. University of Delaware: Archive of Salmon Publishing, Ltd. MS 438, Box 10, F220.

Leland, Mary, 'Giving a Voice to Women Writers', *The Irish Times* 30 May 1985: 10.

Lendennie, Jessie, Interview with Megan Buckley and Julia Walther, Cliffs of Moher, 4 March 2008.

McBreen, Joan, 'Women's Poetry in Contemporary Ireland: The Upstairs Room', delivered at the First Annual Kerry International Summer School, 2-11 August 1994: 1-22. University of Delaware: Archive of Salmon Publishing, Ltd. MS 438,Box 5, F119.

Madden-Simpson, Janet, 'Womenwriting: The Arts of Textual Politics', *Personally Speaking: Women's Thoughts on Women's Issues*, ed. Liz Steiner-Scott (Dublin: Arlen House, 1985): 177-188.

Ó Cuilleanáin, Cormac, 'Irish Publishers: A Nation Once Too Often', *Crane Bag* 8:2 (1984): 115-123.

'Reading the Writing on the Arlen Wall', *The Irish Times* 22 June 1979: 12.

Rose, Catherine, 'Notes on the Competition', *The Adultery and Other Stories* (Dublin: Arlen House, 1982): 108.

---, Interview with Julia Walther, Dublin, 9 September 2008.

'Short Story Prizes for Women', *The Irish Times* 13 October 1987: 9.

Smyth, Ailbhe, 'Ireland's New Rebels', *The Women's Review of Books* 4:7
    (1987): 16-18.
'Social Whirl Dept.', *Books Ireland* 28 (1978): 175.
Stopper, Anne, *Mondays at Gaj's: The Story of the Irish Women's Liberation
    Movement* (Dublin: The Liffey Press, 2006).
Women's Education Bureau (WEB), Spring Newsletter 1987. University of
    Delaware: Archive of Salmon Publishing, Ltd. MS 438, Box 10, F220.
'Women's Press Renaissance', *Books Ireland* 21 (1988): 41.

8 | 'Judgemental oul' hoors': Catholicism in the work of Marian Keyes

Lisa McGonigle

The Catholic Church earned much censure from the Irish Women's Liberation Movement for its dictates on female sexuality and reproductive rights, leading Francis Mulhern to describe Irish feminists as 'the exposed vanguard in a prolonged struggle to end clerical usurpation of women's reproductive rights and thus to open the way to a fully secular public domain' (155). The availability or otherwise of contraceptives, the emotive abortion and divorce referenda of the 1980s and 90s and the tragic events in the lives of a number of individual women - Ann Lovett, Joanne Hayes, the X-case) - described by Siobhan Kilfeather as 'the human costs of Ireland's Catholic ethos' (111), all focused attention on women's sexual and reproductive autonomy or the withholding thereof. Reflecting the striking degree to which these 'questions of socio-sexual control' (Smyth 34) featured on the political agenda of the second half of the twentieth century in Ireland, and the manner in which Irish feminists resisted and challenged the inscription of Catholic doctrine in social policy through activism and intellectual discourse alike, is the *Field Day Anthology: Volume V, women's writing and traditions*. Alongside its sister volume IV, Volume V was commissioned after the first three volumes of the anthology - the product of an all-male editorial committee - were, when viewed from a feminist perspective, felt to elide both female voices and cultural movements of feminist concern. It accordingly contains a section entitled 'The Politics of Sexuality' which demonstrates how, as Roy Foster terms it, 'procreation became politics' (42) from the 1960s onwards.

The supplementary *Field Day* volumes were published in 2002 but by 2004, however, Gerry McCarthy argued that they already presented an outmoded picture of Irish women's writing and concerns when contrasted with the rapidly expanding body of Irish 'chick-lit', women's popular fiction:

> Those volumes [of the *Field Day* project] are already out of date. They have an explicitly political and feminist subtext: their editors are conscious of reclaiming literary ground for women. The new generation of writers has left all that behind. Their work is free-spirited and hedonistic, post-feminist and post-ideological. These writers, and their mainly female readers, are on the same wavelength: they no longer worry about the battle of the sexes. They are too busy enjoying the spoils of victory.

Rebecca Pelan similarly discerns a depoliticization in this recent outpouring of chick-lit, arguing that there has been 'a considerable shift from the focus of earlier works, which generally concerned issues of family (usually dysfunctional) and religion (together with its impact on sexuality), as well as a variety of societal ills', with writers such as Marian Keyes instead showcasing 'an Irish-style *Sex and the City* sassiness, a breezy preoccupation with looks, men and careers' (xiii). Particularly when viewed from the outside, Irish chick-lit appears to have cast off the concerns of the past and instead constitutes part of a global 'new girl order' (Hymowitz), a worldwide economic shift having led to a generation of financially independent and cosmopolitan 'singletons' in the wake of Bridget Jones. One Spanish critic, for example, argues that:

> Cathy Kelly's and Marian Keyes's novels do not present a particularly Irish setting but are part of an international cultural trend. The only references to Irish culture and reality are names and places, and so these novels erase any other trace of cultural identification proposing a universal model of behaviour for 'modern' women in developed countries (Barros del Rio).

A Canadian commentator similarly claims that 'what is remarkable about the novels of [Marian] Keyes and [Cecilia] Ahern is how completely the old Ireland, the impoverished Ireland of saints and martyrs and sinners and drunks, is absent from them. Their stories, which never mention religion, could be set in any affluent western city' (McStoffman).

However, although the work of Keyes, one of Ireland's most successful chick-lit writers, may resonate with an international audience, it nonetheless retains a keen cultural specificity particularly in its engagement with the politics of sexuality and the operations of gender, rendering Keyes far from 'post-ideological' and significantly affecting the description of her as 'post-feminist'. Keyes, admittedly, remarks that her own understanding of the term 'feminism' has evolved: 'I used to describe myself as a post-feminist. I had picked up this notion that all the work ... had been done by those wonderful women in the Sixties and Seventies' (Glover). However, although her generation 'were told that the battle of the sexes was over and we were all equal now' she nonetheless 'couldn't help noticing that women are still second-class citizens' in many ways (Klein). As an example of this she points to the disparagement of chick-lit as 'forgettable froth' while male writers are vaunted for their work within a similar emotional range, 'oh you silly little woman with your little fluffy stories about shoes and romance ... as if men have the monopoly on intellectual criticism' (Carey, Karras). Reappropriating the chick-lit tag, Keyes views it as having the potential to be an 'empowering' genre, 'about the conflicts and confusions of our post-feminist world, where we're told we're equal, but we know we're not' (Lavery). 'Post-' here operates as a temporal marker vis-a-vis Second Wave feminism and the struggles of Irish women's movement throughout the 1960s and 70s rather than indicating a cultural state in which issues of gender inequity and inequality are simply consigned to the past.

Keyes's feminist awakening and how, as she herself puts it, she has become 'more politicized' (Lavery) throughout her literary career, is evinced in her evolving choice of subject material, with Mary Ryan observing that her work 'tackles issues such as domestic violence and rape at full force, creating strong ties between Irish chick-lit and feminism' (98). In *This Charming Man* (2008), for example, a journalist draws attention to how 'one in five Irish women will experience domestic violence at some stage in their lives' (179) but how 'rapists and wife-batterers rarely got anything but joke sentences from a sympathetic, almost entirely male judiciary' (168). *The Brightest Star in the Sky* (2009) similarly explores the societal prejudices and systemic difficulties faced by victims of rape. A character, Maeve, is assaulted by a former boyfriend and propelled into 'a whole world she'd known nothing about ... Cold metal. An internal examination. Swabs and photos. An STD test. An Aids test. Too soon, of course, to do a pregnancy test. Feet back up in the stirrups for another internal. [Her husband] holding her hand. Checks for bruising, tearing, internal bleeding (532). When these harrowing procedures are complete, the attending garda asks her if she's 'sure [she] didn't just, you know, get a bout of the guilts? One last go, for old times' sake, then got afraid that hubby there might get wind' (536). When Maeve makes clear that this was not the case she is then asked 'Are you sure you want to go ahead with this? Taking it further? ... Because it'll ruin his life, you know. Just so as you know' (536). In contrast to this concern for the perpetrator, scant sympathy is shown to Maeve. When she confides in close friends about the rape, she is met with scepticism and disbelief: 'how could he rape you? He used to be your boyfriend ... that's a terrible thing to say. He could sue you for that' (538). And whereas Maeve suffers panic attacks and debilitating anxiety as a result of the rape, the strain on her marriage eventually impelling her husband into a suicide attempt, the case does not even proceed to prosecution as 'the DPP thinks there isn't enough evidence to get a conviction' (537). As Diarmaid Ferriter reports, Ireland in the first decade of the twenty-first century had the lowest rape conviction rate in the European Union (189).

In exploring the challenges facing 'post-feminist Irish women', Keyes notes that 'many of our concerns transcend nationhood and are shared with women of a similar age in the rest of the developed world' (2005b). However, she adds that:

> Irish women are also different from other post-feminist women ... we're still shaking off the shackles of a deeply misogynistic and controlling church, where battered women were told to return to their abusive husbands because 'what God has put together, let no man put asunder'. A country where, although contraception is legal, abortion is not only illegal but unconstitutional (2005b).

Keyes elsewhere points to 'the fact that in our constitution, which is the foundation of the state, it literally says the woman's place is in the home' (Jolly). As 'an attempt to pass from an imagined idea of Irishness to the realized state of Ireland', the 1937 Constitution was both legal charter and moral blueprint and though Patrick Hanafin observes of Article 41 - which recognizes woman's 'life within the home' - that 'it is at the symbolic, rather than at the strictly legal, level that such provisions are of importance ... the very persistence of such provisions in the Constitution [nonetheless] lend tacit support to the notion of patriarchy' (149; 159). Keyes also describes herself as being 'incredibly uncomfortable with any remnants of the theocracy that Ireland was until relatively recently. I much prefer Ireland being a secular country and secular countries don't have the laws of particular religions enshrined in their constitutions' (Carey) and is unequivocal in her antipathy towards the Catholic Church. When asked to name her 'real-life villain' she responded 'I'm not keen on the leaders of most organized religions, but being a recovering Catholic, I'll choose one and go for the Pope' (Philby) and has repeatedly referred to 'the damage done, in particular to Irish women' by the 'misogyny and hypocrisy' of the hierarchy, leaving her 'repelled by the cruelty of Catholicism. Women in Ireland have thirteen children. It is very misogynistic' (O'Connell).

In his essay 'The Irish Mammy', Joseph O'Connor quotes Margaret McCurtain's remark that in such a cultural climate, 'around Irishwomen, as in a cage, were set the structures of family life' (299). A stock figure in Keyes's work is likewise that of the 'Irish Catholic Mammy', a woman of a certain age whose subjectivity is defined by her maternal duties and family role. In *The Other Side of the Story* (2004), Gemma describes her mother, Maureen, as an archetypal 'Irish Catholic Mammy' who 'won't miss Sunday Mass even if she's got rabies and is foaming at the mouth – she'll simply bring a box of tissues and brazen it out. If her leg falls off, she'll hop. If her other leg falls off, she'll walk on her hands while still managing to wave graciously at neighbours' passing cars' (57). Gemma recollects how growing up in the cul-de-sac where her mother still lives, 'all the neighbours were women of Mam's age and older and they were called Mary, Maura, May, Maria, Moira, Mary, Maree, Mary, Mary and Mary. Except for Mrs Prior who was called Lotte but that was only because she was Dutch' (Gemma's mother generously concedes of Mrs Prior, 'I'm very fond of Lotte, even if she is a Lutheran' (57)). Elizabeth Cullingford notes that in post-independence Ireland, women's 'life within the home' was 'invested ... with a constitutionally approved aura of Marian sanctity' and this is reflected in these women's names (251).

When after thirty-five years of marriage, Maureen's husband abruptly leaves to have an affair with his considerably younger PA - 'the tedious predictability of it all' (15), as Gemma bitterly notes - she is distraught. Requiring tranquilizers and anti-depressants, she is initially unable to even to attend to such basic tasks as washing and dressing, leading Gemma to move back home. Twelve months later, however, her husband arrives 'at the front door with three shopping bags full of his stuff and asked Mam ... if he could come back' (526) and by the time Gemma returns to the house that evening 'he was settled in his chair, doing the crossword [and] Mam was in the kitchen cooking up a storm' (527). When Gemma upbraids her mother for not reproaching her father in the slightest about his previous infidelity and desertion, her mother responds in a 'devout and unreachable' (527) tone that 'I made my wedding vows before God and man ... he's my husband. I took my marriage vows in a *church*' (527-28). Gemma reflects that such vows had 'made martyrs and eejits of generations of women' (527) and seethes with resentment that 'thinking of herself as a dutiful wife, instead of a woman with feelings and rights, meant that Dad was able to slot right back into the life that she'd kept warm for him' (528), corroborating Gerardine Meaney's argument that Catholic configurations of womanhood rendered Irish women 'unable to accept themselves as thinking, choosing, sexual, intellectual, and complex ordinary mortals and instead cling to a fantasy of women as simple handmaidens of the Lord' (cited in Inglis 2005: 25). However, although Gemma is 'infuriated ... beyond belief' (528) she recognizes as that 'there's no reasoning with that sort of lunacy' (527) she must accept her mother's passivity and instead concludes 'thank God I'm an atheist' (528) if such self-abnegation and doormatting is the result of piety.

Keyes contends that although 'for Irish people of a certain vintage, devout Catholicism is still the order of the day ... Ireland, in the new millennium, is straddling a spiritual faultline' and that 'for younger compatriots, anything goes' (2000b). This generational divide towards the respect ceded to the Church is also evident in her short story 'Late Opening at the Last Chance Saloon', set against the divorce referendum of 1995. The central protagonist complains to her mother about '"All that praying you made us do...And making us go to Mass. And starving us on Good Friday ... And making us feel ashamed of our bodies and guilty about absolutely everything"' ... Nuala glowed with pride. Truly, she had been the best of Catholic mothers' (184). In contrast to such devotional fervour, the younger characters reject the hegemony of the Church, referring to the clergy as 'hypocrites and perverts' (183) and asking in disgust 'what kind of a country ... says it's OK for men in dresses to sexually assault little boys?' (182). As Joe Cleary observes, a crucial difference between the abortion and divorce referenda of the 1980s and the 1990s was that in the latter decade the 'scandals' and revelations of clerical child abuse 'discredited the authority of the Catholic hierarchy that had earlier given a lead to such campaigns', thereby lessening the public's receptiveness to pastoral guidance on issues of personal morality (15).

The young women equally object to the moral high-handedness of the anti-divorce campaigners. The 'No' lobby is scathingly described as:

> Judgemental oul' hoors. Offer it up, they say. Let him ride rings around himself and publicly humiliate you and you'll get your reward in the next world ... I can't believe the attitude in this country ... where people think that if your husband belts you black and blue that you have to put up with it – for batter, for worse. You can be damn sure that if any of those Good Catholics ever got a good thumping they wouldn't be preaching 'stand by your man'

(186-87).

For Keyes, the hallmark of Catholicism is this judgementalism, also embodied by Chaquie, a minor character in her novel *Rachel's Holiday* (1997). *Rachel's Holiday* documents the eponymous heroine's descent into and recovery from substance abuse with a sizeable part of the text taking place in a drug and alcohol treatment centre. Rachel's roommate in the treatment centre is a 'blonde, glamorous woman' (77) called Chaquie - pronounced 'Jackie' but expressly spelt otherwise as she feels 'Jackie's so common when it's spelt J-A-C-K-I-E' (78) - who appears to be an impeccable exemplar of Catholic orthodoxy and middle-class respectability. 'I didn't see you at Mass this evening' she comments 'purse-lipped' (157) to Rachel, before starting 'on another of her hobby-horses. This time it was the evil of mothers who work' (157). She is elsewhere heard:

> Complaining loudly about unmarried mothers being given free condoms to stop them expanding their families ... 'It's disgraceful,' she fumed. 'Why should the taxpayers' money be spent on giving them free french letters? They shouldn't need anything at all. Do you know what the best contraceptive is? ... The word 'no'! It's as simple as that, just two little letters, n and o. No. If they had any morals at all ... (302).

'I knew her sort', Rachel initially thinks to herself, 'she was a member of Right Wing Catholic Mothers Against Pleasure, or whatever they were called' (160) and although she develops a 'strange, grudging fondness' for Chaquie as the novel progresses, this is because Chaquie's 'in-yer-face right-wing views' (350) and her 'insistence that she was a good, respectable, upper-middle-class citizen' (349)' are shown to be a blind for her alcoholism and the 'pain and insecurity rampaging about below her sleek, glamorous surface' (350), not because Rachel – or indeed, Keyes – comes to align herself in any way with Chaquie's 'judgemental, Catholic stance' (350). The equation of Catholicism with judgementalism also permeates Keyes's novel *Sushi for Beginners* (2000), set in the glossy world of Irish women's magazines. As Ireland undergoes an economic boom and Celtic Tiger consumerism overtakes Catholicism as the dominant cultural force, while certain of the lifestyle magazines – '*Hibernian Bride, Celtic Health, Gaelic Interiors, Irish Gardening*' (6) – increase in circulation, it is gleefully reported throughout the text that the *Catholic Judger* is instead 'about to fold...sales are way down' (6) throughout the text, eventually going 'to the wall' (62).

The young women in 'Late Opening at the Last Chance Saloon' are equally jubilant when they learn that a 'yes' vote in the divorce referendum has been secured. Not only will this allow vulnerable women to extricate themselves from violent or abusive relationships but they also interpret the introduction of divorce in symbolic terms as 'a triumph of civilization and modernism ... now Ireland will be able to hold its head up in the real world, without having to apologize for its medieval laws' (188-89). Keyes herself similarly viewed the introduction of divorce as 'a huge step forward. It meant that Catholic priests were no longer running the country' (Doherty 1998). In her association of the Church with a retrograde oppressiveness which modern Ireland is leaving behind, Keyes aligns herself further with the Irish feminist tradition. The introduction to the 'Politics of Sexuality' section of the *Field Day* anthology, for example, similarly frames the debates and schisms in Irish society 'over women's sexuality, reproduction, the structure of the family and the place of women within it' as 'major battles between tradition and innovation' and the X-case in particular as 'a battle between a conservative, Catholic Ireland and a compassionate modern nation' (Barry and Wills 1411). Joe Cleary observes that:

> Given the oppressive nature of the Irish state as it developed after independence, and the pervasive equation of women with tradition in Irish nationalist and clericalist culture, it was virtually inevitable perhaps that Irish feminism would largely endorse modernization theory. Because Ireland was construed as an oppressively traditional society, modernization by convergence with 'the Western world' was viewed by contrast as an emancipatory process that would liberate Irish women ... Modernization theories and 'second wave' Irish feminism are not only historically coincident with each other, both gaining momentum in the 1960s and 1970s but they also share a structure of feeling in which contemporary Ireland is viewed as a 'traditional' society now undergoing an exhilarating liberation from the past (15-16).

Cleary and others urge for this binary view to be replaced by a more nuanced examination of the changes in Irish society and a recognition that a wholesale disparagement of the past and embracing of the modern brings with it issues of its own. Terry Eagleton, for example, describes 'tradition' in Ireland as signalling 'an oppressive church, a stifling patriarchy, dancing statues of the Virgin, Gaelic chauvinism, and the contract for building new roads going to whichever relative of the minister is currently most strapped for cash' (1998: 313), but cautions that 'modernization ... means sweat shops and shattered communities as well as enlightened values, pollution and migration alongside Thai cuisine ... Temple Bar is no more a solution to the riddle of history than the Tubbercurry Legion of Mary' (2001). He contends that 'a truly modern nation would be one which felt able to recall its history without either tearful sentimentalism or glib derision', though mischievous derision might better describe Keyes's response when asked if she missed the 'old Ireland' (2001). 'Yes', she quipped 'yes, I like to think that in the old Ireland I'd have been condemned from the pulpit and exiled which would have been fun' (Klein).

Tearful sentimentalism for the Catholic past, meanwhile, becomes comedic fodder. *Rachel's Holiday* is one of a series of novels Keyes has written about the five daughters of the Walsh family, presided over by Mary 'Mammy' Walsh.[1]

Mammy Walsh is described by one of her daughters as 'the woman who cried when divorce came to Ireland and said it was the end of civilization as we knew it' (2002: 387) while another recollects that if she or her sisters 'asked for two Paracetemol for our sore throat/stomach ache/broken leg/perforated duodenal ulcer' (2005: 61), their mother's response would be 'Offer it up ... Think of Our Lord suffering on the cross' (2005: 61). In the novel *Angels* (2002), the family visit Los Angeles and attend 'Mass, LA style' (427) with 'lots of singing and melodramatic acting-out of the readings' (428). Mammy Walsh announces to the congregation 'We're from Ireland (427)', her daughter Maggie understanding the unspoken subtext as being '*we're REAL Catholics*' (427). Not only is Irishness synonymous with Catholicism but 'authentic' Catholicism is predicated on self-flagellation and guilt as mastered by the 'über-Catholics from Ireland' (428): in contrast to the 'unbridled zeal' and 'upbeat and celebratory mood' (428) of the service in LA, Maggie recalls Irish Mass as 'a miserable priest droning at a quarter-full church, 'Blah blah blah, sinners, blah blah blah, soul black with sin, blah blah blah, burn in hell' (Keyes: 428). As Tom Inglis observes, this was a 'culture of self-denial, the rhetoric and practice of foregoing pleasure' holding sway (2005: 24).

Of all sinful pleasures, those of sexual overtness and transgression appal Mammy Walsh the most. When she discovers one of Rachel's flimsy G-strings in the washing machine, she explodes in disgust, shouting 'you brazen HUSSY! That might be the kind of thing they wear in New York, but you're not in New York now and while you're under

---

[1] *Watermelon* (Dublin: Poolbeg, 1995). However, the edition cited here is that published by Arrow Books: London, 2005. *Rachel's Holiday* (London: Penguin, 1997). *Angels* (London: Penguin, 2002) and *Anyone Out There?* (London: Penguin, 2007).

my roof you'll cover yourself like a Christian' (1997b: 576). On another
occasion she admonishes for Rachel for 'the right show you made of me
with your drugs carry-on' (543) but when Rachel later apologizes for
'embarrassing you by being a drug addict' (561) her mother concedes
'Sure, it could be miles worse. Hilda Shaw is having a baby. Another
one. And she's *still* not married. And, wait till you hear ... Angela
Kilfeather is after deciding she's a lesbian ... a drug addict is nothing
compared to that' (561). Though Mammy Walsh and Rachel then 'laugh
tearfully' (562) and reconcile and this is a lighthearted moment in an
emotionally demanding text, Keyes is nonetheless adroit in identifying
a cultural consciousness in which the transgressions causing the
greatest disruption to the social order were sexual ones (see Inglis
2005).

Keyes also describes her own mother as an Irish Catholic mammy:
'Devout. The rosary beads. Prays for us all ... Any time anyone gets a
new car it has to be christened by holy water from Knock. She has the
perm, the cardigan, the handbags and neat shoes. The huge disapproval
of promiscuity and people drinking too much' (Swarbrick). She has
similarly spoken about her mother's discomfort with the sexual content
of her work and how her mother 'begs me - begs me - to take out the
bad language and the sex. Begs me ... She's got a big thing about blow
jobs. She doesn't actually believe they happen' (Deveney). However, the
sexual frankness of Keyes's writing is both deliberate and significant.
Her first novel, *Watermelon*, was published in 1995 and in 2006 she
remarked that 'in the early days, I didn't know what I was writing
because the word 'chick-lit' wasn't invented then. I just knew that I
wanted to write a book about women like me: basically, Irish women
that are sexually active. It was the first time in popular commercial Irish
fiction that women were writing about sex' ('How Marian Lives to Dye
Another Day'). She relates this reticence about sex to the hegemony of
the Church, describing the 'constant message of Catholicism' as that
one is 'burdened' with 'original sin ... You are born defective and you are
a woman, so you must be modest. To come out of that with any kind of
sexuality intact is a triumph' ('How Marian Lives to Dye Another Day').
Watermelon thus parodies and dismisses 'that nonsense about men
being ... well ... different from us, dear. They have ... needs ... dear, in
the same way that animals do' (44) by depicting Irish women as having
needs and desires of their own, rather than simply being the chaste

repudiators or joyless recipients of animalistic male lust.[2]

Fintan O'Toole claims of Irish culture of the Celtic Tiger years that:

> The most thoroughly globalized brand of Irish culture in the boom years was also the most conservative. Aspects of Irish culture were commodified as never before in boybands, popular women's fiction and Irish dancing shows. At least the first two of those, however, tended to be peculiarly archaic ... One of the real markers of this was sex. It is a lavish understatement to say that Irish sexual mores changed in the 1990s ... [however] what the boybands and much of the chicklit shared was a strangely antiseptic, coy sexuality (186).

O'Toole points to Cecilia Ahern as an exemplar of this sexual conservatism, shying away as she does from anything approaching explicitness in her work. However just as *mná na hÉireann* are not one homogenous whole, neither are Irish chick-lit writers. If, as one reviewer remarked, 'the action always stops well short of the bedroom door' (Sutton) in the bestsellers of Ahern - who describes herself as a 'modern Catholic' - then Keyes's characters, such as Lola in *This Charming Man*, sneak into the bedroom of a potential lover, speculate on 'the things that must happen in this room' and are urged by their friends to 'Look in [the] drawer beside his bed ... Go on, see if he's got condoms in it. I bet he has (262)'. Lola later reports back to her friends that her new partner is a 'great man for different positions' (294), indeed, his sexual athleticism is such that she 'would be just starting to get into rhythm and enjoy herself when she would be picked up, twirled about like majorette's baton and entirely repositioned' (298). 'How hard is it to just get a normal shag?' (294) she asks, exasperated. Throughout her work Keyes explores a variety of activities and proclivities across the sexual spectrum, including passionate intensity where 'lust just *exploded* within me ... My head swam with shock and pleasure' (1997, 57), an emotionally unengaged rebound relationship in which 'Friday nights ... had become a regular thing *and* we usually managed a quick mid-week ride. [It] was great fun and there was no pesky churning-stomach, wobbly-kneed, tongue-tied stuff you get when you're mad about someone' (2004, 354), the availability of 'special underwear ... to tuck in your man-bits so they won't be poking out through your ... dress' (2008, 284) for cross-dressers, and a same-sex liaison which firmly

---

[2] In her article on Irish chick-lit Mary Ryan cites Donna Ferriss's observation that instead of 'presenting their protagonists as subordinate to male advances, chick-lit authors present women as sexual agents'; Mary Ryan, 'A Feminism of Their Own?: Irish Women's History and Contemporary Irish Women's Writing', *Estudios Irlandeses*, Issue 5, 2010: 92-101: 94.

obliterates one character's 'subconscious prejudice that all lesbians look like Elton John' (2002, 190). As Kathy Cremin notes, 'the evolution of popular Irish women's fiction throughout the 1990s permits us to reflect on ... changing attitudes to gender and sexuality' (Cremin: 62-3) and how the desexualised Irish mammy has been thoroughly displaced.

Imelda Whelehan observes that although the protagonists of chick-lit texts are almost exclusively sexually active young women, certain topics remain curiously occluded from the genre, namely 'periods ... bad sex, abortions, and sexually transmitted diseases' (219). She suggests that the absence of unsatisfactory sex from the genre is because its inclusion could be considered 'too feminist, too strident' (219). Keyes, however, is unflinching in describing not only those encounters where 'as soon as he entered me, I started to come. And come and come. It went on forever ... my body contracted with waves of pleasure' (1997b: 59) but also 'those nightmare sex sessions when you both realize about three seconds into it that it's a terrible, terrible mistake ... [but] you can't pretend that you've just seen someone you know on the other side of the room ... you can't just look at your watch, gasp and mutter something incoherent about your flatmate having no key to get it ... you're there for the duration and you've just got to grin and bear it' (1997: 539-40). Neither such experiences nor the 'sickening period pains' (1997b: 283) by which her protagonists are occasionally beset prove taboo for Keyes. The absence of STDs from her work similarly emanates less from a sense of propriety and more from her characters' fastidiousness in observing 'the condom ritual. You know, rustling round in a drawer for it, the crinkling of the wrapping paper being undone, saying "is that the right way? Or does it go the other way?"' (2005: 326-27) even in the most torrid of moments.

However, there is one notable exception to such heedfulness throughout Keyes's work. As previously mentioned, Keyes has written a series of novels about the five Walsh sisters and Maggie, the second eldest daughter, is looked upon by the others as 'the 'good' daughter' (1997b: 468), a 'lickarse' (1997b: 592), the 'most dutiful of us all' (2005: 43). Rachel reports of their childhood that Maggie's primary school teacher had 'never met such a well-behaved little girl in her thirty-eight years of teaching' (1997b: 307) and describes Maggie as 'the only one of us who spoke to our neighbours, happy to discuss hip replacements, grandchildren's First Communions, the unusually wet weather and the availability of Tayto in Chicago' (1997b: 22). Maggie, for her part, describes the family as operating at 'maintenance level dysfunction' (2002: 24) and the collective credo of her sisters being 'The More

Dramas the Better' (2002: 24). She is only occasionally bothered by how her sisters unfailingly 'referred to me as clean living and sporty ... and painted a picture of me that was years, probably decades, out of date' (2002: 23) and acknowledges in the opening lines of *Angels* - narrated from her perspective - that she'd 'always lived a fairly blameless life' (1), later reiterating that she is 'bad at being bad' (430). She recollects how 'the one time I tried shoplifting, I got caught ... The day I bunked off school ... I got caught' (430-31) and text moves towards the revelation that, as a seventeen year-old, 'the one time I had unprotected sex ... I got pregnant' (431).

Maggie withholds this information from her parents as she feels they would be shocked to hear of her predicament. She was, she explains, 'the well-behaved one, my parents' comfort, the one daughter they could look at and not have to say, 'Where did I go wrong?'' (432), whereas 'if someone wild and breezy like [her older sister] Claire had gotten pregnant at seventeen, it would be as if everyone had almost expected it from her' (2002, 432). Claire for example - who upon being abandoned by her husband and left alone with a newborn baby vows to rear her child on 'feminist diatribes ... out with *The Little Mermaid* and in with *The Female Eunuch*' (2005, 51) - describes abortion as 'something I feel very strongly about' (2005, 506) and rails against 'the crowd who get all sanctimonious and self-righteous and say that abortion is murder' (2005, 505) with 'SPUC stickers [on] the back window of the car' (2005, 505). Maggie remarks that Claire was 'very vocal about women's rights and what bastards the priests were. In fact she used to go on so much about the right to abortion that Mum often sighed, 'That one'll get up the pole and have an abortion just to prove a point' (435). For Maggie, however, having an abortion is not a political statement but a desperate release from a crushing bind. Echoing Frederica Mathewes-Green's famous remark that 'no woman wants an abortion as she wants an ice-cream cone or a Porsche. She wants an abortion as an animal caught in a trap wants to gnaw off its own leg', Maggie describes how she 'thrashed around like an animal in a trap, torn asunder and trapped ever deeper by the ugly realization that no matter what choice I made, it would have terrible implications that I'd have to live with for the rest of my life' (433). Nonetheless, feeling 'young and incapable, barely mature enough to take care of myself, never mind a helpless scrap of life' (433), she decides that 'not having it was the best - or least bad - option' (434). She describes the psychological 'fall-out' (444) from the abortion which follows, how she was wracked by 'every emotion from guilt to curiosity, shock to regret, self-hatred to wretched relief' (444). In subsequent years when friends considering abortion would turn to her for advice, her counsel would be that 'it was their body and they had the right to choose ... But ... they shouldn't expect to emerge unscathed from the experience' (444).

Keyes explains that she didn't want to 'to come across as being blasé about [abortion]. It's probably the worst thing that can happen to many women, having to make that choice. I didn't want to trivialize it, and say 'ah sure, hop off for an abortion in your lunch hour' (Carey). Nonetheless, she stresses that 'we've got to face the fact that it happens' and points to a 'huge blind spot in Ireland, pretending that it's not going on, and of course it happens all the time' (Carey). Whilst contending that 'popular fiction is not really the place for polemic' (Carey), she nonetheless concedes that she was slightly 'agenda-driven' when writing about abortion in *Angels* and wanting to 'show that it happens to 'good girls'' (Hayden) such as Maggie. Luke Gibbons contends that the task fell to Irish culture to 'discharge the excess that could not be accommodated within the language of broadcasting, journalism or indeed the courtroom' (215) by providing 'the scandals' with fictionalized treatment but what Keyes attests to in *Angels* is not the 'sensationalized test cases' which gripped the media in the 1980s and 1990s but the largely unchronicled experiences of the thousands of Irishwomen who travel to Britain for abortions every year.[3] The depth of the emotion, however, not only personal but also political, aroused by the issue of abortion nonetheless permeates the text. Maggie, who describes herself as a 'a foul-weather Christian, and only prayed when I was afraid or when I desperately wanted something' (426), recounts how:

> Occasionally, anti-abortionists paraded through the streets of Dublin, campaigning to make abortion in Ireland more illegal than it always was, carrying rosary beads and waving placards with pictures of abortion foetuses. I had to look away. But when I listened to them condemning abortion so vehemently, I wanted to ask if any of them had ever been in my situation. I would've bet money that they hadn't. And that if they had, their commitment to high-minded principle might have wavered (439).

Although Keyes cannot automatically be conflated with her first-person narrators, she nonetheless acknowledges that this is her own voice in the text: 'that's just how I feel about the men who tell women

---

[3] In 2008, 4,600 women gave addresses in the Irish Republic when presenting for abortions in England and Wales.
http://www.dh.gov.uk/prod_consum_dh/groups/dh_digitalassets/docume nts/digitalasset/dh_099714.pdf

not to have abortions. It's terribly wrong for one group of people to force their morals on another group of people, and judge them, when they know nothing about what it feels like to be in that situation and will never have to put their own opinions to the test' (Carey). In *Watermelon* Claire similarly challenges the reader to 'show me a man who's pregnant, penniless and partnerless and *then* invite him to stand on the soap-box and tell me that he thinks abortion is completely wrong. Hah!' (506). Just as how the 'No' lobby in 'Late Opening at the Last Chance Saloon' were described as 'judgmental oul hoors', here it is the misogyny and judgementalism of the rosary-bead bearing 'pro-life bullies' (444) which proves particularly unpalatable for Keyes.

Ann Dooley describes Irish chick-lit as the product of a 'post-Catholic' climate, reflecting an Ireland which is now 'the most libertine place in Europe' where 'anything goes' after the erosion of 'the authority of the church and the family' (McStoffman). Keyes's landscape may be considered post-Catholic in that Catholicism neither feeds into her protagonists' codes of personal morality nor a potent political force in the more widespread social milieu. The Irish mammy, if viewed affectionately, is a comic anachronism against the social and sexual liberalization which has taken place. Nonetheless, the unfond eye Keyes casts over any lingering traces of the Catholic ethos and the strength of the antagonism she demonstrates towards the Church compromises any description of her chick-lit novels as a celebratory free-for-all. Her championing of Irishwomen's sexual and reproductive freedoms is both a reflection of the societal changes which have occurred and exploration of issues of continued feminist concern.

Bibliography

Barros Del Rio, Maria Amor, 'How to disguise fairy tales in 21st Century Ireland: a feminist analysis of Marian Keyes's and Cathy Kelly's blockbusters', *Estudios Irlandeses,* 0, 2005: 12-21.

Barry, Ursula and Wills, Clair, 'The Republic of Ireland: the politics of sexuality 1965-2000', *Field Day Anthology of Irish Writing: volume V, Irish women's writing and traditions*, eds Angela Bourke et al. (Cork: Cork University Press, 2002): 1409-15.

Bourke, Angela, Siobhan Kilfeather, Maria Luddy, Margaret MacCurtain, Gerardine Meaney, Máirín Ní Dhonnchadha, Mary O'Dowd, and Clair Wills, (eds), *Field Day Anthology of Irish Writing: volume V, Irish women's writing and traditions* (Cork: Cork University Press, 2002).

Carey, Anna, 'Love, marriage and surviving heartache', *Sunday Tribune*, 24 May 2002: accessed via Lexis-Nexis 21 July 2011.

Cleary, Joe, 'Introduction: Ireland and modernity', *Cambridge Companion to Modern Irish Culture*, ed. Joe Cleary (Cambridge: Cambridge University Press, 2005).

Cremin, Kathy, 'The dispersed and dismissed: the world of Irish women's bestsellers', *Critical Survey*, 15, 2003.

Cullingford, Elizabeth, *Ireland's others: ethnicity and gender in Irish literature and popular culture* (Cork: Cork University Press, 2001).

Deveney, Catherine, 'The other side of the story', *Scotland on Sunday*, 20 May 2006: accessed via Lexis-Nexis, 21 July 2011.

Doherty, Amanda, 'Closing the chapter on my alcoholic haze', *Sunday Mirror*, 24 May 1998: accessed via Lexis-Nexis, 21 July 2011.

Eagleton, Terry, 'A side-splitting spoof', *Irish Times*, 3 March 2001: accessed via Lexis-Nexis, 21 July 2011.

---, *Crazy John and the Bishop and other essays on Irish culture* (Cork: Cork University Press, 1998).

Ferguson, Harry, The Paedophile Priest: a deconstruction. *Studies*, 84, 1995, 247-257.

Ferriter, Diarmaid, 'Women and political change in Ireland since 1960', *Eire-Ireland*, Spring/Summer 2008: 179-204.

Foster, Roy, *Luck and the Irish: a brief history of change 1970-2000* (London: Penguin, 2007).

Gibbons, Luke, 'Projecting the nation: cinema and culture', *Cambridge Companion to Modern Irish Culture*, ed Joe Cleary (Cambridge: Cambridge University Press, 2005): 206-24.

Glover, Gillian, 'Anxiety of a best-seller', *Scotsman*, 7 June 2004: accessed via Lexis-Nexis, 21 July 2011.

Hanafin, Patrick, 'Legal texts as cultural documents: interpreting the Irish Constitution', *Writing in the Irish Republic: literature, culture, politics 1949-99*, ed. Ray Ryan (Basingstoke: Macmillan, 2000).

Hayden, Joanne, 'The Marian kind', *Sunday Age*, 28 March 2004: accessed via Lexis-Nexis, 21 July 2011.

'How Marian lives to dye another day', *Sunday Independent*, 18 May 2006: accessed via Lexis-Nexis, 21 July 2011.

Hymowitz, Kay S., 'The New Girl Order', *City Journal*, http://www.city-journal.org/html/17_4_new_girl_order.html: accessed 21 July 2011.

Inglis, Tom, 'Origins and legacies of Irish prudery: sexuality and social control in modern Ireland', *Eire-Ireland*, 40: 9-37.

Jolly, Lynn, 'Ireland hard on women, soft on rape', *Mirror*, 6 April 2007: accessed via Lexis-Nexis, 21 July 2011.

Karras, Aspasia, 'Chew on this', *Sunday Times (South Africa)*. 18 September 2005: accessed via Lexis-Nexis 21 July 2011.

Keyes, Marian, *Angels* (London: Penguin, 2002).

---, *Anyone out there?* (London: Penguin, 2007).

---, *The Brightest Star in the Sky* (London: Penguin, 2009).

---, 'Father Ted loses his sheep', *Sunday Times*. 30 January 2000b: accessed via Lexis-Nexis, 21 July 2011.

---, 'It's been one week since her last confession', *Irish Times*, 1 October 2005b: accessed via Lexis-Nexis, 21 July 2011.

---, 'Late Opening at the Last Chance Saloon', *If Only*, eds Mary Maher and Kate Cruise O'Brien (Dublin: Poolbeg, 1997).

---, *The Other Side of the Story* (London: Penguin, 2004).

---, *Rachel's Holiday* (London: Penguin, 1997b).

---, *Sushi for Beginners* (London: Penguin, 2000).

---, *This Charming Man* (London: Penguin, 2008).

---, *Watermelon* (Arrow Books: London, 2005).

Kilfeather, Siobhán, 'Irish feminism', *Cambridge Companion to Modern Irish Culture*, ed. Joe Cleary (Cambridge: Cambridge University Press, 2005): 96-116

Klein, Marcia, 'Spinning yarns in a post-feminist world', *Sunday Times*. 10 June 2007: accessed via Lexis-Nexis, 21 July 2011.

Lavery, Brian, 'The subtle sisterhood', *Sunday Times*. 2 April 2006: accessed via Lexis-Nexis, 21 July 2011.

McCarthy, Gerry, G. 'Women on the verge of a big shake-up', *Sunday Times*, 7 March 2004: accessed via Lexis-Nexis, 21 July 2011.

McStoffman, Judy, 'The new face of Irish letters', *Toronto Star*, 17 March 2004: accessed via Lexis-Nexis, 19 May 2010.

Mulhern, Francis, *The Present Lasts a Long Time* (Cork: Cork University Press, 1999).

Nolan, Emer, 'Postcolonial literary studies, nationalism and feminist critique in contemporary Ireland', *New Hibernia Review,* 42, 2007: 336-61.

O'Connell, Alex, 'Craicing good read', *Times*, 2 October 1999: accessed via Lexis-Nexis, 21 July 2011.

O'Connor, Joseph, *The Irish Male: his greatest hits* (Dublin: New Island Press, 2009).

O'Toole, Fintan, *Ship of Fools: how corruption and stupidity sank the Celtic Tiger* (London: Faber, 2009).

Pelan, Rebecca, *Two Irelands: literary feminism north and south* (Syracuse: Syracuse University Press, 2005).

Philby, Charlotte, 'Marian Keyes: my secret life', *Independent*, 5 December 2009: accessed via Lexis-Nexis 21 July 2011.

Ryan, Mary, 'A feminism of their own?': Irish women's history and contemporary Irish women's writing', *Estudios Irlandeses, 5*, 2010: 92-101.

Smyth, Ailbhe, 'States of change: reflections on Ireland in several uncertain parts', *Feminist Review* 50 (1995): 24-43.

Sutton, Henry, 'The sins of the father', *New Review*, 13 April 2008: accessed via Lexis-Nexis, 21 July 2011.

Swarbrick, Susan, 'Every morning I wake up in fear', *Herald (Glasgow)*, 19 April 2008: accessed via Lexis-Nexis 21 July 2011.

Whelehan, Imelda, *The Feminist Bestseller: from Sex and the Single Girl to Sex and the City* (Basingstoke: Palgrave Macmillan, 2005).

9 | The Mother-daughter Relationship in Contemporary Plays by Women

Mária Kurdi

Referring to Nancy Chodorow's assumptions about the risks of the mother-daughter bond Gayle Austin reminds us 'that mothers experience a greater continuity with girl children than with boys, and that daughters experience a sense of merging with their mothers that persists into later life'. The closeness is also a source of ambivalence because of the daughters' trying to break the bond', the critic continues, which has implications for the history of theatre in that '[s]tories of mothers and daughters told from the women's point of view are extremely rare in drama'. It can be observed, Austin goes further, that '[w]hile plays in which fathers and sons fight and are then in some way reconciled or separated by death serve to ease the oedipal tensions the son (playwright and audience member) may feel, the dramatizing of unresolved (and possibly unresolvable) preoedipal tensions between daughter and mother may be too painful, or too profoundly repressed, to be shown by the daughter.'[1]

Although the critic, coming from America, has mainly the American scene in mind, her general description of the possible route of the Oedipal scenario into drama applies to the history of Irish theatre as well. While dramatizations of the father-son conflict are quite typical of the male-authored canon from the early twentieth-century onwards, women playwrights have been reluctant to tap into the problematics of the mother-daughter dyad before the 1980s. In fact, mother characters are remarkably absent from their plays. If an offstage mother is briefly

---

[1] Gayle Austin, *Feminist Theories for Dramatic Criticism* (Ann Arbor: The University of Michigan Press, 1990): 66-67.

brought into focus, references to her are not for the sake of depicting a sustaining and harmonious bond with her daughter. In Teresa Deevy's *Katie Roche* (1936) the middle-aged Stan Gregg makes it clear that his interest in Katie is fuelled by her resemblance to her short-lived mother with whom he was hopelessly in love when he was young. Stan measures the daughter against her mother, whom he valued for meeting the expectations of his own social class: 'she was a wonderful woman; she spoke like I do, or Miss Gregg. ... she was a lady; she had none of your ways'. The implied parallel denigrates the daughter as a flawed copy of the mother. Katie's memories of her mother are conspicuously influenced by the patriarchal authority through such comparisons, and she is led to develop a sense of humiliation and self-effacement: 'Tis a shame for me, honest', Katie replies.[2] Being merged with the mother certainly has its inherent difficulties and disadvantages for her.

In the 1930s, when Deevy's play was conceived, the nationalist ideology of the new post-independent state upheld a de-realized image of motherhood, 'venerated in its social and religious aspects, but also ruthlessly demonized if it occurred outside the legalities and control of church and state', Gerardine Meaney claims. The demonization had strong links with what the critic describes as 'the culture's paranoia, a paranoia that sought to exclude the sexual, maternal, nurturing, ever-hungry body.'[3] Stan Gregg does not remember Katie Roche's mother for her beautiful body or any feature of individuality, but for fulfilling an ideal, that of middle-class propriety, held so important in the evolving new state. Woman was regarded not as a subject but much rather as a symbol representing national and religious ideals. In more general terms Moynagh Sullivan argues that 'it is this very confinement to such a symbolic position that has prevented the representation of mother as woman, mother in relation to daughter and daughter in relation to mother'. The 'place of the mother' (as Luce Irigaray calls it) being 'the only space available to woman', Sullivan explains, the 'daughter and the mother are collapsed into the one place, the place of the (phallic) mother, without separate names, meanings and a symbolic arrangement with which to recognize, identify with and thus individuate from one another.'[4] The use of the present tense in

---

[2] Teresa Deevy, *Katie Roche. Three Plays* (London: Macmillan, 1939): 13-14.
[3] Gerardine Meaney, *Gender, Ireland, and Cultural Change. Race, Sex, and Nation* (New York: Routledge, 2010): 10.
[4] Moynagh Sullivan, 'I am, therefore I'm not (Woman)', *International Journal of English Studies* 2.2 (2002): 127.

Sullivan's essay indicates that woman's position is still recognizably defined as well as constrained by the heritage of the discursive structures of patriarchy. If they lack subjectivity, mothers tend to provide a model for their daughters which involves the seemingly contradictory, yet intertwined demands of selflessness on the one hand and readiness to enforce discipline in the family on the other.

An inquiry into the long-lasting impact of the ideologically sanctioned conventional image of Irish motherhood on individuals necessitates the reconsideration of the family as a crucial environment. The period of the 1980s, Ivana Bacik writes, 'can be seen as a decade of contradictions in Ireland, politically repressive, but culturally exciting with signs of change to come.'[5] Admittedly, it introduced an era in which more and more diehard taboos in Irish life became openly discussed and challenged across pieces of journalism, literature and drama, including the family, as a result of the increasing willingness and need of the society to confront the ghostly phenomena underlying its cultural heritage in order to be able to move on. Since then, a range of disturbing facets of family life have pervaded the work of several contemporary Irish female authors, notably the persistent maternalization of women, the various manifestations of gender inequity and the long repressed horrors of domestic violence. Closely related to these concerns, the mother-daughter bond is a domain which many women are likely to experience as fraught with tension and a problematic background to self-development. According to sociological studies from the 1980s and 1990s, female generations tended to have different expectations as to the duties of women in the family and towards one another.[6] In literary representations the issue is necessarily bound up with the portrayal of motherhood, often depicting the ways in which it still carries remnants of the conservative ethics and divisive practices of the past and obstructs the strengthening of supportive intergenerational relations.

The distinctive quality of contemporary Irish drama by women, Lisa Fitzpatrick claims, lies in the efforts to 'disrupt[s] hegemonic narratives' while seeking 'to incorporate previously invisible and inaudible female

---

[5] Ivana Bacik, 'From Virgins and Mothers to Popstars and Presidents: Changing Roles of Women in Ireland', *The Irish Review: Irish Feminisms* 35 (Summer 2007): 104.

[6] See Pat O'Connor, *Emerging Voices: Women in Contemporary Irish Society* (Dublin: Institute of Public Administration, 1998): 126-127.

experience.'[7] Prominent within the patriarchal heritage that several women playwrights contest is the idealized, dematerialized image of motherhood and its restricting effects on female subjectivity. Anti-nationalist and feminist views on the implications of the maternal discourse display remarkable similarities. In *The Mother/Daughter Plot* Marianne Hirsch assesses and interprets feminist theories to provide reasons for the daughters' 'discomfort with the maternal' and their preference of the 'paradigm of sisterhood'. In her argument she first mentions 'the perception that motherhood remains a patriarchal construction and that the mother is an empty function connects the figure of the mother with continued bondage to men and patriarchy'. Awareness of this can even lead to matrophobia on the daughter's part. Hirsch quotes Adrienne Rich, according to whom '[t]he mother stands for the victim in ourselves'. Second, Hirsch discusses the discomfort with maternal vulnerability and dependency as facilitators to mould 'the image of self-creation' in feminist writings. Third, the critic defines the discourse of the body as a terrain in which signs of alienation from the maternal may be identified and resolved. Most importantly for the present investigation, Hirsch's final remark points to the ambivalent connections of motherhood with power, entailing rivalries and competitions among women that might actually result from such an uneasy pairing.[8] Female power is, admittedly, understood as emulating patriarchal authority and agency in the course of subordination to and unquestioning compliance with them.

Focusing on the hidden, disturbing or even shameful aspects of motherhood and their entanglement with the daughters' lives, the maternal appears as dysfunctional in several Irish dramatic texts, inviting a complex analysis. By the construction of incompetent maternal figures and unbalanced daughterly attitudes, Irish female playwrights expose an array of ideologically embedded constraints and practices operating in the society for public scrutiny, demythologizing at the same time the traditionally respected but nowadays rather contentious institution, the nuclear family. Owing to its specific modes of representation drama foregrounds embodiment and acts of performance. Sue-Ellen Case argues that critical approaches to the genre in our time regard female bodies 'as a site where contesting

---

[7] Lisa Fitzpatrick, 'Disrupting Metanarratives: Anne Devlin, Christina Reid, Marina Carr, and the Irish Dramatic Repertory', *Irish University Review* 35.2 (2005): 320.

[8] Marianne Hirsch, *The Mother/Daughter Plot: Narrative, Psychoanalysis, Feminism* (Bloomington and Indianapolis: Indiana University Press, 1989): 164-166.

discourses converge, rather than as a site of shared identification as 'women.'[9] The present paper explores the dramatic portrayal of the tensions and conflicts which undermine the mother-daughter relationship in women authors' works through mimetic or diegetic performance and embodiment to negotiate their potentially traumatizing effects. Presuming that this relationship is complicated by the father figures' experience in the wider patriarchal environment, attention will be paid to their presence as well. A selection of plays from the Republic of Ireland written over the last two decades will be under investigation, considering also the ways in which the mother-daughter genealogy makes visible a range of issues characteristic of the relevant macro- and micro-communites.

Miriam Gallagher's *Shyllag* (1993) is a drama written in the monologue form which usually highlights personal memories, in this case evoked by a number of voices. Tellingly, the protagonist is named Allwych, thereby identified as every(wo)man. She narrates her own story, which is basically a tragic one about the loss of her daughter, Shyllagh. Representing women in general, Allwych introduces herself as holding a dual position in multiple ways. On the one hand, her narration unveils the ambivalence latent in being both daughter and mother. On the other, her role as Travelling Player signals the duality of being an actress who plays to please the conventional needs of various audiences, and the fact that Allwych is also a woman experimenting with new ways to refashion her sense of home and achieve subjecthood in the patriarchal world. These dualities combine with and reinforce each other set against not only male dominance as present in scattered reminiscences about the peremptory mode of her husband's familial communication, but also the demanding attitudes of maternal authority. The play introduces Allwych's mother as a figure of firm ideas about her daughter's duties and future, who demands the girl to be silently obedient: '[b]e true to your destiny. ... Keep smiling and you'll see (*pauses*).'[10] Her assertion of maternal power goes hand in hand with disregarding the daughter's individuality, taking her as a mere extension or copy of herself, who should fulfill the mother's cherished dreams about securing a good place in the society. Interpreting the ideas of Irigaray on the 'phallic mother' Jane Gallop writes that 'the daughter's obligation to reproduce the mother, the mother's story − is a

[9] Sue-Ellen Case, *Feminist and Queer Performance: Critical Strategies* (Houndmills, Basingstoke: Palgrave Macmillan, 2009): 107.

[10] Miriam Gallagher, *Shyllag. Fancy Footwork: Selected Plays* (Dublin: Society of Irish Playwrights, 1997): 379.

more difficult obstacle than even the Father's Law ...'[11] Necessarily, Allwych's refusal to honour this obligation by obediently following the mother's orders instead of trying to find her own route deepens the ambivalence of their relations to extremes. Allwych's recollections of the mother's admired beauty are contrasted with those of her rebellion against the motherly prescriptions in the choice of a husband below the social standards she was expected to keep up to. The mother's reaction reveals disappointment over the daughter's unwillingess to use marriage as a means of conforming to her fantasies about rising in the world: 'What sort of life is that? — in a pub? In Clapham? ... I thought you'd wed a prince.'[12] Not surprisingly, the marked gulf in their outlook on female opportunities and duties leads to an unmendable emotional break between the two women.

Yet the drama shows that to reproduce the mother's story proves too strongly ingrained in woman's fate under patriarchal conditions. When she is mother of a young adult girl, Allwych commits a mistake which surpasses her mother's former lack of understanding in its consequences. Allwych alienates her daughter from herself also by pursuing a dream, this time about the star role of the Queen in *Hamlet* she wants to continue playing even when Shyllag, her daughter, would like to have it. To the suggestion that she may be old for the part she replies, laughing: 'Hah! What an idea! A Queen my dear never ages. She is always a Queen.'[13] Irigaray argues that women share the assigned role of commodities in the world governed by patriarchy, and 'no longer relate to each other except in terms of what they represent in men's desire, and according to the 'forms' that this imposes upon them. Among themselves, they are separated by his speculations.'[14] Women's investments to earn the admiration of men might easily result in collision and rivalry with other females, even within the family. Due to her insistence on playing a superior feminine role, and the jealousy unfolding from their competition for the favours of the same man, Shyllag abandons Allwych for ever, presumably by committing suicide. In the monologue the experience of this enormous loss is suggested to be intricately bound up with the personal vanity and selfish ambitions that women often develop at the expense of considering the interests of other women, be they daughters or peers, to manage in a male

---

[11] Jane Gallop, *Feminism and Psychoanalysis: The Daughter's Seduction* (London: Macmillan, 1982): 113.

[12] Gallagher (1997): 387.

[13] Ibid. 412.

[14] Luce Irigaray, 'Women on the Market', *Literary Theory: An Anthology*, eds Julie Rivkin and Michael Ryan (London: Blackwell, 2004): 809.

dominated world by fulfilling an esteemed iconic position like the Queen's role for Allwych.

Gallagher's play addresses the traumatic effects of mother's and daughter's separation from each other by their accepting or resisting patriarchal values in a way that the monologue evokes the larger canvas of European history rather than Irish social realities as the background. A couple of dramatic works by women from the same decade, the 1990s, deal with the problematic nature of the mother-daughter relationship as part of broader issues on the home front, involving the society's failure to offer sufficient care for young people, girls in particular. *Danti Dan* by Gina Moxley (1995) consists of a chain of fast-paced scenes which are punctuated by scraps of popular music, creating an atmosphere rendered idiosyncratic by the rhythms of youth culture. All the five characters are young people in their teens, and the absence of adults suggests that they do not receive enough proper guidance. In her afterword to the play Moxley remarks that in rural Ireland, where the action takes place during the summer of 1970, most parents were not prepared to acknowledge how far their children responded to the new challenges of a fast changing world, first and foremost to the sexual revolution.[15] The play focuses on the young girl protagonists' discovery of sex, which is to be held in secret given the dominant conservative discourse on sexuality in their community. Routinely, severe parental restrictions are exercised to monitor their behaviour, which, however, the action reveals as disturbingly paradoxical and leading to undesired effects. Sixteen year-old Ber's pregnancy is represented in the context of rigorous maternal control unhappily combining with the failure to give her a workable knowledge about sexuality and the reproductive functions of her body. Dolores, Ber's younger sister's fear that 'Mammy'd kill me if she caught me with Tampax ... 'Cause you are not a virgin anymore after them or something like that'[16] tellingly illustrates the incompetence of their mother to offer the girls some useful education in matters of female healthcare. Relations between daughters and mother are reported to be strained at best. Ber and Dolores mention their mother as an agent of authority and by no means a source of emotional and intellectual support, who is inhumanly rigid 'like a bear' and will 'lacerate us for being late.'[17]

There are hints in the drama that the off-stage mother character is a

[15] Gina Moxley, *Danti Dan. The Dazzling Dark: New Irish Plays*, ed. Frank McGuinness (London: Faber and Faber, 1996): 73.

[16] Ibid.: 23.

[17] Ibid.: 9.

deeply troubled person herself, subject to the lack of control over her own body because of having grown up in a society where sexual education was 'not an official feature of the primary or secondary school curriculum.'[18] Dolores relates a story of domestic confusion which proves revealing about maternal vulnerability in the family: 'Mammy is in bed sick. Cramps or something. There was blood all over the toilet. She was in there with the holy water bottle, firing it down the jacks as if it was Harpic. ... Then Mammy started bawling crying and went into the bedroom and shoved the wardrobe against the door'. The mother seems to have had a miscarriage, probably induced by herself, and suffers from the consequences in isolation, not asking for the help of her husband, whose reaction to the situation is tightening control over Ber, the elder daughter: 'Daddy said she wasn't going out'. Dolores' summarizing remark, 'Flip's sake, it's like Our Lady's loony bin over there[.]'[19], conveys a sense of hysteria generated by conditions in which the risks and realities of female sexuality are shrouded in mystery rather than discussed openly and honestly. Ironically, Ber's unwanted teenage pregnancy can be seen as the result of not receiving the necessary information from their mother about the bodily processes and responsibilities that sexual activity involves. What the mother passes on to her daughters is the powerlessness and helplessness which stem from the lack of knowledge about such important matters. Ber hopes that marriage will be a solution which gives her the chance 'to move out, to give up work'[20] and secure her feminine identity, but following this conventional pattern promises to be only the repetition of the earlier female generation's way of socialization according to the patriarchal mould. At the end of the play it is already Ber who upbraids the younger characters for their transgressive sexual curiosity; her trajectory from rebellious teenager to performing the vigilant older family member's role is unmistakably illustrated by her fiancé's observation: 'She's the image of the mother when aroused.'[21]

Young Irish women's experience of neglect and even hostility towards them on the part of their mothers is a crucial aspect of Stella Feehily's *Duck* (2003), another play of fast-paced short scenes, this time connected with a sense of loss in urban Ireland during the Celtic Tiger era. In O'Connor's view most 'young Irish women ... are growing

---

[18] Sheila M. Greene, 'Growing up Irish: Development in Context', *The Irish Psyche*, Special issue of *The Irish Journal of Psychology* 15. 2&3 (1994): 365.

[19] Moxley (1996): 32.

[20] Ibid.: 22.

[21] Ibid.: 65.

up in a society which has ambivalent and inconsistent attitudes to them as young women'[22]; they are treated in a paradoxical way by the family. The parents regard them as adults who must realize that they are expected to fare on their own, yet they should obey household orders like children. The two girl protagonists of Feehily's *Duck* are both from working-class families. Cat cohabits with her boyfriend, Mark, in whose wine bar she works long hours, while Sophie is a college student. When Cat's relationship breaks up and she goes back home, her mother, Marion's reaction is ambivalent. Meaney's remark about another text is also illuminating here: '[a] highly polarized construction of mothering' is emphasized, 'in terms of warm nature on the one hand, cold discipline on the other.'[23] First Marion plays the caring mother eager to feed her daughter: 'Go on, have a chop, ... You need your protein Catherine. No wonder you are like a stick'. Such gestures of abstract goodwill are then contrasted with her pragmatic and economically shaped view of having one more person in the house as an obstacle to the fulfilment of her domestic duties: 'Look you can't just expect us to foot the bill you know, for your upkeep, we have got Michael to think of too you know. Things are tight at the moment. We want to get a new car and the repayments will be quite high.'[24]

The contradictory aspects of Cat's mother's attitude undermine the possibility of any sincere communication between the two women. Cat does not give an explanation for having left the flat she shared with Mark, finding it useless to speak about a complicated issue to her mother who protects herself from embarrassing facts like the ups and downs of her daughter's personal life by escaping to comfortable clichés: 'Well I didn't think it was a good idea to be sharing with a man anyway. He was bound to start wanting something sooner or later.'[25] On her part, Marion is unwilling to give a straight and honest answer to her daughter's question whether she is welcome to live in the family home again at all. Taking a close look at Cat's parents, Brian Singleton points to a reversal of gender roles. In the scholar's opinion it is the mother who is 'masculinized in the family home' and acts like the patriarch. The father, Frankie is powerless, who merely 'copies his Marion's ... admonitions and instructions' addressed to their daughter and '[w]e learn of his fondness for alcohol and his predilection for

---

[22] O'Connor (1998): 186.
[23] Meaney (2010): 62.
[24] Stella Feehily, *Duck* (London: Hern, 2003): 79, 80.
[25] Ibid.: 79.

spending a lot of time in Cat's vacated bedroom.'[26] When he lends Cat a little money, he asks her not to tell the mother. It is only in the absence of his wife that he opens up a bit and starts joking, with some bitterness, about his marriage with Marion as an obligatory act, insisted on by her who 'said she'd call the police if I didn't marry her.'[27] Threatened with the institutionalized power of the police Frankie's obedience has deprived him of his manhood in the long run. His fate shows that masculine identity can also suffer distortions by the oppressive patriarchal environment, while Marion fills in the gap in the phallic system and loses access to an empathetic female self.

Complementary to the uneasy silence between Cat and Marion, there is physical violence between Sophie and her mother Val. Sophie lives in the family home, which is anything but a warm nest to prepare her for an independent life. The conflict arising between her and Val is shown to be grounded, similarly to Moxley's play, in the dissatisfaction of the mother with her life despite her dutiful efforts as a home-maker. Having a sense of her own emptiness, Val has no kind words or understanding for her daughter. Apparently, she is not interested in the reasons why Sophie misses classes at college or escapes to the use of drugs and alcohol; rather, she tries to humiliate the girl with a chain of blame and threats of punishment. Val's rudeness towards Sophie proves to be a channel for releasing her anger and frustration generated by the well-founded rumour that her husband is having an affair with a young local woman. Sophie only replicates Val's lack of consideration for other women when she confirms the rumour in a hurtful way to Val: 'I just know he's getting fucked on a regular basis'. The mounting tension between the two women erupts in the exchange of violent acts, instigated by Val, who '*wallops*' Sophie, and continued by Sophie '*knocking her [Val]to the floor*'[28] as the next move. Both women suffer from a sense of failure: Sophie has had disillusioning experiences in her search for selfhood, while Val's selfless 'woman-of-the-house' function has been betrayed by her philandering husband and she has no independent life to resort to. Preoccupation with their troubles linked to the internalized need that they should conform to cultural requirements prevents the two from finding emotional support in the other through the use of a 'woman-to-woman' language as Irigaray

---

[26] Brian Singleton, 'Sick, Dying, Dead, Dispersed: The Evanescence of Patriarchy in Contemporary Irish Women's Theatre', *Women in Irish Drama: A Century of Authorship and Representation* ed. Melissa Sihra (London: Palgrave Macmillan, 2007): 195.
[27] Feehily (2003): 88.
[28] Ibid.: 34.

formulates it.[29] Their aggressive behaviour, in which the mother sets the example, expresses a desperate but senseless competition for domestic control.

The context to the failure of the mother-daughter bond is a changing Ireland in *Danti Dan*, where the parents' traditional attitudes to sexuality have remained out of keeping with the new phenomena that incite teenagers' interest in the body without enough knowledge about it. In *Duck* the Celtic Tiger boom provides a context in which 'the pursuit of economic growth at all costs leads to predictable social problems of alienation, fragmentation, high levels of drug and alcohol use and increasing levels of violence' Geraldine Moane maintains.[30] On the side of individuals this entails self-centeredness and indifference to others, exacerbating rather than smoothing out the inherent ambivalence of the mother-daughter relationship. In contemporary drama, Eamonn Jordan writes, '[v]iolence seems to be increasingly the dominant mode of articulation' largely as a means of 'tapping into a framework of powerlessness and inhibition.'[31] Moxley's and Feehily's respective plays stage female characters who, parallelling male aggression, perform violent deeds. Their violence is fuelled by a keenly felt powerlessness to overcome the above outlined inhibiting states of frustration and communicate with one another as independent subjects capable of understanding and loving care in woman-to-woman relationships.

Discussing the persistent inquiry of Irish literary texts into aspects of the national past, Emilie Pine claims that 'the unstable position of women in the Irish society' and its consequences for motherhood as well as daughterhood are dramatized most forcefully in Marina Carr's plays, where mother characters 'are deeply insecure in their own lives and unable, as a result, to be steadfast anchors in their children's lives'. 'Their self-destruction', Pine continues, 'further links the idea of motherhood with trauma, so that mothers in Carr's work are not only

---

[29] Luce Irigaray, *The Irigaray Reader*, ed. with an introductin by Margaret Whitford (Cambridge, Mass.: Basil Blackwell, 1991): 101.

[30] Geraldine Moane, 'Colonialism and the Celtic Tiger: Legacies of History and the Quest for Vision', *Reinventing Ireland. Culture, Society and Global Economy,* ed. Peadar Kirby, Luke Gibbons, and Michael Cronin (London: Pluto, 2002): 109-110.

[31] Eamonn Jordan, 'Urban Drama: Any Myth Will Do?' *The Dreaming Body: Contemporary Irish Theatre* eds Melissa Sihra and Paul Murphy (Gerards Cross: Smythe, 2009): 23.

haunted, but haunting figures.'[32] Among Carr's plays, especially *Portia Coughlan* (1996) and *On Raftery's Hill* (2000) present maternal characters and mother-daughter relationships which bear the mark of severe deformities. However, to credit Maria Doyle's opinion, 'the playwright's interest is broader than the reconstruction of a particularly female identity.'[33] The above two works offer also portraits of both narrow-visioned and disillusioned patriarchs whose ineffectualness and destructiveness, in direct or indirect ways, contribute to the traumatization or failure of women's relations to one another.

In *Portia Coughlan* the eponymous protagonist, Portia's mother, Marianne, represents motherhood as paradoxical. Through marriage she entered a house which was a festering site of hushed-up problems deriving from incest and anti-tinker racism. Her mother-in-law, Blaize, has treated her oppressively over the years, Marianne complains: 'ya auld witch, sendin' me up to me room when the all the work was done, and Portia and Gabriel with me ... because ya couldn't bear to share your kitchen with a Joyce.'[34] Marianne is not only said to be coming from a family of lower social status than Blaize's, but also to be an illegitimate child of Blaize's own husband. The old woman's humiliating attitude towards her daughter-in-law was an integral part of her efforts to maintain power in the family with which to counteract her own subordination and sufferings from marital disloyalty and domestic violence. In a bitter struggle to strengthen her familial position, she invented ways to oppress her daughter-in-law, a young woman socially more vulnerable than herself. Carr's portrayals of motherhood, Catherine Kelly claims, display 'the cycle of damage ... repeated [and] circularity involved in relationships.'[35] Marianne's treatment of her daughter consists of, for the most part, expressing dissatisfaction with Portia's household and giving her orders, which closely follows the pattern that caused her so much suffering when a young woman. She has learnt to share a characteristic feature of mothers in patriarchy, namely the 'narcissistic' attitude to the daughters, considering them 'as

---

[32] Emilie Pine, *The Politics of Irish Memory: Performing Remembrance in Contemporary Irish Culture* (Houndsmill, Basingstoke: Palgrave Macmillan, 2011): 156.

[33] Maria Doyle, 'Slouching Towards Raftery's Hill: The Devolving Patriarch in Marina Carr's Plays', *Modern Drama* 53:4 (Winter 2010): 513.

[34] Marina Carr, *Portia Coughlan* Rev. edition (Loughcrew, Oldcastle: Gallery Press, 1998): 32.

[35] Catherine Kelly, 'Breaking the Mould: Three Plays by Marina Carr', *Women's Studies Review* 8 (2002): 112.

one with themselves,'[36] that is, beings also without individuality.

Portia rebels against living in compliance with the patriarchal rules her father and husband set for her, and becomes a selfish phallic mother. Cathy Leeney characterizes her as 'the epitome of the unwomanly woman; she is self-absorbed, promiscuous, violent, foul-mouthed, unloving, self-destructive and perhaps worst of all, a bad housekeeper.'[37] It is Portia's way of protesting against the requirement to identify with the patriarchal construction of the mother. An important aspect of Portia's relation with her mother is matrophobia, supported by the childhood experience of Marianne's weakness and ambivalent gestures to recuperate her image as a good (phallic) mother. The humiliation Marianne suffered when sent out of the kitchen together with the twins by Blaize is recalled in Portia's account from the daughter's point of view, for whom the mother appeared monstrous in her unpredictable but also disturbingly contradictory behaviour:

> Portia. Aye, sobbin' into the pillow. That sound, that sound, I think hell be a corridor full of rooms like that one with that sound comin' from every one of them, and then you'd turn on us because we were weaker and smaller than you, but that was nothin' compared with your feeble attempts to love us. We'd sooner have your rage any day! Your hysterical picnics, with your bottle of orange and your crisps –

Her family role of insisting on obedience to rules delimits Marianne's vision to the extent that she has no sympathy for her grown-up daughter's obvious psychic crisis, she just preaches about the normative demand of propriety regarding a woman's behaviour: 'Maggie May rang me up, says ya weren't yourself. When is she, says I? Get down off of that table this minute, young lady!' However, Marianne's attempts to reinforce the discourse of the normal through verbal attacks on her daughter only work to help the anger of the daughter find its outlet in a fit of aggression: Portia *'leaps, a wildcat leap from the table onto her mother, knocks her down, on top of her.'*[38] The eruption of violence between two women, as in Feehily's *Duck*, appears as a performative act resembling animal behaviour to underscore the dehumanizing aspect of the situation in which the

---

[36] Nancy J. Chodorow, *The Reproduction of Mothering. Psychoanalysis and the Sociology of Gender* (Berkeley, Los Angeles, London: University of California Press, 1978): 195.

[37] Cathy Leeney, 'Feminist Meanings of Presence and Performance in Theatre', *Opening the Field. Irish Women: Texts and Contexts*, ed. Patricia Boyle Haberstroh and Christine St. Peter (Cork: Cork University Press, 2007): 95.

[38] Carr: 62-63.

daughter is facing the phallic maternal function instead of the mother as a person.

Sly Scully, Marianne's husband and Portia's father is shown as a man who has lost most of his patriarchal authority to control members of the family, women in the first place, because their messy entanglement with each other, largely rooted in the patriarchal system itself, proves too difficult for him to deal with. 'Ah Jaysus, women, Jaysus'[.],[39] runs his helpless comment on witnessing a hateful row between his mother and his wife. The course of the play's action reflects the decline of his grip on family matters in terms of understanding their origin, nature and depth, let alone changing them in some effective way. Motivated by both social and moral considerations he makes attempts to discipline Portia for appearing to conduct an extramarital affair with a man whose communal position is too inferior in Sly's estimation. Later, as the enraged paterfamilias he attacks his daughter when Portia has narrated the story of how her twin brother Gabriel waded into the water fifteen years before to be drowned, and she did not follow him or prevent him from doing so. However, realizing that his efforts to use authority and restore the kind of order he values as the norm always miss the point, Sly eventually cannot but admit that his perspective is restricted to carry on his traditional role: 'What ya want me to do, girl? I deal with animals, not ghosts. What ya want me to do? Marianne, say somethin' to her – I'm not able.'[40] Sly embodies a patriarch self-dethroned by the failure to comprehend that women have subjective lives with dimensions and complexities which his feigned authority and belief only in the male-created rules and routines of the material world are never able to fathom.

The vicious and destructive family conflicts abundant in *Portia* define the 'domestic sphere [as] a site of danger and violation' Melissa Sihra notes.[41] It is her immersion in such a milieu that provides a clue to Portia's profound anxiety concerning her own maternal competence: 'When I look at me sons, Raphael, I see knives and accidents and terrible mutilations. ... And I have to run from them and lock myself away for fear I cause these terrible things to happen. Quintin is safest when I'm nowhere near him ...'[42] The outbreak of these displaced

---

[39] Ibid. 31.

[40] Ibid. 66.

[41] Melissa Sihra, 'Renegotiating landscapes of the female: voices, topographies and corporealities of alterity in Marina Carr's *Portia Coughlan*', *Performing Ireland: new perspectives on contemporary Irish theatre. Australasian Drama Studies* 43 (October 2003): 22.

[42] Carr: 49.

feelings works as part of her determined rejection of the role of the selfless mother. Her pressing desire is to reunite with her lost self, haunting her as the ghost of Gabriel, her dead twin brother. Christina Wald, who discusses the play in the framework of melancholia, writes: 'Gabriel and the lost union with him becomes an imagined place of fulfilment, a utopia that differs from the rigid (gender) boundaries of her environment.'[43] As a play set in rural Ireland, *Portia* invites an interpretation also in broader socio-cultural terms. By depicting Portia as an unmotherly mother of three, the writer 'indicates ... that "women" and "motherhood" should not be seen as synonymous. Not all women desire or are suited to motherhood.'[44] A strict concept of maternal duties involving obligatory self-effacement and the demand of self-sacrifice might disrupt family life rather than make it a source of self-empowerment. Chodorow argues that the concept of the 'Perfect Mother' is but a fantasy creation developed from patriarchal myths to facilitate 'the cultural oppression of women in the interest of a child whose needs are also fantasized.'[45] Because of the long history of Catholic dogmas controlling people's conscience, 'Irish mothers were judged good or bad, success or failure, under a specifically puritanical patriarchy.'[46] The sense of failure to function as a good mother was likely to generate ambivalence in uncertain women like Marianne. As Chodorow words it, '[t]he victim-mother creates a victim-child'[47] when she inadvertently passes on her sense of frustration to her daughter. Portia's maternal crisis replicates in another form Marianne's failure to fulfill the role of the perfect mother, because of being preoccupied with a pervasive sense of lack in herself.

The Mai and *By the Bog of Cats...* Carr's other Midlands plays abound in surrogate mother figures since the protagonists have lost their respective mothers and are surrounded by older women or female relatives who provide them with often contradictory guidance. The fact that Portia's mother is alive gives the playwright the opportunity to contrast her maternal attitudes with her sister, Maggie May's, treatment

---

43 Christina Wald, *Hysteria, Trauma and Melancholia: Performative Maladies in Contemporary Anglophone Drama* (Houndmills, Basingstoke: Palgrave Macmillan, 2007): 192.

44 Kelly: 110.

45 Nancy J. Chodorow, *Feminism and Psychoanalytic Theory* (New Haven and London: Yale UP, 1989): 96.

46 Margaret Maxwell, ' "The stahe a the country": Female silence and father-daughter incest in Marina Carr's *On Raftery's Hill*', *Irish Studies Review* 15.4 (2007): 475.

47 Chodorow: 86.

of Portia. A childless aunt, not a mother but a woman nonetheless, Maggie embodies an alternative to Marianne who is free from ambivalence. First of all in her marriage: she and her husband enjoy a loving and caring relationship, based on an intimate awareness of each other's needs as equals. Maggie, unlike Marianne, takes note of Portia's dark mood and asks about her personal well-being instead of merely lecturing the younger woman on good behaviour: 'Fierce down in yourself, Portia. ... Raphael treatin' you all right'?[48] Hers is the kind of tenderness and understanding which could perhaps save Portia from deeming this world as no place to live. However, as an ex-prostitute belonging to the given environment Maggie remains a socially marginalized woman who is 'far from the emulated and idealized social model of the mother figure that has been traditionally valorized by the Church and State,'[49] Rhona Trench comments. Obviously, she has no access to power, not even through her husband, a man 'unsoiled' in Portia's eyes and a self-proclaimed 'auld eegit'[50] without any space of authority in the symbolic system. Maggie's supportive motherly behaviour suggests the possibility of an alternative relationship grounded in acceptance rather than just narrow-minded criticism among generations of women. Yet this model could operate only in conditions uninfluenced by the both prescriptive and restrictive standards of patriarchy. The impossibility of the alternative represented by Maggie and her husband to ever gain dominance in the world of the drama is underscored by constructing the two characters as comic, unlikely to be taken seriously.

In *On Raftery's Hill* the female characters are grandmother Shalome and two sisters, forty-year-old Dinah and eighteen-year-old Sorrel, who all live with Red, the girls' father and son of Shalome in an isolated house on a hill. Significantly, the Raftery women not only depend on the paterfamilias but are also tied to him sexually because he dominates them through the bond of incest. In a family where extreme gender inequity is the unquestionable norm, the potentially loving mother-daughter relationship suffers the greatest damage. Moynagh Sullivan's train of thought is illuminating: if 'woman is not constructed [and allowed to function] as a subject, ... an *inter-subjective* relation between [them] is not thus possible.'[51] Dinah's memories of her long dead

---

[48] Carr: 16.
[49] Rhona Trench, *Bloody Living: The Loss of Selfhood in the Plays of Marina Carr* (Frankfurt am Main, etc.: Peter Lang, 2010): 12.
[50] Carr: 60.
[51] Sullivan: 28.

mother are shrouded in bitterness: 'She sent me into the bed aside him. I was lanin on the fridge in the pantry and she comes in behind me and says ouh a nowhere, you're to slape in wud your father tonigh. She didn't want him, so she sends me in. I was twelve.'[52] For being abused and thus losing the independence to choose lovers herself, Dinah blames her mother far more than her father, the real victimizer. According to Dinah's report, Mrs Raftery not only did not try to save her from the fate of gender subordination and the powerlessness it entails, but used her own phallic power of giving orders in the family to offer her daughter's body for the service of patriarchal needs. Margaret Maxwell comments on the scene that '[f]or the victimized Dinah, these memories encapsulate figuratively, as well as realistically, a perceived maternal betrayal, and a wholehearted disillusionment with maternal omnipotence.'[53] It is the psychically distorting effect of this very experience that disables the daughter to relate to her own daughter as a loving and helpful mother.

Trench observes that the drama presents 'a gendered hierarchy ... where female subjectivity becomes subsumed within the family unit' and, as a result, 'the roles of mother, wife, sister and daughter' are blurred.[54] The collapse of these distinct female roles is a sign of the women's lack of subjectivity and agency as well as the impossibility of building a mutually reassuring relationship with each other. There are hints and suspicions in the dramatic exchanges to substantiate that Dinah herself is not just the sister of Sorrel but also her mother, as the outcome of being the daughter-lover of their father. It is the confusion of having bonds with both the sister-daughter and the father-lover that explains why Dinah remains mute and paralyzed to prevent her daughter's rape by the father. Chodorow's above quoted idea about the cycle of victim-mother creating a victim-child applies to this Carr drama too. The sexual abuse of Sorrel by their father is but a repetition of Dinah's own fate, which she passes on to her daughter when doing nothing to interfere with the horrible deed in spite of the fact that she was staying in the house at that time. By this Dinah places herself at the middle of the cycle. She unconsciously repeats the pattern of compliance with the patriarch's needs and wishes that her mother set for her when she refuses Red's sexual approach, thus in a sense sending him to the other daughter.

[52] Marina Carr, *On Raftery's Hill* (Loughcrew, Oldcastle: Gallery, 2000): 56.
[53] Maxwell: 475.
[54] Rhona Trench, 'Staging Morality in *On Raftery's Hill*: A Kristevan Reading', Sihra and Murphy eds: 80.

Similarly to Marianne in *Portia*, Dinah's motherly behaviour is highly ambivalent. On the one hand, she pleads with their father in the interest of keeping the innocent girl out of the incestuous history of the family when she warns him: 'Don't touch Sorrel.'[55] On the other hand, she remains completely passive during the rape of the girl by Red. Added to her silent participation in her daughter's sexual abuse Dinah educates Sorrel that she should not tell the truth but lie about their family situation in defence of the patriarchal rule, which displays her phallic motherhood as not only dysfunctional but morally flawed. After Sorrel dismisses her fiancé for good so as not to have to lie to him, Dinah's comment is the following: 'Ud's not lyin, ud's just not tellin him things. Ud's just sayin the opposite of whah you're thinkin. Most goes through their whole life sayin the opposite of whah they think. What's so different abouh you?'[56] What this amounts to is no less than persuading her sister-daughter to accept the distortions of their way of life as normal or even normative, which involves that the daughter should relinquish her claim to an independent subjectivity and emulate the mother's loyalty to the family at any cost it takes. 'Following Dinah's lead of fabricated respectability', Maxwell writes, Sorrel 'constructs an external (verbal) justification of her father's actions as a means to negate her own emotional confusion.'[57] Implicated in the sin spreading across generations, she is rendered powerless to do anything but rationalize the horror of patriarchal abuse for herself like her sister-mother, which again demonstrates that they both take the same faceless and nameless place of woman in the family, serving interests other than their own.

On Raftery's Hill differs from *Portia Coughlan* in a notable respect. While the latter play highlights two phallic mothers' attempts to undermine the daughter's or daughter-in-law's subjectivity and self-esteem by reinforcing or even exacerbating patriarchal expectations, in the former the psychology of the tyrannical male is paid considerable attention. *Raftery* places the mother-daughter relationship in a broader context by juxtaposing and entangling it with the one between father and daughter. In response to Kristeva, Gallop argues that it is because of fearing the ubiquitous influence of the mother on herself that makes the young woman 'cling[s] to the symbolic so as not to be reabsorbed by the mother'[58] Dinah's childhood memories of her father in *Raftery*

---

55 Carr, *On Raftery's Hill*: 30.
56 Ibid. 56.
57 Maxwell: 473.
58 Gallop: 23.

report about an exceptionally reassuring, loving relationship with Red: 'I went everywhere wud him. ... He knew how to build up a child's heart ... Daddy ... Daddy ... never forgeh him for thah.'[59] Red himself is not free from identity confusion; he is tortured by the suspicion and hints that he was conceived in the incestuous relationship of Shalome and her father, meaning that he never had a real father to serve him as a model of manly behaviour. Displacing his feelings of loss he develops a contempt for the maternal as the root of betrayal and trouble, which is manifested in his attacks on animals like cows with big udders, or his own daughter, Sorrel, a young woman engaged to be married and likely to give birth to children in the future. His sense of weakness urges him to attack those weaker than himself, which compensatory act masks a deeply ingrained ambivalence at the same time. Red is a staggering representative of the patriarch, indicating the loss of ground and the pain of vulnerable masculinity as the internal problems generated by a system of gender inequality and its destructive effects on both sides of the oppressor-oppressed divide. Maria Doyle's contention applies to him too: '[r]e-examining the plays through their representations of maleness ... reveals that masculinity is as fraught a concept in Carr's work as is femininity.'[60] The desperate attempts of Red to keep his patriarchal power by over-exercising it only expose that, like a wounded animal of prey, he has become all the more dangerous for the mother-daughter relationship as the paralyzing entrapment of the Raftery sisters demonstrates.

Irigaray says that '[i]n our societies, the mother/daughter, daughter/mother relationship constitutes a highly explosive nucleus. Thinking it, and changing it, is equivalent to shaking the foundations of the patriarchal order.'[61] Its dramatic representations by woman authors present it as an issue through which patriarchy can be critiqued. Not accidentally in this light, *On Raftery's Hill* has been the subject of more perceptive critical studies recently than earlier. The 2000 debut of the play was a shock for many, audience members and reviewers alike, and elicited contradictory responses. Yet by now it is clear that while the play continues Carr's obsession with the portrayal of gender- and generational issues within the Irish family, it also initiates a new path of dramatizing further, more subtle implications of these issues. The novelty of *Raftery* lies in its focus on the role of damaged masculinity in disabling the creation and sustenance of empowering woman-to-

[59] Carr: 40.
[60] Doyle, 513.
[61] Irigaray: 50.

woman relations. Patriarchy is a system of institutions and discourses which impose standards and requirements that participate, in intricate and contradictory ways, in the shaping, regulating at times also distorting of individual lives, both female and male. Moynagh Sullivan argues that 'the reflexive situating of masculinity' is indispensable for 'an interpretational practice in all of Irish studies'[62] to facilitate the re-examination of the Irish national consciousness in its full depth. The further development and enrichment of this project is already anticipated by some primary literature in the present. Women's drama of the last twenty years has displayed a shift towards a more subtle view of male characters by having them perform their own troubled experience, which complicates their role in the traumatization and failure of the woman-to-woman relationship as they appear in the plays. Undoubtedly, the more widespread use of Irish masculinity studies will be very helpful to enlarge and strengthen the critical arsenal of re-evaluating the dramatic problematization of conflict-laden female relations in conjunction with damaged femininity.

---

[62] Moynagh Sullivan, 'Raising the Veil: Mystery, Myth, and Melancholia in Irish Studies', *Irish Literature: Feminist Perspectives* eds Patricia Coughlan and Tina O'Toole (Dublin: Carysfort Press, 2008): 273.

10 | An Exploration of Intergenerational Influences on Working Mothers

Jacinta Byrne-Doran

Introduction

This essay explores the experiences of mothers working in paid employment outside the home. Intergenerational influences in particular come to the fore in the context of the narratives of the working mothers. The essay draws on a wider qualitative study of maternal employment in Ireland. That study was undertaken as part of a PhD. programme in Social Sciences with the Centre for Labour Market Studies at the University of Leicester. In particular, my essay will focus on intergenerational factors gleaned from data collected in 2009 in Ireland, post 'Celtic Tiger' boom that enveloped Ireland from the late 1990s to 2006. Intergenerational factors are significant for my essay given the overt constraints impacting on women of previous generations working in Ireland. These constraints refer specifically to the gendered division of labour upheld within Bunreacht na hÉireann (the Irish Constitution, Article 41) which placed woman and mother at the centre of the family — that is to say, the traditional family. While family *per se* has change in nature and form (Lunn et al. 2009) it must be reiterated that the wording of Article 41 of the Irish Constitution cited below placed immense pressure on women who were mothers to adhere to socially constructed roles of stay-at-home mother responsible for the private sphere of home and family life including child care and housework.

> ... [I]n particular, the State recognizes that by her life within the home, woman gives to the State a support without which the

common good cannot be achieved. The state shall, therefore, endeavour to ensure that mothers shall not be obliged by economic necessity to engage in labour to the neglect of their duties in the home.

'Socially constructed' in this context refers to the idea that 'people's accounts of themselves are constructed' in their relationships with the world they live in and these constructions manifest as stories (Burr 1995: 8). The experiences of women and mothers are influenced by received cultural ideas of how women and mothers should be. Pertinent to the lives of mothers in particular are socially constructed ideas of 'the good mother' and the 'ideal mother'. Research in the 1950's in Britain conducted by psychoanalyst John Bowlby (1953) equated the good mother with the stay-at-home mother. More recently, and particularly from research work in the United States, comes the ideology of 'intensive mothering' purported by Hays (1996) which calls for women and mothers to invest intensively in both work and home domains; to be both good mothers and good employees. This invariably puts pressure on women who are mothers to seek work outside the home and maintain a work identity that is equally as important or sometimes more important than the role of mother in the home. The emergence of choice or preference according to Hakim (2000) means that women *choose* to pursue, for example, the intensive mothering ideology put forward by Hays (1996).While the intensive mothering ideology may suggest highly focused time with children as good enough this invariably leads to questioning the value of the stay-at-home mother. This in turn brings to the fore the ever present rift between the value of the work of the stay-at-home mother and the mother who engages in paid work outside the home (Dillaway and Paré 2008). Hakim (2000) theorizes that women are not a homogenous group in terms of the lifestyles they lead. The categorization of women, however, by Hakim into those who are work-centred, home centred or adaptive does not consider the question of free choice. It does not take into account the myriad of factors impeding choices. These include issues of access to affordable child care for example. Hakim's model does not consider the women who fall between categories or those who 'choose' differently at different stages of their lives (Cartwright 2004). More importantly, 'Preference Theory' as espoused by Hakim (2000) does not explain the processes of how working mothers choose to work; choices are invariably informed by the presence of structures and opportunities and also the absence of opportunity. Choices, be they free or not, are clearly influenced by the presence of constraints. For example, the choices women make are informed by the presence of young or older children and in 2011 in Ireland by the presence or absence of husbands and partners given that 'more than 40,000 men emigrated last year compared to fewer than 25,000 women' (Central Statistics Office 2009; Sheehan 2011: 11); and that 33% of children are born to unmarried women, while approximately 1 in 5 marriages ends in separation or divorce. These statistics highlight some of the constraints on women's employment pattern that contribute to the broad constraints theory put forward by Crompton (2006) as a critique of Hakim's Preference Theory of work and life choices. In this essay I also examine the influence of intergenerational factors on the choices made by women who are mothers to work outside the home.

Historically, the establishment of the Irish State continued to keep Ireland very much under the conservative umbrella, whereby the Roman Catholic Church and the family were given special status within the Constitution. Historically, structures and institutions like the Catholic Church, therefore, exerted power and influence directly through its teachings and indirectly through its provision of education services (Coolahan 1981) and child and family care services for generations in Ireland (Beale 1986; Kiely 1999). Byrne and Lentin (2000: 13) highlight that 'while Catholicism has impacted on who the Irish were and who we have become, we can only assume that its influence has also extended to how Irish sociology has developed'. This is significant given that Delamont (2003) points to the predominance of male sociologists who have theorized for decades about women. In addition to the impact of religious belief, Government services in Ireland have also failed to afford mothers any place in economic and political roles (Kiely 1999a). In 2008 only 13% of politicians (referred to as Teachta Dála) in Dáil Éireann (Government of Ireland) were women (National Women's Council 2009; Joint Committee on the Constitution 2010). This serves to highlight the lack of women evident in leadership and decision-making positions in Ireland. When women do go out to work, disparity clearly exists. As recently as 2008, women's income was two thirds of men's (Central Statistics Office 2009).

Strangleman and Warren (2008: 26) in their discussions of the sociology of work highlight the fact that 'women's voices were rendered largely invisible in early sociology and women's lives were ignored on the whole by its founders'. This absence of women and mothers, not only in sociological discourses but also in discourses on paid work, is reflected within the literature.

The gendered division of labour referred to above was also clearly reflected in the persistence of the 1929 marriage bar in Ireland which meant that married women could not be employed in the public and civil services until 1973 (Beale 1986; Barry 1998). This historical context is both important in itself and most significant to the sample of working mothers who participated in the research on maternal employment. The significance of this lies in the exploration of mothers' or mother-figures' experiences of work for the participants of the study I conducted on maternal employment, and will be further discussed in the methodology section of this essay.

Related also to the above socio-historical issues are considerations of women's personal lives. This refers in particular to the lack of 'access to contraception, access to information about abortion and the legalization of divorce' (Murphy-Lawless and McCarthy 1999: 71) that impacted directly on a generation of women in Ireland, but so too had an impact on a generation of daughters and sons – specifically daughters in the context of my study. The marriage bar was lifted in 1973 as Ireland joined the European Union (EU) and changes occurred in parallel with entry to the EU. The work of activist groups also played a role in changing the ways women were treated. For example, from the early 1970's the women of Ireland began campaigns of behavioural change which directly clashed with the strict prohibition laws on access to information on contraception and contraception per se. The most noted and dramatic demonstration of this was in 1971: 'the contraceptive train' organized by the Irish Women's Liberation Movement. In this campaign, women defied the laws of the land and purchased contraceptives in Northern Ireland to bring back over the borders to the Republic (Conroy 2004).

These actions bring to the fore the impact of social change and lack of change on the lives of men and women. Focus on the personal lives of women has emerged particularly in recent works by Smart (2007), Hollway (2006) and Gatrell (2008) where the significance of whole lives and the impact of generations of family experiences have been key. Hollway (2006) in *The Capacity to Care* explores the so-called feminine characteristics of humanity and care often espoused as women's attributes. Gatrell (2008) offers an interesting exploration of the history of women's work through the nineteenth century and onwards. In her historical description of the productive years of women through the nineteenth century Gatrell (2008) highlights the choices that were available to women at the time. My use of the word choice is significant in this context because any choice appeared constraining and powerless against the dominant patriarchy. Roles of governess, wet nurses, companions and seamstresses no more so than that of wife and mother all seemed to confine women and mothers to the private sphere of the homes and the household. Contextualizing this against the dominant social backdrop could explain the lack of position of women and mothers in public life in terms of politics, business and education. Gatrell (2008: 115) states that 'women's bodies in the context of leading, well paid and influential roles are in the minority – if indeed, they are represented at all'. It does, however, echo Kanter's (1979) findings of the lack of female role models in the higher echelons of business in relation to power and its use.

These considerations are relevant to any exploration of women's position in society, but are particularly pertinent to my discussion of women in the context of paid work outside the home. Paid work in this context does not just include the concept of professional work. I note for example that the idea of 'professional working mothers' is significant to the work of Grady and McCarthy (2008). By 'professional working mothers' Grady and McCarthy define these mothers as those 'who have remained in employment through the period of rearing their family while also developing and investing in their career' (2008: 600). Some mothers in the sample of working mothers I studied could be described as professional women in the context that Grady and McCarthy refer while others identify with a different trajectory. This trajectory is often disjointed and characterized by periods of time away from the workplace where time is not invested in maintaining a career but establishing and maintaining a family.

Before I explore the narratives of a sample of this maternal employment study it is imperative to trace the methodological justifications for the study of maternal employment and locate the significance of the narratives of working mothers.

Methodology

While this essay in addition to the wider maternal employment study does not purport to one specific feminist approach, it does emphasize the narratives of the participant mothers. Given that one of the foci of a feminist approach highlights the voices of women (Gilligan 1982; Bloom 1998; Delamont 2003) in their lives, the methodology adopted for this study does pay attention to the stories told by the participant mothers.

The social constructionist approach (Gergen 1985) therefore, posits as the backdrop to this narrative exploration and emboldens researchers who seek explanations of the nature of social and lived experience such as Miller (2005) in her study of motherhood. These social experiences exist in a complex social reality where participants construct, deconstruct and co-construct meaningful pictures of their social reality and life experiences. This goes some way to explaining why I chose mothers. I am a working mother and this reality permeates my social, personal and interpersonal life. Suggesting a narrative approach as I did in my study brings to the fore the importance of the subjectivity of lived experiences. The narrative approach is described by Kohler Riessman (1993) as a way of claiming a sense of identity and constructing one's life. These lived experiences, therefore, include the everyday activities and performances that make up our daily routines and constitute our stories of personal and social lives (McLeod 1997).

Using a biographical narrative interview method inspired by the work of Wengraf (2006) in his biographical narrative interview, qualitative in depth interviews were conducted with eleven mothers engaged in paid employment outside the home. Participants were interviewed on two occasions; firstly in Spring 2009 and again in Autumn 2009 giving rise to an expanse of rich narratives which were analysed using thematic analysis (Kohler Riessman 2008). Prior to carrying out second interviews, participants received a copy of their first interview transcripts to read, introducing the reflective process to their participation. First interviews were guided by an interview schedule which included the exploration of participants' mothers' work patterns outside the home among other themes which are beyond the remit of this essay. Second round interviews facilitated the use of one question in line with Wengraf's (2006) Biographical Narrative Interview whereby I asked participants what it was like for them to read their transcript from their first interview.

By adopting this methodological approach, I was able to facilitate the group of working mothers tell their stories and facilitate them in reading their interview transcripts. When I informed my participants that I was planning to use this approach all but one was very interested in reading their interview transcripts. The one participant who did not agree to read her transcript describes the experience as similar to watching herself on a video and DVD and she was not comfortable doing this. This participant clearly reflected on her interview experience and her decision was in turn clearly respected in line with the ethical considerations I adhered to in conducting this piece of research. This participant could be described as engaging in Gidden's (1987) idea of the 'double hermeneutic'; a process of self-reflection that both the researcher and research participants engage in as they try to make sense of their personal lives. The first interviews (those from Spring 2009) were methodically transcribed and returned to participants to read prior to arranging a second meeting in Autumn 2009 to provide a space to explore their reflections of reading their own stories. This facilitated a reflective process within the study given the significance of the phenomenon of self-reflection that Giddens (1991) refers to in the context of modernity and the reflexive turn within the social sciences.

Reflexivity, therefore, is an inevitable part of the research process (Smith 1996). It can be described as the process of looking inward; of self-reflection (Giddens 1991). In my study I am very aware of my motivations to study these women because I too am a working mother. I feel the contribution I make to the practice of sociological research is emergent from my methodological approach in giving back interview transcripts to my sample and re interviewing my participants once they have had time to read their stories. In doing so I am cognizant of how Etherington (2007: 601) defines reflexivity. That is to say reflexivity is a 'tool which allows us (researchers) make transparent the values and beliefs we hold in coming to the research process'. The reflexive tool adopted within this study also facilitates the phenomenon of participants as narrator and interpreter of his/ her own life (Giorgi and Giorgi 2008). For the purposes of this essay I will present the experiences of Deirdre, mother of two who is married and works full time outside the home. Deirdre's own mother worked outside the home. Mary also participated in the study on maternal employment. She works outside the home in paid employment on a weekend shift work arrangement and is mother to three children. Mary's mother did not work outside the home. (All names have been changed to ensure confidentiality).

Generations of Work

Within my doctoral research, work is specifically defined within the remit of the research undertaken. Work, therefore, in this context refers only to paid work outside the home. Work *per se* is complex and can potentially draw on a broad multidisciplinary body of research that has spanned generations of study of work and experiences of work. These include the study of management in work organizations through the work of Schein (1973; 1975) and the work of Fagenson (1990) and Long (1990) on 'ideal' manager characteristics. Hochschild's (1989; 1997; 2003) publications, *The Second shift, The Time Bind* and *The Managed Heart* incorporate the study of work, time and family lives especially the lives of women and mothers. Work, therefore, plays a central role in our lives and also provides us with the forum to perform and fulfil certain roles within our lives. Work plays a significant role in facilitating the development and maintenance of a sense of self and identity (Strangleman and Warren 2008). The functions of work include the provision of a structure and schedule to a working day, the provision of a cohort of colleagues, a focus for career development and the attainment of personal and professional goals (Jahoda 1982; Brenner and Bartell 1983; Fryer 1985; Raddon 1992; McKeown 1998; Goodwin 1999).

In the context of work and work roles, intergenerational factors are deemed significant in the work of Hayghe and Bianchi (1994). In their analyses of married mothers' work patterns they highlight the impact of experiences of working mothers on the younger generation. In particular, the experience of having a working mother impacts on career, family and marriage choices for younger generations of women. While this work is based on analysis of secondary data it is, however, relevant because it locates the study on work experience in one calendar year, that being 1992. What emerged as particularly interesting was the significance of age of dependent children on a mother's work patterns or whether she worked at all. This is still reflected for example in the Irish figures where in 2008 the employment rate was 56.9% for women with children aged 0-3 years of age. This percentage increases somewhat with the increased age of children to 60.0% for women with children age 4-5 years. The percentage figure of 64.6% corresponds to women with children 6 years and over (Central Statistics Office 2009). The study of intergeneration transmission has incorporated large scale studies from the work of Moen et al. (1997) to the work of Thomson (2009), in her paper *Thinking Intergenerationally about Motherhood*.

Moen et al. used a sample of mother-daughter pairs (N = 245) where data was collected in 1956 and 1986 for the mothers and once in 1988 for the daughters. These researchers approached their study using 'a life course perspective', specifically drawing on the work of Bronfenbrenner (1979) and highlighting the interrelatedness of our development and relationships within the systems in which we live. Moen et al. (285) investigated two attitudes, namely, 'mothers' and daughters' gender role ideology and their personal work identities'. These results pointed to the relevance of intergenerational influences between mothers and daughters. It also pointed to the mediating effect of 'the importance of the daughter's own status achievement' (Moen et al. 291). The Moen et al. (291) study highlighted the socialization processes that emerge particularly through 'verbal persuasion rather than role modelling' per se in the study of intergenerational influences. This is a significant finding and is reflected in the ideas outlined in the introduction to this essay regarding the constraining influences on women and mothers in Ireland through the generations. While a generation of mothers may not have worked in paid employment outside the home, they were open to the idea of work and encouraging their daughters to do so. This influential power of the maternal is referred to by Deirdre; one of the participants of the maternal employment study I conducted, as the product of her own mothers' life experiences and perceptions of how daughters were treated throughout the 1950's up to the late 1960's. This brings to the fore the work of Thomson (2009) in her exploration of *The Making of Modern Motherhood (the wider study)*. Thomson draws on the work of a wider study of first time mothers (N = 62) to work with 12 women in intergenerational case studies of participants, their mothers and in some cases their grandmothers. An exploration of the cases is beyond the remit of this essay, therefore, focus will turn to Thomson's (2009) conclusions of the intergenerational factors inherent in experiences from mothers to daughters. The case study analyses highlight the entangled and dynamic nature of motherhood from generation to generation. These entanglements are complicated by differences in socio-historical locations and experiences of mothering in previous and later generations. Thomson's (2009) work serves also to acknowledge the biographies of mothers and grandmothers in different temporal spaces and in different times in her paper *Thinking Intergenerationally about Motherhood*.

Despite the fact that I did not undertake to interview participants' mothers and grandmothers about their experiences of working outside the home, the narratives I present here reflect the experiences of some daughters of mothers who worked in paid work outside the home a generation ago. To achieve this I made use of the reflective methodology within the study by asking participants to reflect on their experiences of their mothers' employment outside the home.

The narratives of two participant mothers within this maternal employment study will be explored in the following section to locate the significance of work in these women's lives.

Second generation of working mothers

Seven maternal grandmothers, (my participants' mothers) worked in paid employment outside the home leaving four participants whose mothers did not engage in paid work outside the private sphere of the family home. Intergenerational issues, therefore, come to prominence in analysis of the narratives. In particular, the influence of mothers is significant. This highlights the roles experienced by the participants in formative years as children and it brings to the fore the division of labour within households, not only in relation to roles and tasks but also in connection with guidance for future lives. There are two very significant levels for this theme which come to the fore in the interviews with the participant mothers. Firstly, the significance of their mothers in their lives and secondly the significance of them as mothers in the roles they are presently in. Regardless of whether participants' mothers worked in paid employment outside the home there still exists a strong influence across the generation from mother to daughter. This influence is evident in the narratives when daughters speak of their own mothers as role models when they are growing up. Participants' mothers are also very significant to their daughters' daily lived experiences as they (the daughters) try to establish and maintain a work identity in parallel with their motherhood role.

Despite what has been described as the lack of role models for mothers particularly, and what is described by Gatrell (2008: 125) as 'heteronormative' culture that still pervades thinking about the role of women and mothers in society, mothers continue to work outside the home. Mothers have always worked. Deirdre explores in her narrative that her mother always worked. She opens her narrative by saying 'I didn't know any different' ...

Deirdre: Yeah, my own mum did. She was a teacher and she always worked from when I was very small. And eh, she eh, was a deputy principal in a primary school. And she had four children and I was the youngest. And... yeah, so she would have always have worked. Yeah, always. (Deirdre, married working full time, mother of two young children)

Later in the interview Deirdre is asked how she feels about being a role model for her own children. I ask the following question: do you feel you're a good role model for your children?

I ask this question because during the course of our first meeting Deirdre praises her babysitter for being just that: a good role model for her children.

Deirdre: Most of the time, yeah. I mean, of course there's times when... I don't think I'm a good role model then. I'm very, very conscious of being a role model for my kids. Because..., I mean, monkey see monkey do. You know, and I don't... ... I mean I want them to be good, solid, well-rounded, balanced people like you know, we all want for our kids. And I'm really aware that what they'll see is what they'll be, you *know ... And I do think it's good for them to see me going out to work, you know ...* (Deirdre)

This brings to the fore the significance of intergenerational issues (White 2010) which influence parenting and career choices albeit often at an unconscious level (Hollway 2006). Deirdre speaks about the influence particularly of her mother and her maternal grandmother on her education and career choices and those of Deirdre's siblings. In the following narrative piece Deirdre makes reference to how she came into her own profession and job by tracing back through generations on her mother's side:

> ... [M]y grandmother always put a huge emphasis on education, em because eh ... she would have been educated to second level herself, but in terms of Third Level, she definitely wanted her girls in particular, yeah, to become ... em, to become teachers and go to Third Level. And I know that my granddad wanted my mum to become a seamstress and to get a trade. And that my grandma fought ... not fought, but debated the issue and won. Em and, you know, really fought her corner for her. (Deirdre)

Relaying how her maternal grandmother fought for her mother's 'right' to gain third level education, Deirdre was very aware of the 'verbal persuasion' referred to by Moen et al. that her mother and her grandmother entered into regarding the importance of establishing a work identity in parallel with motherhood. This brings to the fore the efforts of many generations of women who voiced the need for equality while never losing sight of their responsibilities to family. This is evident in Deirdre's narrative below:

> I know that from a very early age, my mum wanted us all to do teaching. Definitely the three girls. She wanted us to do teaching because she always said that it was a fantastic career for a woman and because you could combine motherhood with teaching. That was her experience, and that was her view. (Deirdre)

Deirdre goes on to say that it was her mother who guided the career choices, she follows by saying 'it was always my mum who would have given us advice in terms of subject choices and education, rather than my dad ... you know, so em... I suppose she would have had more of an impact on, I suppose, all of our choices, career-wise'. This serves to highlight again the role of socialization processes and what Moen et al. calls 'verbal persuasion'.

Four participant mothers did not experience their own mothers working outside the home in paid employment. This is very interesting because this impacted on the participant mothers in very different ways according to their self-disclosures. Reactions ranged from the desire to model their mothers' behaviour with the clear goal of becoming a housewife and setting up home independently. Mary who works outside the home on a weekend shift shares her long time aspirations as being similar to her own mother when she states,

> I didn't have any aspirations toward a big career but... from the time I was a child, I can remember all I wanted to do was get married and have a family...'

(Mary, married, working on part time shift work at weekends, has three children.)

Mary's mother did not work outside the home. When Mary's narrative is reflected back to her she expands further on her narrative to illustrate the influence of having the stay-at-home mother and how this experience impacts on her own experience of working motherhood now. Clearly there exists the pull of the desire to give up work against the feeling of fear of being unfulfilled as a stay-at-home mother. Mary elaborates as follows:

> I think that's... that's the role model I had. My mother stayed at home, had family, stayed at home and looked after us and that was kind of the primary... now if it ever came that we won the lottery and I didn't need to work. I probably would give up work. I still don't know whether I'd be fulfilled then because, although I often say 'Oh, I wish I didn't have to be going into work?', and the nights are very, very hard, for 12 hours, but still I'm glad I do it because I think it's important for me, it's important for the children and I think it's important for my husband, that we all have, you know, the different... I think it's important for him to have to look after the children to see what's involved. It's important for them to be looked after by both and have interaction with both.

Mary's narrative above is a significant testament to how she has reconciled her desire to marry and have a family and her desire to create her own life while acknowledging the role model she had in her own mother. This highlights the significant role played by my participants' mothers in the lives of their daughters and serves as a precursor to the next section on the value of mothers in their daughters' lives as they pursue paid employment outside the home.

Mothers and daughters

Frances and Alison also contributed to the study on maternal employment. They both work in paid employment outside the home, Frances on a part time basis and Alison full time, that is, nine to five; five days per week. They both refer to the need for their own mothers once they became mothers themselves. In her initial interview Frances shares her journey of becoming a mother and her parallel efforts at establishing her career and gain experience and employment in her field. This was achieved through the help of her own mother whose presence represented not only support for Frances as she sought out a work role identity for herself but also represented the provision of care for Frances' daughter.

Frances: Em, but I suppose my introduction to motherhood was kind of a surprise as well, you know that kind of way. It wasn't eh, a 'planned event' ... But I found I was very cut off with no family around me. Didn't really know many people and decided to move back to Ireland, back to [name of home town] And I lived with my parents for a short while until I got on my feet and started part-time work when ... then I was very lucky to be able to do that because my mother started to look after my eldest daughter. So I didn't have to look for childcare outside of the family unit let's say, you know, so... I was very lucky that way that you know, there was family contact, getting to know her grandparents and that. So there was peace of mind there. I didn't have to worry about, you know, if she was sick and wasn't able to go to the playschool, and as she got older, that there was someone there to look after her. (Frances, in a relationship, working part time in administration, has three children)

Frances explains further that her mother and her family as a unit were of immense support to her in her early career where she could go out to work to carve a work identity for herself.

Alison, who works full time and has two children, said in the course of her first interview *'the minute I had children I needed my mother'*. In addition to highlighting the role of mothers in the lives of their daughters for very practical reasons Alison's reflections above highlight just how important generations of mothers are to their daughters. All of the mothers in this study reflected on their lives as they read their interview transcripts in the six months between their first and second interviews. Frances is indicative of mothers who seldom take or get the time to be reflective of their lives as working mothers. The narrative below illustrates this in the context of her experiences as a young woman with an unplanned pregnancy who strove to carve a work role identity for herself with the practical support of her own mother.

Frances: It's funny, I never looked back like that at the whole experience from when I was first a mother all the way through my career up until no... you know, as a whole, so it's been interesting from that point of view to see the progress I've made, and to remember that I was such a young mother as well, you know, that I had so many different obstacles to overcome. Em, so I suppose I'm very proud of my achievements to date, that's the way, and also from the point of view of not just where I've got in my career but also the work balance that I've achieved and being aware of what I am able to cope with from a stress point of view. And what's important to me as well, you know, realizing what my ... where my priorities lie.

The above narrative points to the significance of balance in Frances's life as she reflects on her attainment of work/life balance in her life to date. While Frances's mother did not work in paid employment outside the home, this in turn actually facilitated Frances in establishing a career herself secure in the knowledge that her daughter was being minded by her maternal grandmother. This phenomenon is mirrored for many working mothers who tap into extended family non formal child care arrangements depending on job schedules and work demands. The role of maternal grandmothers in supporting their daughter's work role outside the home is emphasized through the provision of care for their grandchildren, thereby, facilitating inter-generational transmissions.

Conclusions

This essay gave an insight into the stories of four working mothers who participated in a study of maternal employment in Ireland. In particular their experiences were analysed against the context of intergenerational factors. Many of the women in the study modelled their sense of self as a caring mother within the home on their own mothers. This was evident in Mary's aspirations to be like her mother. At the same time their commitment to a work role identity; to the experiences of a capable working mother in paid work outside the home also reflected their experiences of their own mothers who had themselves worked outside the private sphere of the family home. Given that the ages of the participants range from 35 to 50 years, then their mothers were involved in such work through the 1960s and 1970s. The participants' mothers, therefore, are representative of a generation of working mothers who worked despite the identified constraints outlined in the introduction to this essay. The most interesting finding to emerge within this study was just how many of the working mothers' own mothers had worked outside of the home. An initial question explored with each of the participants focused on their memories of their own mothers' roles at work within and outside of the home. The first question in the first interviews asked the participants *'Did your mother work outside of the home?'* Within this study, seven of the eleven working mothers had experienced their own mothers engage in employment outside the home. Given the social and media interest in the number of mothers moving out of the home and into paid work during the *Celtic Tiger Years* coupled with the historical context of the *Marriage Bar* highlighted earlier in this essay this figure of seven out of eleven seems significant. The impact of intergenerational issues emphasized the role of early experiences of seeing a mother going out to work. Experiences of mothers' work points to positive role models and a sense of empowerment for women whose mothers worked outside the home a generation ago. All of the women who participated in the wider narrative study of working mothers/maternal employment chose to work. More than half of these mothers had some experience of their own mothers leaving home to go to paid work outside the home. These findings point, therefore, to the significance of their own mothers' lives and biographies on mothers as they engage in paid work outside the home in contemporary Ireland.

Bibliography

Barry, U., 'Women, Equality and Public Policy', in *Social Policy in Ireland: Principles, Practice and Problems*, eds. S. Healy and B. Reynolds (Dublin: Oak Tree Press, 1998).

Beale, J., *Women in Ireland Voices of Change* (Dublin: Gill and Macmillan, 1986).

Bloom, L. R., *Under the signs of hope: Feminist methodology and Narrative Interpretation* (Albany: SUNY Press, 1998).

Bowlby, J. *Child Care and the Growth of Love* (England: Penguin Books, 1953).

Brenner, S. and Bartell, R., 'The psychological impact of unemployment: a structural analysis of cross-sections data', *Journal of Occupational Psychology* (1983), vol. 56: 129-136.

Bronfenbrenner, U., *The Ecology of Human Development: Experiments by Nature and Design* (Cambridge, MA: Harvard University Press, 1979).

Burr, V., *An Introduction to Social Constructionism* (London: Routledge, 1995).

Bunreacht na hEireann (1937) <www.taoiseach.gov.ie/.../Constitution of Ireland -Bunreacht na hEireann> [Accessed on 23 August 2010].

Byrne, A. and R. Lentin, 'Introduction: feminist research methodologies in the social sciences' *(Re)Searching Women*, eds A. Byrne and R. Lentin (Dublin: Institute of Public Administration, 2000).

Cartwright, S., 'Women's Decisions About Paid Work and Family Life After Childbirth: A critique of the Hakim model' *Current RMIT University Research,* eds S. Charlesworth and M. Fasteanu (RMIT Publishing: Melbourne, 2004): 24-36.

Central Statistics Office *Women and Men in Ireland 2008* (Dublin: Central Statistics Office, 2009).

Conroy, P., 'Maternity confined- the struggle for fertility control', in *Motherhood in Ireland,* ed. P. Kennedy (Cork: Mercier Press, 2004).

Coolahan, J., *Irish Education, History and Structure* (Dublin: Institute of Public Administration, 1981).

Crompton, R., *Employment and the Family* (Cambridge: Cambridge University Press, 2006).

Dillaway, H. and Paré, E., 'Locating mothers: how cultural debates about stay at home versus working mothers define women and home' *Journal of Family Issues* (April 2008) Vol. 29, No. 10: 437-464.

Delamont, S., *Feminist Sociology* (London: Sage, 2003).

Etherington, K., 'Ethical research in reflexive relationships', *Qualitative Inquiry* (July 2007), Vol. 13, No. 5: 599-616.

Fagenson, E., 'Perceived masculine and feminine attributes examined as a function of individuals' sex and level in the organizational power hierarchy: A test of four theoretical perspectives' *Journal of Applied Psychology,* (1990) Vol. 75, No. 2: 204-211.

Fryer, D., 'Stages in the psychological response to unemployment: A (dis) integrative review', *Current Psychological Research & Reviews* (Fall 1985): 257-73.

Gatrell, C., *Embodying Women's Work* (Berkshire: Open University Press, 2008).

Gergen, K., (1985) 'The Social Constructionist movement in modern Psychology', *American Psychologist*, Vol. 40, No. 3: 266-275.

Giddens, A., *Social Theory and Modern Sociology* (Cambridge: Polity Press, 1987).

Giddens, A., *Modernity and Self-Identity* (Cambridge: Polity, 1991).

Gilligan, C., *In a Different Voice: Psychological Theory and Women's Development* (Cambridge MA: Harvard University Press, 1982).

Giorgi, A. and B. Giorgi, 'Phenomenology', in *Qualitative Psychology: A Practice Guide to Research Methods* ed. J. Smith (Los Angeles: Sage, 2008).

Goodwin, J., *Men's Work and Males Lives* (Aldershot: Ashgate, 1999).

Grady, G. and A.M. McCarthy, 'Work- life integration: experiences of mid-career professional working mothers', *Journal of Managerial Psychology* (2008) Vol. 23, No. 5: 599-622.

Hakim, C., *Work-Lifestyle Choices in the 21st Century: Preference Theory* (Oxford: Oxford University Press, 2000).

Hayghe, H.V. and S. Bianchi, 'Married mothers' work patterns: the job-family compromise', *Monthly Labor Review,* June 1994.

Hays, S., *The Cultural Contradictions of Motherhood* (New Haven: Yale University Press, 1996).

Hochschild, A., *Second Shift: working parents and the revolution at home* (New York: Penguin, 1989).

---, *The Time Bind* (New York: Henry Holt and Company, 1997).

---, *The Managed Heart: Commercialization of Human Feeling* (California: University of California Press, 2003).

Hollway, W., *The Capacity to Care* (London: Sage, 2006).

Jahoda, M., *Employment and Unemployment* (Cambridge: Cambridge University Press, 1982).

Joint Committee on the Constitution, *Review of the electoral system for the election of members to Dail Eireann*, July 2010.

Kanter, R., 'Power failure in management circuits', *Harvard Business Review*, July-August 1979: 65-75.

Kiely, G., 'Introduction: From Colonial Paternalism to National Partnership: An overview of Irish Social Policy', in *Irish Social Policy in Context* eds G. Kiely, A. O'Donnell, P. Kennedy and S. Quin (Dublin: University College Dublin Press, 1999).

---, 'The family and social policy', in *Irish Social Policy in Context*, eds G. Kiely, A. O'Donnell, P. Kennedy and S. Quin (Dublin: University College Dublin Press, 1999a).

Kohler Riessman, C., *Narrative Analysis*, Qualitative Research Methods Volume 30 (London: Sage, 1993).

---, *Narrative Methods for the Human Sciences* (Los Angeles: Sage Publications, 2008).

Long, B., 'Relationships between coping strategies, sex typed traits and environmental characteristics: A comparison of male and female managers', *Journal of Counselling Psychology* (1990), vol. 37, No. 2: 185-194.

Lunn, P., T. Fahey and C. Hannon, *Family Figures: Family dynamics and family types in Ireland, 1986-2006* (Dublin: Family Support Agency and The Economic and Social Research Institute, 2009).

McKeown, K., 'Fathers and work', in *Changing Fathers? Fatherhood and Family Life in Modern Ireland* eds K. McKeown, H. Ferguson, D. Rooney (Cork: The Collins Press, 1998).

McLeod, J., *Narrative and Psychotherapy* (London: Sage, 1997).

Moen, P., M.A Erickson, and D. Dempster-McClain, 'Their Mother's Daughters? The Intergenerational transmission of gender attitudes in a work of changing roles', *The Journal of Marriage and Family*, Vol. 59, No. 2 (May 1997): 281-293.

Miller, T., *Making Sense of Motherhood – A Narrative Approach* (Cambridge: Cambridge University Press, 2005).

Murphy-Lawless, J. and J. McCarthy, 'Social policy and fertility change in Ireland: The push to legislate in favour of women's agency', *European Journal of Women's Studies* (1999), vol. 6, No. 1: 69-96.

National Women's Council of Ireland *Submission to The Review of Electoral Reform* (2009) <www.ncwi.ie>.

Raddon, A., 'Mothers in the academy', *Studies in Higher Education* (2002), vol.27, No.4: 387-403.

Schein, V. E., 'The relationships between sex role stereotypes and requisite management characteristics', *Journal of Applied Psychology*, (1973) Vol. 57, No. 2: 95-100.

Schein, V. E., 'Relationships between sex role stereotypes and requisite management characteristics among female managers', *Journal of Applied Psychology* (1975), vol. 60, No. 3: 340-344.

Sheehan, A., 'Twice as many men as women leaving country', *Irish Independent*, Wednesday 2 February 2011.

Smart, C., *Personal Life* (Cambridge: Polity, 2007).

Smith, J., 'Evolving issues for qualitative psychology', in *Handbook of Qualitative Research Methods* ed. J. Richardson (Leicester: The British Psychological Society, 1996).

Strangleman, T. and T. Warren, *Work and Society: Sociological Approaches, Themes and Methods* (London: Routledge: 2008).
Thomson, R., 'Thinking Intergenerationally about motherhood', *Studies in the Maternal* 1 (1) 2009 <www.mamsie.bbk.ac.uk>.
Wengraf, T., *Qualitative Research Interviewing* (London: Sage, 2006).
White, V., *Mother Ireland Why Ireland hates Motherhood* (Dublin: Londubh Books, 2010).

11 | Women Writing Violence

Lisa Fitzpatrick

A number of critics have noted that rape and sexual and domestic violence are amongst the recurring themes in women's dramatic writing (Goodman 1993; Canning 2003), suggesting the importance of these issues to women's lives and experience. The volume of work suggests that sexual violence is a concern for women across cultural borders, though refracted differently through the specific cultural circumstances of different communities of women, other material conditions of their lives, and the cultural conventions and practices available to them. In the Irish theatre, there are representations of gothic families that populate the plays of Marina Carr, and the unthinking, violent contempt dramatized in work like Clare McIntyre's *Low Level Panic*, Stella Feehily's *Duck*, and Abbie Spallen's *Pumpgirl*. Plays by Patricia Burke-Brogan, Patricia Byrne, Stella Feehily, Miriam Gallagher, Gina Moxley, Abbie Spallen, Paula Meehan – to name a few – deal with issues of sexual and psychosexual abuse by placing it on the public stage and writing female characters who speak and name the experiences in a way that potentially encourages spectators to reassess cultural norms of shame and blame, or indeed to feel less alone with their own experiences of violence. In work by Northern Irish playwrights Anne Devlin and Christina Reid, set during the 'Troubles'[1], there is a pervading sense of a violent culture in which women are largely relegated to secondary status within both family and the wider society. This is manifested in the plays in their depiction of women's lack of connection with their own bodies and sexualities and a clear sense of social disapproval

---

[1] 'The Troubles' is the colloquial name for the period of civil unrest in Northern Ireland, lasting from 1969 to the Good Friday Agreement of 1998.

around extra-marital sex (in, for example, *Tea in a China Cup*, *The Belle of the Belfast City*, and *Ourselves Alone*), and in repeated representations of male characters reinforcing their dominance through verbal threats and physical violence. Thematically, gender-based and sexual violence recur as naturalistic representations in the dramatic practice of many Irish women playwrights. Unlike male-authored work, which tends to position sexual violence as a metaphor for the violence in Northern Ireland, women's writing generally tends to address issues of sexual violence as intimate and interpersonal. In examining the representation of rape and violence by contemporary Irish women playwrights, I will be looking in particular at the tensions between the staging of rape from a female and/or feminist perspective, the demands of dramatic form and meaning-making in performance, and the dominant social discourses around rape that shape the reception of the work. The texts under discussion are Marina Carr's *On Raftery's Hill* and *By the Bog of Cats*, Clare McIntyre's *Low Level Panic* which was performed by Glasshouse Productions in Dublin in 1991, and Stella Feehily's *Duck*.

Writing Rape

Violence is, and historically has always been, an intrinsic aspect of theatre and drama. Aristotle's *Poetics* identifies the representation of the painful and monstrous as a source of spectatorial pleasure, but warns that it should not be merely 'monstrous' but should evoke fear and pity in the spectator (xi; xiv). Although conventions of different periods have prohibited the representation of violence on stage, the performance of quite gruesome acts has been commonplace throughout theatre history, and has often been undertaken with considerable ingenuity. In the Mystery Cycles, the scourging and crucifixion of Christ is staged; Marlowe's Faust is dragged by demons into Hell; Gloucester's eyes are put out; Jacobean tragedy is fantastically gruesome, while comedy has historically allowed for the staging of all kinds of physical rough housing. So putting explicit violence on stage to revolt, thrill, and excite the audience is nothing new; and similarly, though the staging of rape and sexual violence may seem like a feminist concern, it has historically been commonplace. Elizabeth Howe notes that after the introduction of female actresses on the British stage in 1660, 'rapes occur regularly in plays right into the eighteenth century. Anne Bracegirdle [a popular actress of the time] actually specialized in having her virgin innocence brutally taken from her'[2]. Rape and domestic violence are common themes in comedy, too, and the representation of violence can be quite explicit. *The Taming of the Shrew* is a palimpsest of earlier folk tales and folk belief about women, in which the abuse of Katherine is staged as comic; bawdy humour in the Restoration comedies often hangs upon the idea that the woman's virtue is a pretence aimed at securing a husband, so that rape is understood only as a forceful seduction, and in melodrama the villain's assault on the heroine's virtue only makes her saviour hero more desirable by comparison. René Branca asserts that 'A staging of an attempted rape would ... draw a crowd' and that posters often used images of distressed or dishevelled young women, clinging to their armed protectors (2005: 34-5). More recent examples from comedy include *The Benny Hill Show*, with its recurring scene of Benny Hill chasing a curvaceous and scantily clad young woman in fast-motion; or rape-jokes in contemporary stand-up comedy. It seems churlishly and humourlessly feminist to object to such material, but it reveals how much a kind of sexual bothering of women is part of our culture of humour, and how insistent is the sense that it is harmless, inoffensive and fun.

The social and cultural changes wrought by the Women's Movement internationally have radically altered the ways in which sexual and domestic violence are represented in public discourses and on stage, and thus its reception by critics and audiences. Nonetheless, certain assumptions about women writers persist, and this is evident in the treatment of women's writings on rape. In particular, women writers' emphasis on the physical, interpersonal and violent nature of rape (rather than its use as a metaphor for public or political struggles) shapes the interpretation of women's writing as concerned with 'realistic' exploration of issues, and therefore often as aesthetically weak, as didactic, or as deeply concerned with 'authentic' reproduction of the actual world. But staging strategies that are not realistic may nonetheless express something that can be recognized as truthful (if not verisimilar), for their representation of emotional or affective responses to violence. For example, Fabulous Beast's 2003 production of *Giselle* represents the rape of Giselle by her brother Hilarion through a series of movements that do not mimic the movements of rape. Giselle is mute due to the trauma of her mother's suicide, but the sense of threat is established by her tense, silent compliance with her brother's demands, which suggests that she knows to fear him. The threat is rendered

---

[2] Elizabeth Howe, *The First English Actresses* (Cambridge, Cambridge U.P., 1992): 43.

sexual by the direction of Hilarion's gaze (at her breasts), and his pointing finger which descends from her mouth to her breasts, and by her frozen immobility. His manipulation of her while she sits on his knee, his turning of her and placing her on her back, and his movements above her, are all sexually suggestive, as is his spitting on her face (an image of ejaculation), and his licking her face. He then prances around her prone body. The movements of the performers communicate a rape or sexual violation to the spectators through the foregrounding of Giselle's fear; her familiarity with this violence; her brother's madness, and her sense of isolation and helplessness which is made more poignant by her inability to cry for help.

Giselle's silence suggests an unspeakable trauma, which language cannot adequately capture or express; it suggests the difficulty of reducing her experience into a readily comprehensible narrative, and it references a number of canonical, silenced female characters: Philomele, whose brother in law Tereus rapes her and cuts out her tongue so she cannot speak against him, or Lavinia in *Titus Andronicus* who is raped, her tongue cut out and her hands cut off, again so that she cannot identify the guilty. The silent Giselle cannot tell anyone what is happening to her: she literally has no words to express her experience. Canning argues that 'making rape something shameful so that women would not dare voice their experiences' led women to believe that 'since they were the only ones suffering, they were responsible'[3]. She argues that dramatic representations of rape have potential as ways for women to speak and name their experience, and to insert a female perspective in the public communal space of the theatre. Both Canning and Goodman see this as empowering and activist, and link female-authored representations of rape on stage to the feminist movement and to the emergence of a feminist theatre movement.

Representing Rape on the Irish Stage

In the Irish theatre, one of the first feminist performance companies was Glasshouse Productions, which staged Clare McIntyre's *Low Level Panic* (along with Eve Lewis's *Ficky Stingers*) in Dublin in the early 1990s. The play centres around three young women sharing an apartment in an unnamed city, and the action takes place mainly in the bathroom as they bathe and dress to go out. The episodic structure and the deft comedy of the dialogue between the friends enhance the

---

[3] Charlotte Canning, *Feminist Theaters in the USA: Staging Women's Experience* (London & New York: Routledge, 1996): 152.

exploration of sexual politics and in particular, the character Mary's emerging awareness of connections between the objectification of women, and the casual sexual violence recently inflicted upon her. The play ran at the Andrews Lane Theatre, and the members of the cast remember that the (female) *Evening Press* critic described the piece as 'cathartic ... and doubly painful because we witness it every day of our lives', while the (male) reviewer for the *Irish Times* described it as 'loaded' and 'clearly a kind of propaganda', 'Brothers, I think this is one for the Sisters'. It is interesting to read this review – which is by Gerry Colgan – in the light of Countryman and Headrick's argument about the international reception of Irish women's writing being troubled by an incongruity between what is represented, and the audience's expectations of Ireland and Irish theatre. *Low Level Panic* unsettles received ideas about sexual assault as a crime committed by monsters in an alleyway, by representing a female experience of the crime and by forcing an audience response through the uncomfortable, audible assault of screaming. Sexual assault is here represented as something that ordinary men do to ordinary women, while the power relations in operation through their taunting of her are also revealed as a form of violence. Caroline Williams, the company's producer, recalls how the review validated and inspired the company: '[Colgan's] review was a clear indicator to the company that there was a belief out there that plays by women were for women, and that a play which explored women's sexuality, pornography, eating disorders and more was marginal because it was not about men ... we found it proof positive that presenting plays by women about women was an important and radical act'[4].

The director, Katy Hayes, identifies two questions that demanded her attention and that 'presented major challenges to our youth and inexperience: how do you show rape on stage that captures the horror, but is theatrically convincing? How do you present a naked woman in a bath in a play about pornography, and avoid titillation?' (136). The issue of capturing the horror of sexual violence while avoiding a gratuitous display of the female body, is one that recurs in representations of sexual violence. In *Low Level Panic*, the female protagonist narrates and enacts a sexual assault by two men, using the movements of her own body and the voices of two men, A and B, who are never seen. The scene takes place on the street, where Mary is

---

[4] Caroline Williams, K. Hayes, S. Quill & C. Dowling 'People in Glasshouse' *Druids, Dudes and Beauty Queens* ed. Dermot Bolger (Dublin: New Island Books, 2001): 137.

unlocking her bicycle late at night, and begins with a monologue in which she considers all the things she could have done differently:

> **Mary:** Maybe if I'd been wearing trousers ... it's not really comfortable on a bike in a skirt: it just makes people look at your legs. But who's around at that time of night to look? Anyway I wasn't even on the bike ... I could have cycled to work wearing a pair of jeans and had my skirt folded in one of the panniers but then it would have been all squashed and that wouldn't have gone down well at all with the management ... Or I could have come to work on the bicycle wearing a skirt and could have changed into trousers to go home given that you're meant to be alright in daylight but you're not safe at night. Or I could have walked to work and got a taxi home and I could have worn whatever I liked ... (86-7).

Eventually she concludes that, no matter what other circumstances she had changed, 'I'd still have been there' (87), acknowledging the irrelevance of what she was wearing and by extension her blamelessness. The scene follows this narrative so that the audience see Mary unlocking her bicycle while, in voiceover, A and B circle her, commenting on the bicycle, asking where she is going, if she has been with her boyfriend, where she is from, and complimenting the bicycle in mocking *double entendres* that are designed to intimidate and disempower her. The stage directions for the attack specify that one man puts his hands on her hips and pushes his fingers into her vagina while the other grasps her breasts:

> The movements are forceful and deliberate. The actress should carry out these actions until it is crystal clear that she is not being felt in a tentative way but is being sexually assaulted. She then holds her arms away from herself, disassociating herself from what is happening to her and screams (89).

The scene ends with Mary 'screaming for everything: to be helped: to release her anger and her fear' (90).

The actor's dissociation of herself from her body communicates some of the trauma of the attack in its physical representation of her desire to escape the restrictions of her physical body and her gender, her alienation or withdrawal from the body that is helpless to defend itself, and her paralyzing sense of being entrapped between social demands (of feminine compliance, submission, and politeness) and her instinct to defend herself. Her distress at the assault is expressed in her screaming, her rage at finding a discarded pornographic magazine in the bin, and her sudden awareness of billboard posters which she now reads as graphic images of sexual violence: she begins to connect the sexual objectification of women to the male violence she experienced.

Marina Carr's 2002 play *On Raftery's Hill* is a kind of gothic family horror that also explores female inarticulacy in response to male violence. In terms of textual analysis, the play offers an example of what Sharon Marcus and Carine Mardorossian in their competing analyses call the 'rape script'. Marcus uses the term to argue that 'the violence of rape is enabled by narratives, complexes and institutions which derive their strength ... from their power to structure our lives as imposing cultural scripts' (1992: 388-9). She identifies rape as one such 'script' – meaning, a range of discourses that the individual is exposed to and shaped by – and as such, she argues that it 'continually scripts these [gender] inequalities anew', that it acts to 'feminize' women in the sense of reinscribing a sense of powerlessness and victimhood which curtails freedom of movement and expression, and imprints the gender identity of 'feminine victim'. Carr's play illustrates the argument in a scene at the end of Act 1, in which Red Raftery rapes his daughter Sorrel, and in which the dialogue systematically strips Sorrel of her ability to speak and so to resist. The scene ends with Red shoving her down on the table and slamming his knife into the table beside her body, signifying rape without actually showing it explicitly.

On Raftery's Hill is set entirely in the kitchen of Red Raftery's farmhouse on top of the eponymous hill where the family live. They are Shalome, his senile mother who is always trying to go 'home' to her Daddy; his son Ded, whom he has terrorized and brutalized to the extent that he lives a semi-human existence with the animals in the cow-shed; his daughters Dinah and Sorrel, the latter of whom is twenty and engaged to a young local farmer named Dara Mood, and Red himself. His wife is long since dead. Red tortures the livestock, slashing the cows' udders, and he is involved in a long-term sexual relationship with his elder daughter Dinah. This began violently in her childhood when the mother sent Dinah in to sleep with her father; but Dinah has long since resigned herself to the inevitability of it, though it remains a source of shame. She says, of herself and her father: 'So we do ud from time to time ... we want ud to stop. Ud's just like children playin in a field ah some awful game before rules was made' (2000: 57-8). Dinah, it gradually becomes apparent, is the mother of Red's younger daughter Sorrel. Mária Kurdi's paper in this collection considers the dynamics of this mother-daughter relationship in some detail; it is enough here to note that the dialogue and action suggest that the family has a long history of incestuous relationships. Shalome's repeated attempts to escape from the Hill to Kinnegar, to her 'daddy', hint that Red himself may be her son by her own father. The first act ends with the rape of Sorrel, and the second act sees the family gradually reveal its secrets to her, and concludes with her troubling decision to break off her engagement and stay on the Hill amongst them.

The rape in *On Raftery's Hill* is the culmination of a long sequence of angry exchanges between Sorrel and Red that takes place late at night. The sense of threat develops quite suddenly, when Sorrel attempts to pass him to leave the room, and he blocks her path. He accuses her of not gutting the hares he caught earlier in the day. When Sorrel states 'I don't know how to gut a hare', Red seizes control of the moment: 'Donten ya? Alrigh, I'll show ya how to gut a hare' (34). The stage directions read: 'Grabs her suddenly and holds her in a vice grip. Sorrel struggles pointlessly against the strength of him' (34). Red implacably cuts off her clothes with a knife, narrating how to skin and gut the hare while Sorrel screams for help to Dinah, Ded, and her grandmother. Red tells her 'Dinah won't come and ya think Ded's comin? (*a mad laugh*) And Granny's noh comin. And your precious Dara Mood can't help ya now.' Sorrel loses speech as the scene progresses: '*Her voice has betrayed her. We hear the odd animal moan or shriek.*' (35). Meanwhile, Red is so much in control that he even pauses and '*looks in satisfaction at his work*'. He then '(... *pushes her across the table, cuts the straps of her slip.*) Now, this is how ya gut a hare. (*Stabs knife in table. Blackout.*) (35).

In staging violence, the creation of a sense of threat can be more effective than the witnessing of the act of violence itself: the capacity of the violence to exist at the edges of human imagination before it is enacted on stage allows the full range of possible horror to exist momentarily for the individual spectator. The fear of what might happen, of the unknown, is greater than the horror of witnessing of an act (which in any case happens to a body one might empathetically identify with, but which is not one's own; and, of course, the act is simulated, however convincingly, and is not actually *real*.) Thus Carr's strategy of proceeding to blackout is one that invokes and exploits the audience's imagination, and the second act, which includes references to Sorrel's injuries – 'There's marks on her as hasn't healed in three weeks', Dinah says (45) – validates the spectator's worst imaginings.

In relation to the rape in *On Raftery's Hill*, there are two key points to raise. Firstly, that Sorrel is silenced by Red, and that he controls the conversation and therefore controls the scene; and secondly, that the knife is a pocket knife, one he has used earlier in the scene to clean his nails. If it were not specified it would be easy to imagine that Red is using a far more threatening object, such as a hunting knife. The small knife emphasizes that Red's power resides mainly in his words and in his socially approved dominance as Sorrel's father and the head of the family. His monologue does not offer Sorrel any opportunity for verbal resistance, and he reduces her – via his language of intimidation and power – to the helpless animal described in the stage directions. As the scene continues, Sorrel increasingly capitulates to Red's scripting of her role, which reasserts his control of her and of her sexuality, both as a physically stronger male and as her father: the attack begins on the pretext that she has been plotting to overthrow him and to install her fiancé in his place as head of the patriarchal family. The scene scripts Sorrel's submission while it performs it, so that her systematic disempowerment is metaphorically represented in the physical stripping of her clothes, reducing her to a silent, and silenced, body. The other characters' refusal to come to her aid also testifies to Red's control of his environment.

Though narratively coherent, in rehearsal the scene uncovers difficulties with the staging of the piece as well as insights into its genre. The initial aim in rehearsal was to explore strategies that potentially implicated the audience ethically in the performance of violence, ways in which Sorrel might struggle out of the proscenium arch, out of the frame of the performance, to appear to appeal directly to the spectators as well as to her family within the dramatic world. Such staging strategies may create a sense of foreboding for the spectator, so that he or she experiences the desire to intervene, and a heightened sense of dread at what is about to happen. The first issue for consideration is the stage directions in the rape scene. The stage directions given in the printed text specify that Red 'grabs [Sorrel] suddenly and holds her in a vice grip. Sorrel struggles pointlessly against the strength of him'. It seems that a degree of submission on Sorrel's part is written imperceptibly into the script, just as it is in the dialogue where Sorrel's screams for help are not answered by the others in the house, and as she realizes she is alone, Red's control of language reduces her to inarticulacy.

Rehearsals pointed to particular ways in which such a scene might reflect – wittingly or unwittingly – normative ideas about gender, about gendered bodies, and about gender relations. The submission of Sorrel to Red's violence fits within popular narratives of rape: the act is represented ambivalently in scholarly volumes on female psychology and sexuality, in film, pulp fiction, romantic magazines and novels, soft and hardcore pornography. This narrative is of rape as a kind of forceful seduction to which the woman submits when she realizes she has no alternative, and in which she finds a kind of masochistic pleasure. Such narratives are so familiar to all of us that they become part of a cultural landscape. The play ends with Sorrel breaking off her engagement and choosing to stay with her family on the hill – and therefore, choosing or accepting a likely sexual relationship with her father. It is arguably the incestuous context that Carr gives to the rape that makes it so repugnant: if Sorrel's rapist was her fiancé, would a conclusion in which they were reunited be so far beyond conventional plot or narrative?

One of the problems with pursuing a kind of realistic staging in which rape is enacted in front of the audience, is that the body of Sorrel is put on display in a way that Red's is not; and the seeming inevitability of the action does not provoke the audience to question the structures that support Red's power over his children. Therefore, the interpersonal violence is foregrounded and vilified, but the systemic violence that underlies it remains invisible. Sorrel's forced inarticulacy is also troubling, as an image of silencing that obliterates her subjective experience. And in fact, the greater the attempts at realistic staging the more the play emerges as a dark fairytale, a story of hobgoblins, or to quote Dinah a horror story of 'children playin in a field ah some awful game before rules was made'. Though apparently naturalistic, at least in some respects the play is anti-naturalistic, grotesque, and monstrous.

Writing Mayhem and Murder

On Raftery's Hill and *Low Level Panic* represent female victims, and, arguably, reinscribe female identity as bound up with victimhood, casting the male as the oppressor. Such versions of femaleness sit in dismal contrast to canonical characters like Pegeen Mike, who is so memorably described as 'a fine, hardy girl would knock the head of any two men in the place', and as 'a girl you'd see itching and scratching, and she with a stale stink of poteen on her from selling in the shop'[5]. In Stella Feehily's *Duck*, the central characters are more glamorous than Pegeen but they share her rambunctious engagement with the world around them. First produced by Out of Joint and the Royal Court in 2003, the play opened in London before touring to Dublin, and was critically well reviewed. It was likened to other work in the contemporary British theatre, such as Simon Burt's *Untouchable*, though it is also reminiscent of Rebecca Pritchard's *Yard Gals*, Enda

---

[5] Synge, J.M. *The Playboy of the Western World* available online at
    http://etext.virginia.edu/toc/modeng/public/SynPlay.html. Last accessed
    01/01/2012.

Walsh's *Disco Pigs*, or other dramas of young women's friendships and journeys to maturity such as Shelagh Delaney's *A Taste of Honey* or Lisa McGee's *Girls and Dolls*. *Duck* stages scenes from the life of two young women, Cat and Sophie, who are both in their late teens. The play traces the girls' experiences as they try to establish a sense of who they are and their place in the world. Sophie is at college, and Cat has acquired a thuggish, drug-dealing boyfriend, Mark, who employs her in his club and offers her to his friend Eddie with the words 'You can have her … She's a hole. She likes it hard' (19). She also has an older lover, the writer Jack, who calls her Gina Lollobrigida and offers her a more romantic image of herself. In *Duck*, violence is brutal, both in the language and in what the characters do to each other; and it represents the female characters as aggressors rather than victims, women who will fight viciously when necessary to defend themselves and their interests. The play opens with the sound of an explosion before the two run on drunk: Cat has just blown up her boyfriend's car by setting fire to the fuel tank. They then fight two men who proposition them and threaten them with rape.

The opening scenes of the play show Cat drunk and retching by the roadside, smudged with ash from her attack on Mark's car, while Sophie attempts to comfort her. As they squat on the pavement they are approached by 'two inner city lads' who 'strut over' and ask 'Are youse queers?' (6). As the dialogue unfolds, the male characters attempt the intimidation through language that operates so successfully in *Low Level Panic* or *On Raftery's Hill*; but the female characters responses in *Duck* are very different. Rather than being embarrassed, disoriented, or reduced to inarticulacy Cat and Sophie respond directly:

> **Sophie:** Right, you can get lost now.
> **Cat:** Yeah, fuck off out of my face.
> *The dialogue continues*:
> **Boy 1:** I like dirty bitches. (*Grabbing his crotch*) Do ya want a bit of that baby?
> **Sophie:** (*Whispering to Cat*) Pull your bag over and stand up with me
> *They get to their feet. Sophie has a bottle of Bacardi breezer behind her back.*
> No thanks, I was about to lick my friend out when you arrived.
> *The girls run, and the boys give chase*:
> **BOY 2:** Get them.
> **BOY 1:** Fuck the shite oura them.

But Sophie smashes the bottle and uses it to cut both boys, shouting 'FUCK OFF FUCK OFF FUCK OFF', telling Boy 1 'I am going to rip your ugly face off'. The fight stops and *'they all look in amazement at Sophie'* (8). The scale of Sophie's resistance frightens the two boys who realize that these women are not the easy prey they expected. They run away, still shouting abuse.

Sharon Marcus's argument that 'the violence of rape is enabled by narratives, complexes and institutions which derive their strength... from their power to structure our lives as imposing cultural scripts' is illustrated in this scene where the female characters clearly do not respond as expected to the men's sexual aggression. They not only resist – they are more frightening than the men, and more reckless in their violence. Such a response attests, amongst other things, to the value they place upon themselves and their own bodily safety and integrity. Cat is too drunk to do much, but Sophie demonstrates a willingness to kill, or at least mutilate and 'rip the face off' her assailants. The volume of her screaming and the fact that she screams her aggression – 'FUCK OFF FUCK OFF FUCK OFF' – rather than crying for help add to the sense of alarm within the scene. While the men's aggression follows a recognizable pattern, similar to the taunting of Sorrel or of Mary, Sophie does not offer the conventional response. Her reaction typifies the qualities of violence: it is sudden, chaotic, unexpected.

Torching Mark's jeep is Cat's revenge for some slight. Like the broken bottle Sophie swings, this action expresses Cat's lack of inhibition and lack of control. She is not afraid, afterwards: despite Mark's violence she seems impervious to the danger he poses to her. Even when he and Eddie break into her other boyfriend's house and attack them as they lie sleeping, Cat remains defiant, challenging him: 'I'm sick to my tits of you / so hurry up and do something cos I'm getting cold' (105). Like Hester Swane in Carr's *By the Bog of Cats*, Cat and Sophie actively resist male aggression, refuse to respond in a passive or submissive manner to threatening behaviour, and commit acts of destruction on stage.

Hester Swane is a murderer: she describes her killing of her brother earlier in her life, and cuts her small daughter's throat on stage in front of the audience. *By the Bog of Cats* is loosely based on the Greek tragedy *Medea*, though it references a number of other canonical texts as well. The central character, Hester Swane, has been abandoned by her lover Carthage Kilbride, who plans to marry Caroline Cassidy, daughter of Xavier a local landowner. Hester's rage at this betrayal leads her to disrupt the wedding by showing up in her own wedding dress, and to burn down the cattle sheds with the animals inside them. Reacting to this violence Xavier Cassidy attempts to intimidate her into leaving the townland, but she resists. When she can resist no longer, she kills the seven year old daughter she has with Carthage, and kills herself. Her motivation for killing the child is complicated: she believes that the child will be in danger from Xavier, since she believes that he abused his own children; she was abandoned by her mother when she was seven, and she can't bear to repeat that history, and the little girl begs to 'come too' when Hester tells her goodbye. But Hester has, previously, murdered her brother to benefit Carthage, so she has a long history of violent action.

As in many plays that deal with rape and sexual violence against women, key moments of the action revolve around who is credible and who is not. In *Low Level Panic* Jo gets irritated with Mary's distress, saying 'Try to stop thinking for once, will you? For five minutes' (101); in *On Raftery's Hill* Red warningly asks if Sorrel is 'goin to start spreadin lies' and in *by the Bog of Cats* Xavier Cassidy uses his shotgun to look down Hester's dress, and tells her, 'I could do what I wanted with ya right here and now and no wan would believe ya' (331). But like Sophie and Cat, Hester fights back. She does not contradict him, because he is correct – he is more credible than she is. Instead she demands 'What're ya goin' to do, Cassidy? Blow me head off?' and she *'puts her mouth over the barrel'* and taunts him, 'G'wan shoot! Blow me away. Save me the bother meself (*goes for the trigger*.) Ya want me to do it for ya?' (331). It is Cassidy, panicked, who struggles to get away from *her*. In responding to the violence with violence, Hester refuses to submit, in contrast to the disturbing sense in which the central female characters in *Low Level Panic* and *On Raftery's Hill* internalize their own helplessness, and become compliant with their attackers in a way that performs female submission. Hester – violent, outcast, labelled mad – finds a freedom to resist those norms and to protect herself, at least temporarily. Ironically, it is her lack of concern for her own safety that protects her from Cassidy. While Cat and Sophie use violence to protect themselves, Hester demonstrates a reckless lack of concern for her own life and safety and in doing so, frightens Cassidy. He glimpses the chaos of violence and retreats. Although she kills herself in the final moments of the play, she dies by no hand but her own, and manages first to create a swathe of destruction all around her.

The murder of the child Josie and Hester's suicide conclude a long sequence in which she reviews her life, beginning with her discussing her grief for her mother with her neighbour, progressing through her conflict with Cassidy, her last conversation with Carthage and Caroline, and her reflection upon the murder of her brother. Finally alone, she '*takes a drink, goes into the caravan, comes out with a knife. She tests it for sharpness, teases it across her throat, shivers.* Come on now, ya done it aisy enough to another, now it's your own turn. *Bares her throat, ready to do it. Enter Josie...*' (337). This sequence, following on from Hester's confession of murdering her brother by slitting his throat and tipping him, still alive, into the lake with a boulder tied to his waist, heightens the tension for the audience. Aware of the character's capacity for violence, the spectators have reason to fear what they will see next. At this point in the play, Hester's death appears inevitable. But the scene is interrupted by the arrival of Josie, allowing for two contradictory reactions: a sense of reprieve, since Hester will not kill herself in front of her child, and a heightened sense of tension for the vulnerability of the child. The ensuing scene – of the child's panic that her mother is 'goin' away ... somewhere ya can never return from' and her frantic demands to come too (338), lead to an horrific moment where, holding Josie in her arms, '*Hester cuts Josie's throat with one savage movement*' (339). She then '*Begins to wail, a terrible animal wail*'. In the premiere production, Olwen Fouéré interpreted this direction to produce a frightening, heartrending scream that continues over a duration to voice the character's grief and despair but also to create an affective experience for the audience who are unsettled by the dreadful sound. Hester's suicide, which follows and is represented in a dance with Death (the 'Ghost Fancier'), is in fact far less harrowing than these earlier scenes.

Conclusions:

By resisting successfully in their various ways, characters in *By the Bog of Cats* and *Duck* disrupt what Mardorossian calls the 'rape script': they resist attempts to reduce them to violated bodies or to inscribe, through sexual violence, their inferior status. The ferocious independence expressed by Hester and powerfully interpreted in the premiere by Olwen Fouéré wreaks havoc on her community, but presents the spectators with a female character who defies male attempts to delimit and define her. She is always outside, in the exterior spaces of the bog, in opposition to the usual situation of female characters within or in connection to a domestic interior space. She is remorseless, scarcely regretting her brutal murder of her brother. She spread mayhem, thereby attacking the very symbols (the hearth; the bridal party) of the patriarchal family.

Violence by female characters is often written and received as evidence of madness or badness. Clytemnestra kills her husband in the bath, where he is helpless, unarmed, and believes himself to be in the safety of the domestic space; Medea kills her sons, also inside the home, to revenge herself upon her unfaithful husband; both are represented in Greek mythologies as sorceresses. Defined as evil characters whose behaviour challenges every sacred belief about womanhood, they are scheming, violent, and destructive of those they should love best and protect. Female violence is often considered more disturbing than male violence because it disrupts normative ideas of gender which force upon women the role of nurturers and carers. It is also particularly disruptive because the world that women inhabit – the domestic world – is supposed to be safe, a haven from the dangers of the unbounded public world. By wreaking chaotic violence within this private world, violent female characters make nowhere safe; they threaten to destroy the patriarchal family and therefore the society it stands for.

Women's writing of rape and sexual violence is thus often problematically received, reduced to anti-male polemic (as in the reviews of *Low Level Panic*) and denied a complex aesthetic interpretation. Yet the issue remains central to women's dramatic writing, whether it is present in the workings of the plot or in small details of the characterization or setting. In Irish women's writing, rape, incest, sexual abuse and domestic violence are all recurring themes, represented in a wide variety of ways and in different genres of writing and performance. Though frequently interpreted as acts of interpersonal violence, these acts are also expressive of social and cultural attitudes, both contemporary and historical. The emphasis on violence and oppression within the family situates women's writing as part of a tradition of drama that focuses on the family and on the domestic space, from the early years of the National Theatre movement and the work of Synge through to contemporary plays by Murphy, Friel, McPherson, Carr, Moxley, and other male and female playwrights.

Yet at the same time, depictions of rape remain problematic because they so often erase the human subjectivity of the victim, reducing her to a cypher or to a body suffering beautifully and displayed for the audience's pleasure in spectacle. Staging violence in an explicit way, which draws attention to struggle, cruelty and pain, inevitably also emphasizes the physicality of the body. Erased or visible, the female body on stage remains problematic.

Bibliography

Aristotle, *Poetics*, trans. S.H. Butcher. Online, available at http://ebooks.adelaide.edu.au/a/aristotle/poetics/. Last accessed 10/03/2012.

Canning, Charlotte, *Feminist Theaters in the USA: Staging Women's Experience* (London & New York: Routledge, 1996).

Carr, Marina,'By the Bog of Cats' *Marina Carr Plays 1* (London: Faber & Faber, 1999).

---, *On Raftery's Hill* (London: Faber & Faber, 2000).

Feehily, Stella, *Duck* (London: Nick Hern Books, 2003).

Goodman, Lizbeth, *Contemporary Feminist Theatres* (London & NY: Routledge, 1993).

Howe, Elizabeth, *The First English Actresses* (Cambridge: Cambridge U.P., 1992).

Marcus, Sharon, 'Fighting Bodies, Fighting Words: a theory and politics of rape prevention' in Butler, J. & JW Scott, eds, *Feminists Theorize the Political* (London & New York: Routledge, 1992): 385-403.

Mardorossian, Carine, 'Towards a New Feminist Theory of Rape' in *Signs*, vol. 27:3, Spring 2002:, 743-775.

McIntyre, Clare, *My Heart's a Suitcase & Low Level Panic* (London: Nick Hern Books, 1994).

12 | Feminism, Gender Roles and Sexualities in Contemporary Productions of Oscar Wilde

Aideen Kerr

In Wilde's 1895 play *The Importance of Being Earnest* Jack Worthing asks Miss Prism 'Why should there be one law for men, and another for women?'[1] This article will investigate how Wilde manipulated many of his dramatic characters and used them as a medium to expose the gender inequality in Victorian society. I will interrogate what Declan Kiberd asserts was Wilde's 'lifelong commitment to feminism'[2] in his personal life and evidenced in three of his plays: *The Importance of Being Earnest, An Ideal Husband* and *A Woman of No Importance*. This exploration will include a study of some of the contemporary adaptations of these plays including Conall Morrison's all-male adaptation of *Earnest* in 2005, Neil Bartlett's 2008 production of *An Ideal Husband* and Rough Magic's 2010 production of *Earnest*. The title of this collection, which celebrates Performing Feminisms in Ireland, allows me to focus specifically on Irish adaptations of Wilde's plays. As I adopt a feminist lens to study these plays and adaptations Gayle Austin's approach is useful in its application to Wilde's construction of female characters on the Victorian stage. Austin's feminist framework 'means paying attention when women appear as characters and noticing when they do not'[3] (1990:2). For this examination I am adopting a material feminist approach; one of the major advantages of material feminism is the prominent position given

---

[1] Oscar Wilde, 'The Importance of Being Earnest' , *The Complete Works of Oscar Wilde* (Glasgow: Harper Collins, 1948): 415.

[2] Declan Kiberd, *Inventing Ireland* (London: Vintage, 1995): 40.

[3] Gayle Austin, *Feminist Theories for Dramatic Criticism* (Ann Arbor: University of Michigan Press, 1990): 2.

to questions of class, race, and sexual preference; these receive little treatment in liberal or radical feminism. Austin suggests that a material feminist framework 'makes it imperative that other categories of oppression be considered, along with that of gender' (6). The material feminist lens is appropriate when considering Wilde, his dramatic output and his personal life, as we must also consider the roles of gender, sexuality and class in this context.

A feminist lens that focused only on gender would be too reductive in its consideration. In contemporary society we need to think about gender and sexuality in a more liberating way and isolating these concepts would also be too definitive. Austin asserts that material feminism: '1. Minimizes biological differences between men and women, 2. Stresses material conditions of production such as history, race, class, gender, [and] 3. Group more important than the individual' (6). Austin's three stages of feminist criticism are a useful tool that can provide an awareness of both the potential and the limitations to studying Wilde's plays in this context; 1. Working within the canon: examining images of women; 2. Expanding the canon: focusing on women writers; and 3. Exploding the canon: questioning underlying assumptions of an entire field of study, including canon formation (6).

The main limitation is obvious; Wilde was a male author not a female one. His unconventional ties to the feminism of his time and his pioneering of gender models that contested the restricted binaries of Victorian gender roles also forecasted what gender roles could be like in the future. As one of the prominent Irish modernists and feminists that emerged during the Victorian period, I will argue that Wilde is a pivotal figure in the history of feminism. I will analyse his personal ties to Victorian feminism as well as studying the subversive nature of the gender roles Wilde creates in *The Importance of Being Earnest* (1895), *An Ideal Husband* (1895) and *A Woman of No Importance* (1893). I will also study two contemporary productions of *The Importance of Being Earnest*: Conall Morrison's all-male adaptation of *Earnest* at the Abbey Theatre in 2005 and Rough Magic's 2010 production of *Earnest* at Dublin's Gaiety Theatre. These productions undermine and replace the original potential of Wilde's subversive female characters in various ways and in doing so they reinforce oppositional gender roles on the contemporary stage. I will also analyse Neil Bartlett's 2008 production of *An Ideal Husband* at the Abbey Theatre Dublin.

One of Wilde's most cherished and influential relationships during his lifetime was with his mother Lady Wilde, who wrote under the pseudonym Speranza. Wilde's mother was a celebrated nationalist writer whose poetic vision of Ireland was widely inspirational in the nineteenth century. She published widely in a variety of areas including poetry, politics and folklore.

As Kiberd suggests Wilde's 'love of her was melodramatic but genuine, as was his repeated espousal in later writings of her doctrines – especially her belief in a woman's right to work and to engage in political activity' (1995:34). Throughout his life Wilde sustained many life-long relationships with women including his wife (despite the scandal), the author Ada Leverson whom he called Sphinx, as well as declaring his admiration for various actresses, particularly Sara Bernhardt. His respect for Sara Bernhardt can be evidenced by his claim that he wrote *Salome* for her: 'At a party at Henry Irving's she (Bernhardt) remarked to Wilde that he should write a play for her one day. 'I have already done so'. As soon as she read *Salome* she decided to play the title role.[4] As a child Wilde's early life was marked with tragedy; his younger sister Isola died when Wilde was just aged twelve. This premature death and the tragic death of his two half-sisters in a fire when Wilde was seventeen may have influenced a more potent connection to the feminist cause throughout his lifetime. Wilde's poignant poem *Requiescat,* written in 1881, reflects his loss felt by Isola's death;

> Peace, Peace, She cannot hear
> Lyre or sonnet,
> All my life's buried here,
> Heap earth upon it (1948: 749).

Following Wilde's death in 1900 an envelope was found in his possession which contained a lock of his beloved dead sister's hair. The influence of these personal relationships can be seen in Wilde's plays; many of his central characters are women and Wilde often privileges an interrogation of female relationships over those of male relationships.

In the years preceding Wilde's popular dramas 1887-1890, he held a three year editorship of the Victorian magazine *A Lady's World*. Before Wilde's editorship the magazine followed and promoted Victorian fashion trends for women, dedicating no space to the discussion of women's issues or publication of articles. He immediately renamed the magazine to *The Woman's World;* this move portrayed Wilde's urgency to use the magazine as a platform to publish and promote women's issues and writing by women. Figure One is the cover image of the

---

[4] Richard Ellman, *Oscar Wilde* (London: Penguin, 1987): 350.

Figure 3: Cover of *The Woman's World*

magazine after Wilde's renaming of it. Stephen Calloway suggests that
this new title denoted Wilde's 'advanced views on female
participation'.[5] According to Wilde's close friend and literary executor
Robert Ross, Wilde renamed the magazine on the advice of his female
friend Dinah Mulock Craik; she was a novelist and poet whose husband,

---

[5] Stephen Calloway, *Oscar Wilde: An Exquisite Life* (London: Stewart, TAbori &
Chang, 1997): 53-4.

George, was a partner in the Macmillan publishing company[6]. Wilde's re-branding of the magazine, inspired in part by Craik, contested the exclusivity of Victorian woman as an expected ideal and privileged a more modern and liberating idea of woman. This idea of the new woman meant that for the first time a female voice could be heard in the public intellectual sphere; publication in the magazine meant a female interaction with public and political issues of the day, formerly a male-dominated sphere. This preoccupation with women's issues and gender roles, as Kiberd acknowledges, is investigated throughout Wilde's plays. Within Wildean studies there is a need to move away from the academic temptation of labelling his plays as mere social comedies; this framework seems to be too reductive for plays that continue to contest the very boundaries of gender and sexuality.

Grosz cites Irigaray who demonstrates that 'the female body is the site for patriarchal power relations, and, at the same time, for symbolic and representational resistances.'[7] Masculine identity and the masculine body exist in relation to the recognition of the female body as other. In the context of Wilde's plays the female body becomes a site upon which restrictive gender roles can be challenged and ultimately reformed. In many of his plays Wilde presents us with a character who appears to be the ideal Victorian woman, for example Lady Chiltern in *An Ideal Husband*, but he subsequently deflates this fictionalized notion and replaces her with a more liberating idea of woman. Irigaray's assertion will be examined in light of a variety of Wilde's female characters who contest the rigid gender binaries in the Victorian world.

The Importance of Being Earnest was first staged at St James's Theatre, London, on the 14th February 1895. The play's two bachelor dandies, Algernon and Jack, invent dying invalids and troubled siblings to account for their desired absence in the city or country. Their deceptive double lives, referred to as 'bunburying', come to a head when they discover that they are brothers. Their respective love interests, Gwendolen and Cecily (Jack's ward), are unconventional female characters whose decisions in the play often dictate the fate of their male counterparts. Similarly, Gwendolen's mother Lady Bracknell is a formidable character who dominates her family, especially her husband. In Wilde's *Earnest* Cecily becomes a site upon which Wilde can contest existing gender roles. By reversing the characterization of

---

[6] Robert Ross, *Collected Works of Oscar Wilde* (London, 1887): 207.

[7] Elizabeth Grosz, *Jacques Lacan: a feminist introduction* (London: Routledge, 1990): 114.

male and female roles in the play Wilde disparages the ascribed and confined roles that exist for the two sexes in Victorian society. For example Lady Bracknell's movement outside of her domestic sphere and her husband's confinement to the home, as well as his absence onstage, suggests that she is the more liberated of the two. Lady Bracknell's female voice dominates the stage in the scenes that she appears in; this is contrasted with the silence of her unseen husband who never appears onstage to claim his identity for himself. In a play that is obsessed with the idea of self-invention Wilde constructs Cecily Cardew in *Earnest* as a bi-gendered model of the future who has the potential to subvert normative gender roles in the theatre. Wilde's adoption of a somewhat inverted female character and body in his plays are a mode by which he contested the patriarchal gender roles in Victorian society.

Although the character Cecily Cardew is identified as female in *The Importance of Being Earnest*, signifiers throughout the play suggest that this character blurs the very lines of gender identity. From the beginning of the play confusion and ambiguity surround Cecily's identity and physical being even before she appears onstage. Jack initially claims that she is his aunt and it emerges eventually that, in reality, she is his ward. The name Cecily evokes a male historical narrative, Cecily having been widely used as a nickname for rent boys in Victorian society. Aside from all-male performances of the play like Morrison's 2005 adaptation, however, Cecily is typically identified as a female body according to costume onstage. But the historical Victorian connotations associated with the name confuse the gender reality of the character onstage. The name Cecily connotes an effeminate homosexual; in other slang the term 'Molly House' identified a private meeting place where men met each other for same-sex liaisons in the eighteenth century.

Jill Dolan claims that

> By questioning the entire apparatus of theater's representation of women, feminists can 'deconstruct gender categories. If we stop considering the stage as a mirror of reality, we can use it as a laboratory in which to reconstruct new, non-gendered identities. And in the process we can change the very nature of theatre itself.'[8]

In order to change the gender roles, norms and expectations on the stage of the future we need to deconstruct restrictive and

---

[8] Jill Dolan, 'Gender Impersonation Onstage' *Women and Performance* 2:4 (1985): 5-11.

heteronormative gender roles and sexualities. As aforementioned, Cecily can be interpreted as a bigendered or epicene character and identity. In *Earnest* her body is a site upon which bigendered experimentation and patriarchal resistance takes place; she assumes both male and female names, characteristics and personal histories so that both male and female genders exist onstage in the one physical form. Cecily could be read as a bigendered model of the future. Sue Ellen Case proposes that 'The feminist in nature can create the laboratory in which the single most effective mode of repression – gender – can be exposed, dismantled, and removed'.[9] Wilde dilutes and dismantles normative Victorian gender roles in *Earnest, An Ideal Husband* and *A Woman of No Importance*.

In the section of Wilde's *Earnest* entitled The Persons of the Play the female characters carry various titles which reinforce their gender status; 'Lady', 'Miss', etc. Cecily Cardew and Gwendolen Fairfax are the only exceptions to this rule. In Cecily's case this could imply that her character occupies a liminal gendered space between male and female. The untitled and youthful characters could also represent a more liberated generation of the future; a generation that do not use gender as a definitive signifier. Jack initially denies that he knows Cecily 'I don't know any one of the name of Cecily ... as far as I remember' (1948: 359). In their previous dialogue Algernon and Jack refer to Gwendolen as 'her'; her gendered identity is explicitly recognized but neither character initially acknowledges Cecily's gendered identity. An explicit gendered identity is denied to Cecily from the very opening of *Earnest*. This reinforces Lizbeth Goodman's proposition that gender and performance are 'unknowns, as concepts to be explored.'[10] Goodman's inspiring interpretation of what gender should be is a liberating and inclusive framework that could also be applied in a positive way to sexuality. Wilde's own bisexual performance of identity as a husband to Constance Lloyd, a father to their children and a secret male lover to Lord Alfred Douglas, reveals the artificiality of compulsory Victorian heterosexuality.

Cecily's invention of a historical narrative is represented by the personal history she writes of her and Algernon's relationship before they have met; this is a meta-theatrical technique that contests the dominant male narrative of the past. In re-writing the past Cecily exposes the absence of complex female characters in the literary and

---

[9] Sue-Ellen Case, *Feminism and Theatre* (London: Routledge, 1988): 131-32.
[10] Lizbeth Goodman, *The Routledge Reader in Gender and Performance* (London: Routledge, 1998): 1.

dramatic canon, which remains subject to the patriarchal framework. Her need to invent a history mirrors the absence of woman in the canon and forecasts the need for more realistic female characters. Cecily's is a quest to re-establish a new voice in the canon and similarly with Wilde's editorship of *The Woman's World*, Wilde's privileging of the female voice over the male is his recognition of gender inequality in Victorian society. Instead of adhering to normative gender roles Wilde's characters try gender on in his plays; gender is a performative experiment that is up for grabs and that has the potential to subvert hegemonic structures.

The implication of the silver cigarette case in *Earnest* implies that Wilde's two main male characters, Jack and Algernon, may be in contact with the Victorian homosexual underworld. Wilde often lavished gifts upon Victorian rent boys; these most often took the form of a silver cigarette case. Wilde is experimenting with the idea of gender and is exploring the possibility of Cecily as a female body on the stage, but with historically male connotations and male characteristics. Judith Butler asserts that we recognize an individual's gender by what clothes they wear and how they wear them. However in the case of Cecily the historical connotations with same-sex passion and the 'normative' male characteristics she assumes, contests Butler's model of gender differentiation. In Morrison's all-male adaptation of *Earnest* these bigendered signifiers are blurred even further and with the absence of the female body onstage Cecily becomes more of a male presence than a bigendered one.

Usually recognized as a female body, Cecily is a site upon which class relations can be contested. Act Two opens with her attempt to rupture Victorian class boundaries:

> **Miss Prism:** Cecily, Cecily! Surely such a utilitarian occupation as the watering of flowers is rather Moultan's duty than yours?
> **Cecily:** I wish you would give Moultan the German lesson instead of me (1948: 375).

Cecily also displays an unconventional and liberal stance on gender equality; 'But men don't sew Miss Prism... And if they did, I don't see why they should be punished for it' (376). Cecily's diary 'usually chronicles the things that have never happened, and couldn't have possibly happened. I believe that Memory is responsible for nearly all the three-volume novels that Mudie sends us' (376). Cecily's acknowledgment of her fictionalized historical past is Wilde's way of comically re-writing or re-establishing the position of women in the literary and dramatic canon. By creating more complex nineteenth century female characters Wilde established a more liberating concept of the woman that challenges reductive notions of woman in the canon.

When Algernon arrives onstage in *Earnest* and doubles as Jack's fictional brother Ernest, Cecily's journal, as well as her bold assertion that she and Algernon met three months before they actually met, is indicative of her power in their relationship. 'I don't think Miss Prism would like my being alone with him. So I had better send for him at once, before she comes in' (378). Their ensuing dialogue portrays Cecily's gender inversion in their relationship; she has assumed the typical role of the dominant male in the relationship. Algernon: 'I thought every woman had a mission of some kind, nowadays'. Cecily: 'Every female has! No woman. Besides I have no time to reform you this afternoon' (379). Cecily assumes female attributes but refuses to be defined definitively as a woman in the restrictive Victorian context. Cecily's refusal to be labelled also reflects Wilde's distinction between the more realistic idea of Woman and the fictionalized 'ideal' 'female' in Victorian society? This belief is also reflected in his re-naming of *A Lady's World* to *The Woman's World*.

Wilde's reversal of a gender power exchange is evident in the relationship between Cecily and Algernon, and Jack and Gwendolen. When Jack proposes to Gwendolen in Act One she is in the position of power while he has exposed his vulnerability. She also unconventionally declares her love for him before he has the opportunity to do so or to propose to her. Gwendolen and Cecily remain powerful in this exchange and it is Jack and Algernon who are subject to their partner's decisions. Gwendolen's reaction to Algernon and Jack's wish to be christened Ernest, provokes the following response: 'How absurd to talk of the equality of the sexes! Where questions of self-sacrifice are concerned, men are infinitely beyond us.' Cecily: 'They have moments of physical courage of which we women know absolutely nothing' (407). This satire on supposedly male courage with reference to Algernon and Jacks christenings mocks the ideal of the Victorian man as well as highlighting the gender inequality evident in Victorian society.

Algernon's declaration of his love for Cecily paradoxically indicates her power in the relationship: 'ever since ... when I first looked upon your wonderful and incomparable beauty, I have not merely been your abject slave and servant but, soaring above the pinions of a possibly monstrous ambition, I have dared to love you wildly, passionately, devotedly, hopelessly' (393). Cecily insists that he repeat these lines twice so that she can copy them into her journal. Her insistence that he repeat the lines while she copies them down undermines Algernon's romantic declaration. His extended declaration of love inspires the following reaction: 'Oh, I don't think that makes any sense at all. The fact is that men should never try to dictate to women. They never know how to do it, and when they do do it, they always say something particularly foolish' (393). Algernon goes on:

> **Algernon:** I love you, I want you. I can't live without you, Cecily! You know I love you... (*Rushes over to her and places his hand on hers.*)
> **Cecily:** (*rising*): Oh, you have made me make a blot. And yours is the only real proposal I have ever had in all my life. I should like to have it entered neatly (394).

While Algernon's confession exposes a certain vulnerability Cecily's concerns are of a superficial nature. Cecily informs Algernon that 'we have been engaged for the last three months' and that she has bought herself gifts from him and written many letters to herself on his behalf (394).

Algernon's acceptance and passivity in the relationship is more typically regarded as characteristically female; this is an inversion of typical Victorian gender roles. The female voice is empowered and the male voice accepts this power reversal absolutely.

> **Cecily:** I wrote your letters for you ... I should have thought you would have remembered the violent letter you wrote to me because I danced with Lord Kelso at the county ball? ... Of course you did. Otherwise I wouldn't have forgiven you or accepted this little gold bangle with the turquoise and diamond heart, that you sent me the next day. (*Shows bangle*).
> **Algernon:** Did I give you this Cecily?... So we have been engaged for three months, Cecily! (395).

Algernon's passivity, as well as Gwendolen's dominance of Jack, provides an alternative framework for heterosexual Victorian couples. Kiberd proposes that in *Earnest* 'Far from the men engaging in the traditional discussion of the finer points of the female form, it is the women who discuss the physical appeal of the men: when Algernon proposes to Cecily, it is *she* who runs her fingers through his hair and asks sternly: "I hope your hair curls naturally. Does it?"' (395). Algernon responds 'Yes darling, with a little help from others' (1948: 395).

Gwendolen also assumes the more typical male role in her relationship with Jack. It is Gwendolen who boldly asserts her love for Jack; she obtains and sustains the power in their relationship:

> **Gwendolen:** ... My ideal has always been to love someone of the name Ernest. There is something in the name that inspires

absolute confidence. The moment Algernon first mentioned to me that he had a friend called Ernest, I knew I was destined to love you.

Jack: You really love me, Gwendolen?

Gwendolen: Passionately ... I adore you. But you haven't proposed to me yet. Nothing has been said at all about marriage ... And to spare you any possible disappointment, Mr. Worthing, I think it only fair to tell you quite frankly beforehand that I am fully determined to accept you (366).

Gwendolen's unconventional assertion of her love for Jack in such a matter of fact style suggests that this relationship will be on her terms, not his.

Lady Bracknell's dominance in the public sphere and the absolute denial of her husband's voice onstage throughout the play is emblematic of Wilde's inverted marital framework. Lady Bracknell initially disapproves and subsequently gives her consent to her daughter Gwendolen to marry Jack, as well as giving Algernon and Cecily her blessing. As Jack's ward, Cecily needs his permission to marry before she comes of age. Jack: 'The moment you consent to my marriage with Gwendolen, I will most gladly allow your nephew to form an alliance with my ward' (412). However Lady Bracknell will not be blackmailed by Jack and her outright refusal of this undermines normative gender roles in the Victorian world. It is also Lady Bracknell who can inform Jack of who he is; Lady Bracknell and Cecily construct the fictionalized versions of a historical past that in time dictate the actions of the male characters as well as the plot mechanisms in *Earnest*. The power and progression of the plot and the action of the drama are often in the hands of Wilde's female characters. The influence of admirable female figures in Wilde's personal life, like Lady Wilde, inspired strong female characters on the stage.

Although *Earnest* opens with an all-male dialogue between Algernon and his manservant Lane, this dialogue is quickly penetrated by Lady Bracknell and her daughter Gwendolen. When Algernon and Cecily meet for the first time we realize that it is Cecily who has constructed their historical narrative; their past relationship. Algernon's acceptance of this narrative from a female perspective in Cecily's case renders the male narrative the submissive narrative, while female narrative is taken as the dominant narrative. Obviously this gendered dialogue is in contrast to the male-oriented canon that privileged male inventions of a fictionalized and often disposable role of Woman. Wilde's outspoken and assertive female characters are a vital alternative to this fictionalized version. Could this be Wilde's implicit way of re-writing women back into the dramatic canon? This is a key concept because as we look to material feminism in the hopes of reforming and restructuring the patriarchal framework we need not just female support and determination but male support for this movement too.

Conall Morrison's adaptation of *The Importance of Being Earnest* was staged at the Abbey theatre Dublin in 2005 and advertised the production as 'a cast composed entirely of men.' In a recent interview with Alan Stanford who doubled as Wilde, Lady Bracknell and Lane in the play, Stanford claimed that the cast were not merely cross-dressing but acting from their male perspective of how they interpret women.[11] By replacing Wilde's female characters with male actors within Stanford's framework, the all-male cast of *Earnest* reinstates the privileged male gaze while undermining the importance of Wilde's original female characters. The all-male cast plays on Wilde's same-sex relations with men during his lifetime as is emphasized by Stanford's wearing a green carnation in the play; this flower was a code of recognition amongst the homosexual community in London in the 1890s. The opening of Morrison's production emphasizes this aspect of Wilde's personal life. It is three months before Wilde's death in 1900 and the setting is a Parisian cafe the Brasserie Dauphine. Stanford drinks absinthe, is dressed in Wilde's typically dandyish costume: a black velvet suit, stockings, and he wears a peculiarly long womanly wig which allows for the easy transformation from Wilde to Lady Bracknell. Wilde is initially abused and then adored by a group of playful male youths who surround him in admiration and obvious flirtation. The music in the cafe resurrects the nostalgic memory of his 1895 play *Earnest* from which the play itself unfolds.

In Morrison's adaptation the violent removal of the female body also removes all potential to resist and reform restrictive gender roles. Not only does this version of *Earnest* become a narrow framework for an all-male performance, it undermines the original potential of Wilde's female characters to subvert gender norms. The original potential of the female characters to subvert is itself subverted by the presence and replacement of a male body onstage. Cecily is no longer the site for representational resistances to patriarchal power relations but a symbol of male power and patriarchy. The adaptation fails to engage with Wilde's representation of women and concentrates on an all-male perspective: seen as the actors are acting out their *male* interpretation

---

[11] Author's interview with Alan Stanford, Dublin, January 2011.

of women, as Stanford says. This exclusively male performance could also be dangerous in alienating the female members of the audience. As aforementioned the all-male cast accentuates Wilde's same-sex desire for other men during his lifetime. The beginning of Act Two of Morrison's *Earnest* portrays this desire; Stanford (presumably playing his role as Wilde) walks across the stage to a young man who removes his shirt to expose his upper body, he hands his shirt to Stanford and the pair walk off together stage right. This act plays on the circle of men involved in the 1895 Wilde trials. Morrison also adds kisses between the actors into his adaptation; for example Jack and Gwendolen kiss and Algernon and Cecily kiss. This plays on the all-male desire of the adaptation as well as (possibly inadvertently) emphasizing the absence of the female body on the stage.

In Morrison's *Earnest* Wilde's female characters are replaced with male actors dressed in drag, making the female characters seem ridiculous in comparison to the male characters or to their representation in conventional productions of the play that include male and female actors. Stanford's male performance of Lady Bracknell deflates her subversive dominance and reverses the shift of the female gaze, reinstating the male gaze once again. Patrick Moy's role as Cecily and Tadhg Murphy's role as Gwendolen inverts the original potential of the characters to challenge the patriarchal framework, and instead empowers an exclusively male discourse. The dominant role of Lady Bracknell and the roles of Cecily and Gwendolen in Wilde's play are reversed in this adaptation; the male bodies occupy the former female vehicles of subversion; this mirrors the patriarchal framework of the contemporary world. Although the male performances of these female roles can seem entertaining on a superficial level, after an analysis of the production their roles become problematic. Moy and Murphy play their parts with a high-pitched, giddy and child-like absurdity, which deflate the importance of Wilde's female characters and renders them harmless. The female characters then are constructed onstage through an all-male performance and through an all-male gaze.

For audience members who are unfamiliar with Wilde's play Morrison's adaptation portrays *Earnest* as a farcical social comedy which promotes the importance of the male voice and satirizes the absurdity of the female voice. Wilde's alternative to the heterosexual marital framework evidenced by the female desire of Ernest in the play is replaced by male desire. In its alienation of more realistic female roles on the stage Morrison's adaptation reinforces the binary oppositions of gender in the contemporary world. The production implies that there is no need for female actors in *Earnest*; the male actors' smooth transformation from male to female roles implies this. For example Stanford assumes the role of Lady Bracknell by wearing a tablecloth as a skirt and a lampshade cover as a throw around his shoulders. If the adaptation had included male and female actors who had cross-dressed then the production may have been a more gender liberating experience. The simultaneous cross-dressing of gender roles would have played on the performative aspect of gender and by playing the 'other' gender perhaps the gap could have been bridged between both genders on the contemporary stage.

The play on gender throughout *Earnest* implies that there is a need for gender to be an inventive and inclusive framework; Wilde's blurring of gender distinctions calls for a reformation of the polarized Victorian gender roles. The 2010 Rough Magic cast of *Earnest* in Dublin's Gaiety Theatre undermined this potential to subvert normative gender roles by playing the female roles superficially, whimsically, or in Stockard Channing's case, (she played Lady Bracknell), weakly. The pivotal role of Lady Bracknell was deflated by Channing's subdued performance; some of her lines were barely audible so that in place of Lady Bracknell's dominance was Channing's laconic delivery, which excited some critical comment by reviewers. In this production Wilde's female characters seem more like conventional Victorian women who play conventional gender roles. Lynne Parker directed this production and seems to have decided on an interpretation of *Earnest* as farcical social comedy with much of the darkness of the characters removed. In other interpretations of *Earnest* the potential to recognize Cecily as a force to subvert the patriarchal framework can inspire the feminist movement. The downplaying of the strong female characters in Rough Magic's production of Earnest emphasized the need for more complex female roles on the stage. Again, rather than the female being a site of patriarchal resistance as Irigaray proposes, in this production Cecily represents the dominance of the patriarchal framework. Parker's adaptation did not emphasize the unconventional inversion of gender roles in the play and in that sense her adapted characters were somewhat less radical than Wilde's original characters.

Visually, the production aesthetic drew upon an eclectic range of sources to combine clashing costumes from various epochs with a set design that was decorated with various scaffolds and rustic Celtic prints that hung from the flies. Apart from these scaffolds and prints the stage setting was bare, in sharp contrast to the elaborate costumes. But despite some disappointment at Channing's performance and the interpretation of the play, the production was inspiring in its offstage female participation in theatre and suggested the growing numbers of women involved in theatrical endeavours; the director, lighting designer and costume designer were all women.

Miss Prism is portrayed as the fictionalized version of an 'ideal' Victorian woman in *Earnest*. Wilde quickly deflates the notion of the 'ideal' woman; on discovery of Miss Prism's controversial involvement in Jack's background she is exposed as a hypocrite; 'you have fallen lately, Cecily, into a bad habit of thinking for yourself. You should give it up. It is not quite womanly ... Men don't like it' (391). Wilde's deflation of the 'ideal' woman is also evident in his characterization of Lady Chiltern in *An Ideal Husband*. The idealization of this fictionalized version of woman is dismantled when Lady Chiltern's rigid Victorian rectitude is exposed as vacuous and she adjusts her ideals for the convenience of her husband's fraudulent past. In her discussion about resisting the canon of American drama Gayle Austin suggests that some of Eugene O'Neill's female characters in *A Long Day's Journey into Night* (1956) 'are constructed offstage through the men's dialogue' (1990: 32). I want to suggest that in *Earnest* Lady Bracknell's husband, predominantly referred to only through recognition of his relationship with Lady Bracknell and Gwendolen, as a husband or father (for example 'Papa'), is constructed offstage through the *women's* dialogue. He is referred to only once as Lord Bracknell in the course of the play by Lady Bracknell; his absence throughout the play means that he never claims his title or his identity for himself. He is essentially constructed through the female gaze. The privileged female gaze in *Earnest* is juxtaposed against the absence of the universal and fictionalized 'Woman' constructed through the male gaze in most literary and dramatic history.

Neil Bartlett, the director of the 2008 Abbey production of the play recognized a mistake production companies can make when adapting Wilde's plays; 'For a play that is usually (wrongly) categorized as a Society comedy, it gives a fair impression of having been written in blood.'[12] His production of *An Ideal Husband* opened at the Abbey Theatre, Dublin, on the 14th August 2008 and was designed by Rae Smith. Smith adhered to Wilde's original direction in designing a traditionally rich Victorian set design and costumes. The set designs provided the audience with signifiers about what setting they were in and what kind of performance they could expect. In this production of

---

[12] Abbey Theatre Programme (2008): 3

An Ideal Husband the predominant colours of each act reflected the
disparate themes of the play. In Act Two the Chilterns' morning-room
was characterized by the colour white, which suggests an innocence and
purity to the household, but the very sincerity of this colour mocks the
Chiltern's supposed morality as their wealth is based on fraud. Chiltern
represents the ideal Victorian mode of masculinity which Wilde
debunks, and his satirization of the fictionalized Victorian woman is
realized. Wilde's deflation of the idealized Victorian husband implies
that there is an alternative framework that must be considered.

Act Three was set in the library of Lord Goring's house and this
setting was dimly lit and black and red in colour. This setting
acknowledged Chiltern's scandal and anticipated Mrs Cheveley's
attempted blackmail of Lord Goring. The marketing angle of the 2008
Abbey production accentuated the biographical strands of *An Ideal
Husband*. The marketing campaign described the play in the following
words: 'Oscar Wilde was a man who knew all about leading a double
life. *An Ideal Husband* is Wilde's painfully personal portrait of a
marriage wrecked by double standards' (Abbey Programme 2008: 3).
The quote inextricably links the portrayal of the Chilterns' marriage to
Wilde's own marriage. The threatening line 'We have all to pay for what
we do' in blood red across Wilde's face on the black and white image of
him on the front cover of the 2008 programme evokes the 1895 trials
and labels him as convict. This labelling is problematic in the context of
contemporary society as the programme suggests that although
homosexuality was decriminalized in 1993 Wilde is still associated with
his conviction of 'gross indecency'. In the play Sir Robert Chiltern's
plea, which warns against the dangers of adulation, mocks marriage
and the idealization of the Victorian husband:

> **Chiltern:** There was your mistake ... Why do you place us on
> monstrous pedestals ... All sins, except a sin against itself, Love
> should forgive ... Women think that they are making ideals of men.
> What they are making of us are false idols merely ... Let women
> make no more ideals of men! let them not put them on altars and
> bow before them, or they may ruin other lives as completely as you
> – you whom I have loved so wildly – have ruined mine! (552-3).

In this extract Sir Robert addresses not just his wife but society as a
whole; he forecasts the consequences of concealing the truth behind a
mask which will, by the laws of gravity eventually fall from one's face.

The promise of marriage concludes both *Earnest* and *An Ideal
Husband* but no wedding takes place onstage in either play, nor does
either play conclude with a post-marital scene. Could this be Wilde's

refusal of accepting the 'gift' of woman from one man to another? Levi-Strauss argues that 'marriages are a most basic form of gift exchange, in which it is women who are the most precious of gifts' (Austin 1990: 44). In Levi-Strauss's framework women exist as the ultimate object of an all-male exchange in a patriarchal framework. Wilde's consistent refusal to stage marriage must imply, to some significant extent, a disapproval of this exchange. Rubin goes on to define the position of women in marriage: 'If it is women who are being transacted, then it is the men who give and take them who are linked, the woman being a conduit of a relationship rather than a partner to it' (Austin 1990:44). In *A Woman of No Importance* and in *The Importance of Being Earnest* it is the men who are the desired objects of exchange, not the women. Gerald is fought over by his mother and by Lord Illingworth (his birth father, though this fact is concealed from Gerald) and Gwendolen and Cecily quarrel over their beloved Ernest. In Morrison's adaptation this heterosexual reversal is replaced by an all-male desire and in Parker's production it is played down to the point that audience members might not pick up on it.

Cecily and Gwendolen's melodramatic mix up over their engage-ments to Ernest is to illustrate the unconventional inversion of gender power in the play. It is Cecily and Gwendolen that argue over the fictional Ernest and swear to protect or 'rescue him at once' from any 'unfortunate entanglement' (399). Although it is Algernon and Jack who deceive Cecily and Gwendolen, on discovery of that deception it is Cecily and Gwendolen who have the power; their decisions will ultimately dictate the outcome of their situations. It is the fictionalized Ernest who is the object of exchange; this is Wilde's subversion of the conventional institution of marriage and his satire of the Victorian idealization of the family. Wilde's inversion of the idealization of the Victorian husband or father figure is evident from Act One of *Earnest*; Algernon says 'All women become like their mothers. That is their tragedy. No man does. That's his' (371). Wilde's emphasis on the female figure, in particular the mother figure, reflects an alternative to the Victorian father figure as well as the admiration Wilde had for his own mother Lady Wilde. This early quote from Algernon also sets up the inverted gender paradigm from the beginning of the play and forecasts the stage dominance of Wilde's female characters.

Within the Christian marital institute in the Western world and in heteronormative Victorian society women are perceived as objects of approval or exchange; this is evident in the idealization of the family unit. In Austin's analysis of the female characters in Arthur Miller's

Death of a Salesman she claims the son Happy 'will bring home a woman for his parents in exchange for their approval of him' (Austin 1990: 50). In Wilde's plays the women are the desired object of societal acceptance; marriage is the ultimately acceptable position in society. Marriage was the very medium by which one could enter and be accepted into society. In *An Ideal Husband* Lord Goring's father emphasizes the importance of him getting married, and Lady Bracknell warns Jack about mocking society and being on the outside. She suggests that marriage could be used as a tool for advancement in society.

If we look at the history of the canon of literature and drama there is a need for women to be subjects onstage, not objects; female roles were too often brides to be, helpless widows, infantile or even insane characters. Wilde's female characters provided a stepping-stone towards gender equality on the stage; his creation of more complex female characters called for a re-negotiation of past and future roles for women. In many of Wilde's plays it is his male characters that are the objects of exchange. In *A Woman of No Importance* Gerald Arbuthnot is Lord Illingworth's object of desire while Gerald remains under the control of his mother. He is an object of exchange between his mother and his father; this narrates an alternative to the patriarchal marital exchange. It is also Gerald's mother who conceals the truth about his identity and past from him; she is in the ultimate position of power and manipulates the narrative history of Gerald's past. Gerald's mother Mrs Arbuthnot claims her son as her own; in this sense he is the object of desire and exchange between them; 'You have no right to claim him, or the smallest part of him. The boy is entirely mine and shall remain mine' (489). In this play of gender subversion it is Mrs Arbuthnot who has left Lord Illingworth. 'You forget, Rachel, it was you who left me. It was not I who left you' (489). Lord Illingworth advises Gerald:

> **ILLINGWORTH**: Society is a necessary thing. No man has got any real success in this world unless he has women to back him. And women rule society. If you have not got women on your side you are quite over ... to the philosopher Gerald, women represent the triumph of matter over mind – just as men represent the triumph of mind over morals ... The history of women is the history of the worst form of tyranny the world has ever known. The tyranny of the weak over the strong. It is the only tyranny that lasts. (493-94).

Wilde's reference to the tyranny of the weak over that of the strong refers to the patriarchal framework that still dominates in contemporary society.

One of the main aims of Victorian feminists was the quest for 'the restitution of conjugal rights... [Victorian law] in effect gave a husband custody of his wife's body by ordering an errant spouse to return home.'[13] Wilde's denial of marriage onstage in his plays could be interpreted as a rejection of the Victorian law that dictates male governance over the female body. The exchange of Wilde's male characters in the plays is a parody on the exchange of women in marriage. Shanley admires the political activism of the feminists but concludes that 'Although they procured many of the changes that they sought in marriage law, no piece of legislation ever fully reflected the principle that the only proper basis for marriage law was full legal equality between husband and wife' (4). Gender equality in marriage was never realized in Victorian law. The idealization of the Victorian family unit and the domestic sphere is reflected in popular Victorian mantras and ballads; '"Home Sweet Home", the enormously popular ballad song first heard in the 1870s, and mottoes such as "East, west, home's best", "Bless our home", and "Home is the nest where all is best", which adorned the homes of many working-class houses, reflected the firm hold of the ideal in the Victorian imagination' (4-5). The idealization of the home, the domestic sphere and consequently the role of Victorian mother and wife created gendered expectations that fostered binary gender roles in society. It is important to note that these three plays feature only one married couple and that is Sir Robert and Lady Chiltern, and Wilde undermines their Victorian rectitude, satirizing the institution of marriage. The plethora of bachelors and single female characters throughout his plays that remain unmarried deflate the idealization of the Victorian family unit, and suggest a more liberal framework that does not alienate the individual as extremely as this heteronormative framework does. The single life lived by many of Wilde's characters provides an alternative framework to marriage as well as reflecting the narrow framework of compulsory Victorian heterosexuality and marriage.

Act Two of *A Woman of No Importance* is characterized by an exclusively female dialogue; Mrs Allonby notices 'What a comfort it is to have gotten rid of the men for a little' (477). Mrs Allonby reflects on her thoughts about marriage: 'I don't think we should ever be spoken of as other people's property. All men are married women's property. That is the only true definition of what married women's property really is. But we don't belong to any one' (478). Mrs Allonby's is an amusing and

---

[13] L. Shanley, *Feminism, Marriage, and the Law in Victorian England* (London: I.B. Tauris & Co., 1989): 3.

liberating idea of marriage that advocates the treatment of men as the object of exchange between women; this incident can also be connected to the treatment of Gerald in the play, as well as Ernest in *The Importance of Being Earnest*. Wilde's overt refusal to stage marriage before the curtain falls suggests the offstage potential to reform the restrictive role of women in Victorian society.

Wilde's plays display his interest in female relationships; for example the importance of Cecily's role in *Earnest*, Wilde's emphasis on mother-daughter relationships for example Lady Bracknell and her daughter Gwendolen, as well as the developed characters Mrs Cheveley, Lady Chiltern, and Mrs Arbuthnot, and the list goes on. This unconventional privileging of female relations on the stage would have been conceived as effeminate, since effeminacy was often recognized in Victorian society as spending too much time with or on women. Wilde's penchant for exploring female relations on the stage is an alternative and a refutation of Freudian and later Lacanian theory that focused on phallocentric and oedipal relations. In Wilde's plays it is more typical for female rather than male dialogue to dominate the stage. The women are the subjects in these plays not the objects, although the threat of marriage at the conclusions of the plays reinforces the reality of gender inequality in the Victorian world. Wilde's fascination with female relationships could reflect a protracted desire to imagine the mother-daughter relationship that his own mother would have had with his sister Isola, who tragically died while Wilde was a boy.

Wilde saw the potential in drama to subvert the dominant framework that could lead to a reformation of modern gender roles in Victorian society. In contemporary society we generally consider gender and sexuality in a more liberating way. With theatre comes the possibility to re-imagine new gender roles and in order to do this we need to discard reductive labels that isolate the individual from hegemonic society. As long as the patriarchal framework is the dominant discourse in society then restrictive gender roles, expectations and 'normative' sexualities will dictate heteronormative patterns of behaviour. We need to fracture the discourse that gives birth to unrealistic and unhealthy gender roles and expectations; only then can gender equality be realized on the global stage. As contemporary feminists we need to persevere in our interrogation and invention of a more realistic female narrative that shatters the patriarchal invention of fictionalized Woman evident in the male-dominated canon. Perhaps future productions of Wilde's plays will help us to invent gender roles that challenge the patriarchal framework in the same way as his plays inverted and contested Victorian gender roles.

Bibliography:

Austin, G., *Feminist Theories for Dramatic Criticism* (Ann Arbor: University of Michigan Press, 1990).

Bartlett, N. Abbey Programme: *An Ideal Husband* (2008).

Calloway, S., *Oscar Wilde: An exquisite life* (London: Stewart, Tabori, & Chang, 1997).

Case, S.E., *Feminism and Theatre* (New York: Methuen, 1988).

Coppa, F., *Palgrave Advances in Oscar Wilde Studies,* ed. Frederick S. Roden (Basingstoke: Palgrave Macmillan, 2004)

Dolan, J., 'Gender Impersonation Onstage: destroying or maintaining the mirror of gender roles?' *Women and Performance* 2:4 (1985) 5-11. Ellmann, R. *Oscar Wilde* (London: Penguin, 1987).

Goodman, L., *The Routledge Reader in Gender and Performance* (London: Routledge, 1998).

Grosz, E., *Jacques Lacan: a feminist introduction* (London: Routledge, 1990).

Kiberd, D., *Inventing Ireland: the literature of the modern nation* (London: Vintage,1995).

Ross, R., *Collected Works of Oscar Wilde: Reviews* vol. 13, London, 1887.

Shanley, L., *Feminism, Marriage, and the Law in Victorian England 1850-1895* (London: I.B. Tauris & Co., 1989).

Wilde, O., *Complete Works of Oscar Wilde* (Glasgow: Harper Collins, 1948).

13 | 'Le Monkey Homosexuel': the role of Ruth McCarthy's queerzines in Northern Ireland in the 1990s and 2000s.

Alyson Campbell and Suzanne Patman

Ruth McCarthy has been a lesbian/feminist/queer activist in both the North and South of Ireland for over twenty years. Working in the arts, and notably through her co-founding and artistic directorship of OUTburst Queer Arts Festival, she has been instrumental in helping forge queer visibility and community in Belfast. The socio-political climate in Northern Ireland, which has seen OUTburst flourish since its inception in 2007 is, in many ways, radically different from the environment into which she settled in the early 1990s. While gender and sexuality debates are still lagging behind in Northern Ireland as a result of an equal opportunities agenda that has been dominated by religious and sectarian concerns, one area that has changed irrevocably is the communication made possible by the advent of widespread access to the internet. It is easy to forget that before this technological revolution, creating networks for non-normative representation and collaboration was a very different and challenging affair. It was in this context that McCarthy initially produced her queerzine *Muffmonsters on Prozac* (1996-8) and later *Howl* (2001-4). The latter was also the name of a monthly queer club night in Belfast McCarthy initiated and ran with Carol Byrne, Amberlea Trainor and Helen Toland.[1]

In this interview we trace the genealogies of McCarthy's zines, looking at the motivations and methodologies behind a collaborative

---

[1] *Howl* took place in various venues, beginning with Morrisons on Bedford Street, Orpheus on University Street and finally at the Pavilion on the Ormeau Road.

project that was an irreverent but vital response to a prevailing culture of conservative heteronormativity.[2]

It is, above all, the lo-fi, do-it-yourself nature of the work that comes across as McCarthy's driving force. The DIY approach espoused by zinesters is considered by Doreen Piano as part of a third wave feminist 'resistance to mainstream culture as well as a form of creative and political expression'.[3] This resistance is epitomized by McCarthy's recurring character, 'Le Monkey Homosexuel,' who appears with the launch of *Howl* and acts as a trickster figure throughout this *samizdat* work. As Lewis Hyde notes,

> trickster is a boundary-crosser... We constantly distinguish – right and wrong, sacred and profane, clean and dirty, male and female, young and old, living and dead – and in every case trickster will cross the line and confuse the distinction... Trickster is the mythic embodiment of ambiguity and ambivalence, doubleness and duplicity, contradiction and paradox.[4]

Without using the term, this definition opens up the trickster to analogies with the boundary-blurrings and resistances of queer. If McCarthy self-identifies as lesbian and feminist, her methodologies for social, cultural and political change are absolutely embedded in queer thinking and practices. She is concerned with the margins of both feminist and lesbian, gay, bisexual and transgender (LGBT) experience, resistant to what Lisa Duggan has notably called the 'homonormative' strains of LGBT mainstream culture and the dominant voices of middle-class liberal feminism.[5] McCarthy's 'Le Monkey' is an ambiguous, gender-amorphous, fluid and unruly conduit encouraging readers to engage with 'disruptive imagination' as a way to create new cultural conditions.[6] While she shudders at the comparison, we suggest McCarthy herself can be seen to have played the role of 'Le Monkey

---

[2] Interviews by email 9, 12 and 15 January 2011, and in person 6 February 2011 in Belfast.

[3] Doreen Piano, 'Congregating Women: Reading 3rd Wave Feminist Practices in Subcultural Production', *Rhizomes*, 4, Spring 2002, E-journal, http://www.rhizomes.net/issue4/index.html, 18/02/2011. Unpaginated, parag. 4.

[4] Lewis Hyde, *Trickster Makes this World: Mischief, Myth, and Art* (New York: North Point Press, 1998): 7.

[5] Lisa Duggan defines the 'new homonormativity' as 'politics that does not contest dominant heteronormative assumptions and institutions but upholds and sustains them', in *The Twilight of Equality?: Neoliberalism, Cultural Politics, and the Attack on Democracy* (Boston: Beacon Press, 2003): 50.

[6] McCarthy takes the term 'disruptive imagination' from Hyde's *Trickster Makes this World: Mischief, Myth, and Art*.

Homosexuel' in Northern Irish culture, using this playful position to produce subversive, productive, queer dissent.

Figure 4: Le Monkey Homosexuel and Revolution Through Bad Dancing (Ruth McCarthy)

While McCarthy is now an established figure in the arts/community scene, she first came to Belfast in the early 1990s when there were very few established institutions available for the expression of lesbian or

queer voices.[7] This gap fostered the small but thriving grassroots
network of which McCarthy became an important part, notably through
her zines. Through what Chris Atton sees as zines' ability to assist in the
creation of an 'alternative public sphere' and disruption of traditional
hierarchies by their 'horizontal channels of communication,'[8]
Muffmonsters and *Howl* facilitated in McCarthy's case a dialogue
between organizations as disparate as the lesbian community in Belfast
and anarchist collectives in London, as well as other zinesters around
the world. Reviewing *Muffmonsters on Prozac*, music magazine *Melody
Maker's* Paul Rothwell (himself producer of a zine, *Shaved Anus*) noted
the 'hilariously restructured kitsch cartoon strips' and suggested it was
'pretty damn close' to the 'best queerzine around.'[9]

Muffmonsters on Prozac and *Howl* are typical of much zine culture
in that they 'experiment with writing styles, cartoons, designs, pranks,
and political diatribes that are not intended to please, and in some cases
are constructed to shock the readership.'[10] They were sporadically
written, with contributions from many others, and ranged in size and
content. The first issue of *Muffmonsters* was a collaborative effort
between McCarthy and Queen's University student Fiona McNally, and
explicitly challenged the impositions and rules of 'identity', as McCarthy
says in her introduction:

> Maybe you're odd too. Maybe you're happy being 'queer'. Mis-
> shapes/oddballs/mind-fucks/weirdos/subversives/shit-
> stirrers/freaks/lessies/faggots (labels, labels, everywhere ...)[11]

It also offered a contemporary political commentary: Margaret
Thatcher, Clause 28, Barbie and Camille Paglia are all satirized, both in
polemical discourse and surreal cartoon form, as is the political
situation in Northern Ireland. The overwhelming thrust of the issue is
the presentation of personal opinions and perspectives that sit outside
mainstream sets of ideologies. As noted by commentators on zine
culture, the 'D.I.Y. ethic encourages active participation in the
production of critical beliefs and practices in place of consumption of

---

[7] As well as being Festival Director of OUTburst Queer Arts Festival, McCarthy
has been on the Board of Directors of LASI (Lesbian Advocacy Services
Initiative) and works with a number of LGBT groups in Northern Ireland.

[8] C. Atton, 'A Reassessment of the alternative press', *Media Culture Society*,
1999, 21:51, 54, 55.

[9] P. Rothwell, 'zine by Zine', *Melody Maker*, 3/08/96: 27

[10] D. Collins, '"No Experts: Guaranteed!": Do-It-Yourself Sex Radicalism and
the Production of the Lesbian Sex Zine "Brat Attack"', *Signs*, Vol 25, No 1
(Autumn, 1999): 68.

[11] McCarthy & McNally, *Muffmonsters on Prozac*, Issue 1, 1996, (unpaginated).

established political norms or representational media'.[12] The drive to voice her own ideas and, in turn, to encourage others to do likewise, sets the tone for McCarthy's work over the next fifteen years.

Figure 5: Le Monkey Homosexuel dans le Marching Season (Ruth McCarthy)

The second issue of *Muffmonsters* appeared a year later, in August 1997, written in collaboration with Terry McGaughey, aka 'Fagboys on Losec', as well as other contributors, and was given a second publication run in the face of demand. The irreverence became even

---

[12] Collins: 68.

more heightened, strengthened by anti-consumerist sentiments, and the zine continued to comment on current issues such as 'body facism' and the rise of the internet. 'Regular features', such as music reviews, became established, but these remained resolutely personal in tone and the zine as a whole, with its homages to Noddy and Xena the Warrior Princess's subtextual affair with Gabrielle, never verged towards the serious or pretended to mimic the mainstream.

August 1998 saw the third and final issue of *Muffmonsters*, this time solely produced by McCarthy herself. This issue is more personal and less overtly polemic, but maintains its wit and social commentary. It is also notable for its greater engagement with organized community activities: there is a review of the venue Queer Space and references to the activities of QueerAction. This more embodied engagement with the 'queer community' was expressed through McCarthy's Howl project – an alternative music queer club and the playground of 'Le Monkey Homosexuel'. The club night was accompanied by *Howl* the zine, a small publication of often only a few pages, that could be distributed at the venue and described itself as 'Queer like a jam and monkey sandwich'.[13] The first issue sets out the Howl 'manifesto', a typically playful yet subversive list:

> MUSIC is like a box of chocolates. Pretty fucking delicious (Except for the coffee cremes)
> Respect the DJs. Buy them drink. Admire their freckles. But DO NOT ask them to buy techno or house. They CAN and WILL bite.
> HOWL is queer. Queer is homo/trans/hetero/a/sexual. If you are offended by same sex advances or displays of affection/lust, you will probably be better off somewhere that is else. Homophobia is for sissies.
> Sharing is a beautiful thing. Like new born puppies or dead fascists or a long lost Pixies track. Share with us your ideas for HOWL and world peace.
> Leave your designer mind at home and say hello to your imagination. It's pretty ...'[14]

---

[13] McCarthy, *Howl*, issue 1, 2001, front cover.
[14] Ibid., (unpaginated).

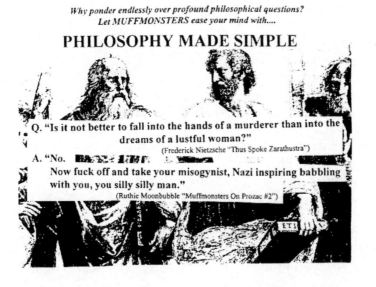

Figure 6: Philosophy Made Simple (Ruth McCarthy)

This ethos fits with the DIY impetus not only to do it oneself, but to foster an environment where others do it themselves too. It also exemplifies what Piano sees as 'a tenet of third wave feminism: the commitment to anti-exclusionary practices through the practice of self-reflexivity, political intervention, and anti-essentialist practices'.[15] By destabilizing aspects of the conformist Northern Irish community through humour and by exposing conventions to an albeit gentle ridicule, McCarthy has acted as one of what Hyde calls the 'creators of culture.'[16] Le Monkey has been the public face of a 'disruptive imagination'[17] but it is McCarthy's voice that has quietly but insistently fuelled a discussion of the contradiction and paradox that continues to play out in Northern Ireland. Her involvement in the arts community specifically, and political activism in general, may now have the respectability of funding, wide community support and a level of media visibility, but her aims appear to remain fundamentally the same: 'shining a light on the absurd and on the socially unacceptable things that we are supposed to not say out loud.'[18]

---

[15] Piano, para. 15.
[16] Hyde: 8
[17] Ibid: 13
[18] Ruth McCarthy, interview with author, 6 February 2011, Belfast.

Alyson Campbell: When did you come to Belfast? Why did you come? What was it like?

Ruth McCarthy: I moved to Belfast permanently in 1991. I'd been in a relationship with a woman here while I was at college in Limerick, so I was up visiting quite a lot during the previous two years. When I finished college I just wanted to get out of Limerick so it seemed the sensible place to move to. In the middle of the Troubles. That says a lot about Limerick ... Belfast was still pretty much lockdown city with self-imposed city centre curfew at night. Gates still up on Royal Avenue and like a ghost-town after 6pm.

In terms of social queer life, there was one gay bar at the time, the Crow's Nest. Mixed, a bit rough at times, not so many lesbians. There were lots of little *ad hoc* events as well in places like the Queen's University Students' Union, the Crescent Arts Centre, etc. Not a big LGBT rights movement but a fairly busy and growing one. I think that was the first year of PRIDE here. The lesbian feminist community was very active and involved in quite a bit of grassroots activity: Reclaim the Night, feminist cabarets, that sort of vibe. Think a slightly less organized and more socially-orientated *Spare Rib*. Lesbian Line was pretty key at the time, as was a pre-internet *Women's News* magazine, predominantly run by lesbian women. Having come from Limerick where we had very little by way of a lesbian political or social life, I think I got involved in everything I possibly could. Some of the women were amazing and I pretty much got my feminist education from being around them.

In terms, though, of actual wider culture – I was interested in music, books, art – there wasn't really an outlet for that in the LGB social scene, so it was like having two different identities that were important to me. I was involved in organizing lesbian events at that stage but it was more in the background. I didn't have a whole lot of confidence and would have run with whatever other people were into. I wasn't into obscure or transgressive stuff but lesbian culture was still pretty fixed in terms of what kind of music you listened to or books you read. I liked alternative humour, comix, music ... didn't have much of that in Limerick but there was a little more of it in Belfast, so I started to get a bit more into that with gigs etc. in the early to mid 90s.

AC: What made you start to make zines? Had you always written/drawn?

RMcC: For as long as I remember I was always drawing and making up stories. I loved art and it was just my 'thing' from about 6. At school I did the school magazine a couple of times and did little cartoons about teachers. Nothing too controversial, I was way too polite at the time and the nuns would have throttled me for anything too cheeky. I went to art college in Limerick from 1988 – 1991, doing Fine Art/Printmaking. I loved black and white, loved illustrative type work. I was mediocre at best, I didn't work very hard but did do a decent thesis on lesbian

Figure 7: The Bawdy Shop (Ruth McCarthy)

imagery in fine art. At that stage I wouldn't really have known what a zine was, though I had completely fallen in love with a self-published magazine, *Shocking Pink*, produced by radical young dykes in England.

I loved the irreverence of magazines like *Viz* that were really very laddish, so to have that kind of brazenness and humour in a political context for dykes was amazing. So I knew 'that's what I want to do!' but I wouldn't have called it a zine or have seen anything else remotely like it. There would have been music zines here at the time but I wasn't really aware of them. There wasn't a hierarchy, but there were some zines that were seen as key. *Outpunk* was a huge influence. *Holy Tit Clamps, Shaved Anus, Vaseline Zine*, which was from Club V in London – the only alternative queer club – that would have been a huge influence on me starting Howl, for instance.

I did also love things like *Class War* newspaper in a strange way; it was very daring with its covers, usually some sort of violent but comical death of a Royal or political leader. And, just to go backwards a bit, I totally loved the political cartoon books my dad would have when I was still in Limerick: *Private Eye, The Phoenix* – a sort of Irish version of *Private Eye* – and random collections of cartoons from *The Irish Times* or whatever. I was reading those when I was 13/14 and didn't get half the humour, but I loved that medium and poking at the establishment with clever humour. Now that I think of it, that's absolutely where the interest came from.

There was a woman from Larne who lived here years ago called Gill McKnight. Gill is now a writer of brilliantly trashy lesbian pulp romance/adventure novels, which she writes from her home on Lesbos.

Gill did a cartoon strip, 'Saphhowoman and the Great Belfast Dykes', as a regular thing in *Women's News* mag and was the nearest I had to someone to share alternative cultural references with. The cartoon strip was great actually. You could recognize nearly all of the women in it as actual local dykes. We weren't really good mates or anything but she was funny and a bit cheeky, so after a few evenings yapping away we decided to make our own little comic book with lesbian pastiches of old girls' comics and some light satirical cartoons and articles. As with many great ideas, we were all talk but never really got round to it. I made a cover with the name on it ('Non-scene Femme') and drew a few frames of a cartoon where kd lang was a vampire but that was it.

About 3 years after that I met a sort of punk/skinhead gay man called Martin who had a band called The Golden Mile and did a zine called *Swedish Nurse*. It was mostly about left-field and alt music but he was very openly gay and did not shy away from that in his zine. He was totally unlike all the other gay men I knew. Very, very cool. At that stage I already knew I was going to make my own comic or something akin to a magazine but finally got what a zine was with Martin. I hadn't

seen specifically queer zines at that stage but decided to make one.

I think I felt a little bit on my own with being a dyke but not always agreeing with or liking certain aspects of lesbian 'culture'. Or wanting something different or more challenging from it. A bit more rock and roll than guitar ballad, if that makes sense. More Patti Smith than Tracy Chapman. But I also always had this odd duality thing where my drive was to be 'bold' and push the boat out, while at the same time feeling this strange need for approval or not to upset anyone. Probably the nuns. I wasn't shy but I was severely lacking in confidence. And didn't really have any older real life role models or mentors for support, I think that was part of it. So I think zines appealed to me because I could just let myself off the leash but could still hide behind the fact that it was small scale, quite intimate, not putting my neck out to an uncomfortable degree. I'd also been dealing with severe anxiety and depression for a number of years and, with hindsight, I think I needed a bit of an outlet for a lot of things. I think there was a bit of a message in a bottle element to it. A bit of a reaching out to make sure that I wasn't on my own. Not that the content always reflected that, it wasn't at all confessional or personal that way and it was very up-beat. But feeling isolated was definitely part of the motivation behind doing zines.

I think I had already started to draw some cartoons in 1995 when I met Fiona McNally, a lesbian feminist 2nd year lit student at Queen's. We became really good friends and I talked her into co-producing things for the zine. It was pretty much a sit-up-all-night cigarettes and coffee and politics thing. We just worked ourselves up, went out and spray painted queer slogans, came home and wrote and drew. I put the zine together, did all the 'silly' content and Fiona did random semi-academic rants which, to be honest, I didn't fully understand. When *Muffmonsters on Prozac* came out I was on the dole and totally broke, so two older lesbians who worked for a charity organization let me photocopy the first 100 copies in their office. I didn't think people would 'get' it at all. I don't know why because it wasn't that radical or at all offensive, but there really was nobody else saying anything like it here. But the response was brilliant.

AC: How did you organize distribution of the zines?

RMcC: There's an interesting argument that comes up now so much of this stuff is online, you know, the authentic thing. But if I had been able to get out to 10 million people instead of 100, because I could only afford to print up 100 copies, what would I have done? I do love the medium, I love having a solid in-your-hand paper thing that ends up in Australia or ends up in wherever, but it's interesting. Years ago the choice wasn't there, and distribution started off as very limited. It wasn't just restricted to Belfast though, it went to Cork, and anywhere there was alternative bookshops. The Key Co-op in Cork stocked it, Doctor Roberts the record shop here [Belfast], an alternative bookshop in Derry and Books Upstairs in Dublin. So shop-wise, there were maybe about five shops that stocked it. It might have been on sale at a zine shop in Greenwich Village as well, but most of it was mail order and I had a PO Box to write to, that we also used for a number of organizations like the Gay Switchboard who wouldn't want to advertise their address. There was no mailing list or anything, we had no idea about distribution, but it was a trickle effect because once you started getting into reviews in other zines – and this was slow too because most zines weren't regular - people might start to show some interest. And three or four years later I'd get someone write to me looking for the last issue. So with the first one we printed 100, and then 50 or 75 more, and then I think we went for 200 with the second and third. You did swaps a lot – if anyone did their own zine they'd send you a copy of theirs and you'd send them yours – but you would occasionally get a pound in the post stuck to a postcard. And there was a thing where American political prisoners got zines free, which could be a bit more problematic for people here with the idea of political prisoner being a bit more loaded than some American anarchist trying to free a budgie somewhere, you know?

Distribution wise you never knew where things would end up. I remember getting a letter from a guy in the Czech Republic who did a zine called the Salivation Army, and I'd never sent anything there at all. God knows how he got a copy, or how they ended up in Australia, or some bizarre State in the US. When magazines calculate their circulation rate they multiply the actual purchasing figures because the theory is that for every copy that's sold another four or five people read it. If you were to do that with zines it would be quite interesting because you don't know how many people have seen them, despite the limited print runs.

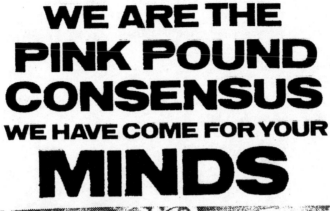

Figure 8: The Pink Pound Consensus (HOMOCULT)

AC: Did the zines get any recognition as something different on the scene?

RMcC: There were quite a few reviews and articles over the years. Because there was nothing else in Ireland like it at the time any gay media just picked up on it. It could have been the biggest pile of shite, and a lot of it probably was, but it was just that there was no alternative queer voice so that was a big thing. There was an article in *Diva* magazine, but because I'd talked about how I'd started out while having some issues with depression she kept describing me as 'mentally ill', which really pissed me off. It was mostly reviews in the alternative media and other zines, like 'Queerzine explosion' (an insert into *Factsheet Five*) but some of *Muffmonsters* has also been made available online at the queerzine archive project[19]

AC: In terms of responses from readers – are there any that you think shed light on the impact of the zines?

RMcC: We didn't get tons of letters, maybe about twenty odd letters over the period of time. There was one from a couple of people in Cork who'd seen it and were just like 'Oh my God, there's other people out there who are wanting something different'. Because really, honestly, queer had just not hit Ireland. Gay was just about getting there. So the response from people was that, and you can see from the article in *GCN* [*Gay Community News*] that they were very excited that there was a different type of voice.[20]

But the thing with zines was that it was – elitist isn't the right word – but it was what I see as the 'antenna' thing, trying to find people, trying to reach out, to broadcast to the other people you were trying to find, not just to everyone. The net has really changed that now but what mattered to me most was the response from other people who were doing zines. The ultimate thing was for me when someone would say 'do you want to write an article for my zine' or saying that they'd write an article for mine. There was a whole scene in London; Queeruption was a big thing, which was my eye opener. When Terry and I were doing this we were very much in isolation but we heard about this thing in London called Queeruption, and we didn't really know anyone in London but decided to just go over. The 121 Centre in Brixton was an anarchist squat and they had the first UK Queeruption there. It was like S&M workshops in the basement and sex parties – which we refused to go to – and shoplifting workshops and all that. It was the first time I saw David Hoyle, and apparently they'd all saved up their dole money for weeks to give him a few quid. He took it from them and burnt it on stage. Fabulous. And it was the first time I met a lot of people whose zines I'd gotten. So even though we were over here we managed to become part of that scene. And even though zines may not have had a

---

[19] The queerzine archive project, www.qzap.org.

[20] The *Gay Community News* article (author unknown) states that 'Muffmonsters on Prozac is a magnificently motivated mind-blowing magazine', *GCN*, December 1996/January 1997: 13. The article draws attention to the lack of lesbian activity – both social and political – in Belfast at the time.

huge effect on wider culture, they made it possible to create a network of people who were doing interesting things and who are still doing really interesting things. It was a loose network that then influenced other networks. Like the Riot Grrl thing, it never intended to take over the world, it intended to empower through a ripple effect with people. That London thing had an impact on me, and I was able to come back here and have a bit of an impact on other stuff, and that might have had an impact on a few other people who are now doing stuff. That's kind of what zines did, they were never intended to change the world, it was much more 'is there anybody there?' I think.

AC: How did Howl begin?

RMcC: The club Howl then began in March of 2001. I've got a picture of a young Beth Ditto there when we'd been going about a year and a half, and we later did a punk jubilee night where we had a piñata of the Queen, which I remember made my Dad very nervous, about beating the Queen in Belfast. It started as a club, and there would have been four of us doing it. The last zine I'd done was in about 1998, so I'd taken a break for a while and when we started doing Howl I thought, let's do a zine every month – which everybody thought was a bit ambitious, but it was only meant to be a small thing. So I kind of put it together and contributed most of the content. I was working at the BBC at the time and I used to do most of the scripts for Eamonn Holmes and light entertainment afternoon programs for housewives and then I'd be like, queer stuff! And my boss caught on that I was photocopying these in the BBC as well and he'd talk about the 'little magazines' I was doing. Working there was my first 'proper job', even though I was nearly thirty, and I felt like Howl was my outlet from being a corporate whore.

There were a couple of Howls where we didn't do a zine, but we'd always have something for people; there were badges at one point and then we had a monkey stamp. We had a record label as well, Howl Records; we had 7" vinyl and the monkey is on the label.

AC: Where did the idea of Le Monkey homosexuel come from?

RMcC: Le Monkey was born around 2000. Looking back now, the very first time I drew Le Monkey (who is gender neutral, so I never say he/she – I'll use 'LM') was in a 'silent' strip and LM didn't have a name. I have that in a sketchbook. The timeline is completely skewiff because I don't put dates on things and am very disorganized. I wasn't planning on it becoming a regular character but I liked the way LM looked and it's what I would scribble when on the phone or doodling during meetings, quite subconsciously.

I love monkeys. It's always been a 'thing'. I love the boldness and the disregard for being 'proper'. Monkeys throw shit, scratch their asses, steal things – and at the same time manage to be totally adorable and totally get away with it. I think it's that duality thing again. Total anarchy and absolute sweetness wrapped up in fur. Putting that in a queer context seemed fitting.

The image of LM is very simple and cartoony, not at all sophisticated. I love taking simple innocent things and re-appropriating them. I love that John Waters kind of vibe that is tender and sweet and innocent but dirty and untidy, shining a light on the absurd and on the socially unacceptable things that we are supposed to not say out loud.

The name 'Le Monkey Homosexuel' came from me being utterly rubbish with languages. I was terrible at French and Irish at school. Awful. I couldn't grasp it at all. I remember one particular encounter with my French teacher, a nun, where she completely humiliated me for not being able to say 'The owl has grey eyes' in French. How absurd is that?! This led to my (defiant) love of making up my own 'languages', cobbled together from half remembered Irish and French words, with disco sound effects thrown in for good measure. This was the language that Le Monkey spoke. It made perfect sense, I mean you could understand what LM was saying, but it was complete rubbish. I still do this with friends. It's incredibly childish and amuses me greatly.

When I started doing HOWL Le Monkey just took on a life of its own. And people seemed to really like it. People actually talked about Le Monkey Homosexuel. Now when I say 'people', you're talking about a small group of people. But in my little circle, Le Monkey ruled. HOWL lasted four years and we decided to finish on a high, while it was still good. On the very last night, it was decided that we would kill Le Monkey off. We borrowed a real coffin, put a big toy monkey in it, had a 'wake' and carried the coffin out on our shoulders at the end of the night. I was really sad about it. I didn't want LM to be killed off really but I went along with it because Le Monkey had sort of taken on an identity beyond me by becoming the 'face' of the club.

So that was the end of Le Monkey. Though I still comfort myself by believing that 'Le Monkey is not dead, just sleeping'.

AC: In what ways do you see Le Monkey as a trickster figure?

RMcC: Well, just to establish first that it wasn't created with that level of intellect or consideration. I never sat down and started drawing a 'trickster' figure. It just happened. I've been totally enthralled by mythology for as long as I can remember. And looking at those stories as an adult, you really can't get much more deviant, bizarre and fantastic. Scatological, sexually transgressive, totally beautiful and quite often outside the 'rules' that we impose on ourselves socially. But at the same time having this wonderful truth and morality to them. Love that.

It's only in recent years that I've become more familiar with the trickster figure in a specific sense but I think that many of the characters I loved (and was often frightened by) in those stories were incarnations of the trickster. Not just in old mythologies but in modern comedies, books, films, etc. My idea of the trickster is a sort of anarchic character who breaks taboos, poops on the status quo, challenges the established order of things and is a little bit naive and reckless with itself. I think I'm inherently trickster in nature but it's always a bit of a struggle to let that out. Damn you, Catholicism. I don't see Le Monkey as some sort of revolutionary or avant garde figure, it really wasn't as daring or shocking as that in a wider sense. If I was doing it now it would be a little more teetering on the edge, I'd have more confidence with it. But on a personal and very local level, there was definitely a bold playfulness to it at the time. Not quite a 'Fuck you', more of a 'Belfast, I moon you and your Emperor's Clothes! Gay culture, I pee in your perfectly manicured garden'. Le Monkey said things out loud that I was thinking and I'm sure it was often what other people were thinking too because they got it.

The trickster thing, when I think back on it now, was always the thing I loved in mythology. The magical shit-stirrer. I picked up that book, [Hyde's] *The Trickster makes this World*, and I got it. That's what I always wanted, but I never would have deliberately done it, it was always accidental. I had no idea what I was doing most of the time.

OH LOOK! I SHOULD HAVE
EQUAL RIGHTS COZ I CAN'T
HELP BEING THE WAY I AM

PITY ME, NICE POLITICIAN
MAN! I HAVE NO SAY IN
MY DEVIANT WAYS!

HA!
PISH AND SHITE...

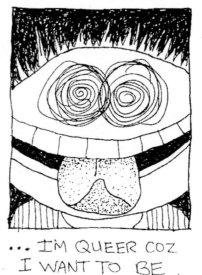

... I'M QUEER COZ
I WANT TO BE.

Figure 9: Queer Coz I Want to Be (Ruth McCarthy)

When you look at the zines and you look at *Queer with Class* the stuff I
was doing wasn't that incendiary, it really wasn't, but in context it was

provocative.[21] It would be a vanity to say I was setting out to be the Trickster, it was purely accidental, but it did kick certain things off. I do think it changed things a little bit here, Howl and the zines, none of it changed the world or ever will but the ripple thing, you know? In terms of the Trickster thing it did jar the status quo here a little bit.

The trickster figure often steals things that don't belong to it – talents, energies, cultures, masks – and creates something new. Mixing Daniel O'Donnell and beat generation jazz, that sort of thing. Or creates a disruption. One of my favourite LM incidents was when the other HOWL women decided to adopt a monkey for me at Belfast Zoo as a birthday present. They filled in the form and, when asked what name the monkey was to be given, wrote 'Le Monkey Homosexuel'. They got a message from the zoo to say that this was not appropriate because 'there would be children reading the name on zoo signs'. It may seem like a small thing but it says so much. There was no big political agenda behind it – it was done with a certain naivety that was very Le Monkey. It's the innocence of trickster that I love most; behind all the disruption and anarchy there is love of life and life-force that it can't help. There's no nastiness to it, no deliberate meanness. That's the spirit of Le Monkey I think. Take 'em down with love.

AC: Was the monkey a way to say things you couldn't say as Ruth?

RMcC: Absolutely. I'm very like my Ma in a way, always the peacekeeper, and I think over the last few years that's changed, but I do still find it difficult to say things. And I don't have very much in common with a lot of the people in the established gay community here, and they're amazing people who have brought in a lot of important changes but I think I've gone beyond the gay. The monkey was a cheeky way of saying things. I remember the girls bought me a toy monkey and I'd have it on the desk at work and when people would come in it'd be like 'the monkey needs to say ...' and it would be like the monkey said it not me. You ask me if I see myself as the Trickster figure, and that's kind of a funny thing, I don't really see it in that way, and feel like it's a bit embarrassing. But what I recognize that I connect with about the Trickster is a lot of the time the Trickster isn't doing stuff that's good for it or deliberate but that just happens out of its own giddy persona and that's what I identify with. It's not like Hyde talking about Duchamp and Ginsberg who changed things by being really bold. What I got from *Trickster Makes This World* is that the Trickster is really all about

21 Homocult, *Queer with Class* (Manchester: MS ED (The Talking Lesbian) PROMOTIONS, 1992).

shame. What the Trickster does is always things like shitting, it's all the things you're not supposed to talk about, and at the end the book talks about how to be creative you have to lift the blanket or the veil of shame and it's when you do that that you unearth things. So for me, on a personal journey with all this, absolutely, to be able to turn around now and say the things that would have only come out of Le Monkey's mouth ...

AC: How does your involvement with OUTburst connect with your earlier work, in the sense of disrupting the status quo?

RMcC: It's important to say that I didn't come up with OUTburst. I was invited along to some of the planning and because I'd just finished with the BBC and I was free and had some energy I took on some of the organizational stuff and because of the position I was in I was able to do some of the running with it. So in some ways yes, the experience that I'd had with this other stuff gave me the confidence, and a lot of the people I'd met gave me access to programming stuff and an awareness of a wider scene. It was the more grown up continuation I guess. Zines are a very youthful medium. I might contribute to one now, but I wouldn't be interested necessarily in creating one. OUTburst for me is the same sensibility, and in terms of the Trickster stuff it's that sense of pushing things on, and maybe that is the main thing with it – lifting the blanket of shame and moving away from that gay thing of apologizing, still using the heterosexual touchstones. I think OUTburst doesn't do that and maybe that is the sensibility I bring to it. Maybe that is my role in OUTburst.

So yes, OUTburst is the natural progression of all this for me, and I can even see where I might go next because I think there are some things in the world that might need changed. And I'm always thinking about the next thing.

AC: What queer things do you see happening next in Northern Ireland?

RMcC: I think there's a lot of things happening off the back of OUTburst now, like the book club group; there are people who are queer thinking, who might have been put off by the gay stuff, who are finding others who want to think a bit differently. People want to do stuff that's beyond LGBT issues, like Spirit Level Activists, who want to go out on the streets with zines or pamphlets. Now people are self-organizing things like poker tournaments and theatre evenings and things around food, which is socializing obviously but also capacity building and it will lead to something else. There are a lot of creative people within those groups, and there'll be an excuse to get together and I think there's going to be a whole new creative scene, which is really exciting. The next step then I think will be a step away from LGBT stuff, not as a divisive thing, but just as a step beyond. It's like feminism or anything else: we got a lot of equal rights in a world that wasn't equal, but now there's less of a single issue focus. And that's the thing about the Trickster, the different levels of trickster: there's the single issue Trickster, then the ones that are just always looking towards the periphery. Gay isn't irrelevant in Northern Ireland yet; some of us are lucky to live in a bubble that we've made for ourselves that's fairly safe, but most queer people in Northern Ireland, particularly rurally, don't have that, but they're getting there. There's a queer centre in Strabane now, for example. And so there is room to think about what's next. There may be a point where I say enough and just go and do some gardening, but I know that I will still be looking for what needs to change. There's work here still to be done but there are more people now I think who will speak out loud. And that ripples not just coming from me or from OUTburst but from lots of people and lots of influences. When I did the very first zines, I remember, it was like a message in a bottle. You had all these ideas and nowhere to send them. But maybe OUTburst gave people a place to send some of those ideas to.

Bibliography

Atton, C., 'A Reassessment of the alternative press', *Media Culture Society*, (1999) 21:51, 51-76.

Collins, D., '"No Experts: Guaranteed!": Do-It-Yourself Sex Radicalism and the Production of the Lesbian Sex Zine "Brat Attack"', *Signs*, vol. 25, No 1 (Autumn, 1999): 65-89.

Duggan, Lisa, *The Twilight of Equality?: Neoliberalism, Cultural Politics, and the Attack on Democracy* (Boston: Beacon Press, 2003).

Hyde, Lewis, *Trickster Makes this World: Mischief, Myth, and Art* (New York: North Point Press, 1998)

McCarthy, Ruth & Fiona McNally, *Muffmosters on Prozac*, Issue 1, 1996.

McCarthy, Ruth, *Howl*, issue 1, 2001.

Piano, D, 'Congregating Women: Reading 3rd Wave Feminist Practices in Subcultural Production', *Rhizomes*, 4, (Spring 2002), E-journal, http://www.rhizomes.net/issue4/index.html, 18/02/2011.

www.qzap.org, queerzine archive project. Last accessed 01/07/2011

Rothwell, P, 'zine by Zine', *Melody Maker*, 3/08/96: 27.

Unknown, 'Muffmonsters on Prozac', *Gay Community News*, December 1996/January 1997.

14 | Protests, parades, and marches: activism and extending abortion legislation to Northern Ireland

Fiona Bloomer

Introduction

An average of 20 women a week leaves Northern Ireland (NI) to seek abortions in Britain (www.fpa.org.uk, 2010). In Ireland the figure is 85 (www.ifpa.ie, 2010). Both of these figures are likely to represent an underestimation. Based on data provided by abortions service providers to the Department of Health in Britain, they are extrapolated from the address provided by the client, who for various reasons may be unwilling to provide her home address. Nor do these figures capture the data related to women who seek abortion abroad. Such dramatic figures motivate the Alliance for Choice movement to campaign for the extension of the 1967 Abortion Act to NI, and for both parts of Ireland to move into the mainstream of European abortion rights.

The Alliance for Choice movement was founded in 1996 and its most recent period of activism began in the months preceding a proposed debate in Westminster in 2008. The debate centred around a tabled amendment to the Human Fertilization and Embryology Bill (HFEB), by Diane Abbot MP, which sought an extension of the legislation to NI. In response a wide ranging campaign was set in motion in order to raise awareness amongst MPs, trade unions and the wider public. The Alliance for Choice campaign took a strong pro-choice approach, focusing on the issue of equality with women in the rest of the UK. The campaign included lobbying activities, public protests, petitions and seminar sessions. Despite the withdrawal of the amendment to the HFEB in late 2008 the movement has continued with its campaign, including preparation of a submission to the United Nations Convention on the Elimination of all forms of Discrimination Against Women (CEDAW) under the Optional Protocol procedure, requesting the Committee to undertake an Inquiry into abortion in NI.

The awareness raising nature of the movement has continued to grow, focusing on a range of activities from lobbying at party political conferences, a pilot training programme for the women's sector and documentary film nights showing how abortion is dealt with in South Africa, Poland and the United States of America (USA). Additionally motions have been tabled at trade union conferences, and the organization, at the invitation of the trade union movement, took part in the ICTU-led May Day parade through the streets of Belfast attended by thousands and watched by thousands more. The movement also sought support from sister organizations in the Republic of Ireland and in Britain, sharing information, ideas and providing mutual support as well as engaging with locally based organizations including the Belfast Feminist Network.

This essay will review the actions of the Alliance for Choice movement, with particular attention to the role of women in the movement. It will consider their motivations for participation in the movement and reflect on the impact of the movement in achieving its goal of gaining an extension of the abortion legislation to Northern Ireland. Additionally the essay reflects briefly on the background of abortion access internationally, the Northern Irish context and then focuses on primary research conducted with members of the Alliance for Choice group. A variety of data collection methods were utilized including semi-structured interviews, conducted on a face to face and email basis, participant observation at Alliance for Choice events and analysis of material from the organization's website, leaflets and social network site. The essay is largely descriptive, reflecting on the story of recent campaign activities; substantive space is given to the voices of the activists themselves as they articulate their motivations and assess the impact of the campaign.

Access to abortion – the International Context

Statistics show that worldwide abortion services are available to 60% of women of reproductive age (15–44). Those women facing restrictions largely reside in developing countries:

> In Africa, 92% of women of reproductive age live under severely restrictive laws; in Latin America, 97% do. Ironically, the abortion laws governing most of the countries in these regions are

holdovers from the colonial era, imposed by European countries that have long ago abandoned such restrictive laws for themselves. (Cohen, 2009:4; see also Boland and Katzive 2008; Lamas, 2008)

In referring to the USA, Baker (2008:72) commented that even in states where abortion legislation is present, access can be highly restrictive:

> ... some hospitals do not provide abortions, largely for religious reasons, which forces women to travel to other places at greater expense to obtain these services. This situation encourages illegal abortions and also opens the jurisdiction to accusations of inequalities in access to health services.

Particular groups are vulnerable to lack of access such as minority ethnic groups whose healthcare is federally funded, or whose first language is not English and who cannot speak the language; and those whose health insurance does not pay for abortions (Hessini et al. 2008:40). In recent years challenges in accessing abortion services have also been highlighted in European countries such as Poland (Kramer, 2009, 2010; Mishtal, 2009, Girard and Nowick 2002) and Portugal (Manuel and Tollefsen, 2008); Villar, 2002). For example, Hannafin (2009) found that access to abortion in Italy was restricted due to fear of negative impact on the doctor's career, with pressure and verbal abuse also identified as key factors in medical staffs' reluctance or refusal to perform abortions.

Access to Abortion – A matter of human rights

Commentators trace the current focus on access to abortion services as a rights based issue back to the late 1960s. Recognition over the negative impact on women's lives to restrictive practice and cultural barriers to abortion was highlighted by the United Nations (UN) in this period when it changed its focus on family planning away from one of population control to one of human rights (Baker, 2008). Over the coming decades the UN became more vocal in urging governments to take action to improve access to quality family planning services (UN, 1994, 1995). Its voice in this matter was seen as empowering women in reproductive matters (Baker 2008:65). The UN's powers however have largely been confined to urging governments to take action to provide access to safe abortion 'where it is legal' as opposed to requesting changes to legislative frameworks (Baker 2008:71; see also Center for Reproductive Rights, 2003). As Mullally (2005:79) observed

> this limited recognition of women's reproductive rights has been difficult to secure and is the subject of an ongoing struggle, both at

national and international levels.

The key driver for reform varies between countries, often depending upon contextual factors specific to individual countries. Countries such as Nepal and Swaziland have instigated reform of abortion laws in recognition of women's rights. In Colombia, Peru and Poland advocating human rights was a key initiator of reform (Cook and Dickens, 2003:3). Worldwide over the last two decades 36 countries have reformed their abortion laws (Boland and Katzive, 2008) although some have introduced restrictions e.g. Nicaragua, El Salvador and Poland (Cohen, 2009).

In contrast in Sub-Saharan Africa a specific focus on reproductive rights standards led to reform of the law, this focus on reproductive rights was also highlighted when the European Parliament voted to support a report by the Committee on Women's Rights and Equal Opportunities on the matter (Boland and Katzive, 2008:117 and Center for Reproductive Rights, 2004; European Parliament, 2002).

Cook and Dickens (2003:43) in considering the drivers for reform state that these changes

> ... have been aided, and occasionally triggered, by richer varieties of pragmatic research in the social and public health sciences, and by the growing influence of feminist theories or explanations, about law, social organization, and politics. The statistical and related data have interacted with feminist explanations of the gendered nature of restrictive abortion laws and practices, to reveal the devastating impact on women's lives of unsafe and unplanned pregnancy, and denial of access to legal abortion services.

The influence of the UN and other campaigning bodies at international and country-level has seen success, however provision of abortion services is one which remains highly controversial (Baker, 2008), with Ireland, north and south proving to be classic examples.

Ireland/ Northern Ireland

The controversial debate surrounding access to abortion in Ireland, North and South, is one which has raged for decades. In Ireland abortion is only permitted in cases where the woman's life is in danger (Best, 2005; Mullally, 2005). A recent European Court Ruling recommended clarification of the law but did not find that the current legislation contravened human rights, at least in 2 of the 3 cases heard, nor was the decision unanimous (de Londros, 2010). The severe restrictions in Ireland have led women seeking abortion services to travel elsewhere (Rossiter, 2009). Gilmartin and White (2011) note that the ability to travel is dependent on a number of factors not least of which are finances.

Northern Ireland's legal stance on abortion dates back to legislation from 1861, the Offences Against the Person Act, which stipulates that it is a criminal offence to unlawfully procure a miscarriage (FPA et al., 2010:14). Whilst abortion laws underwent significant reform in England, Scotland and Wales in the late 1960s, in Northern Ireland reform did not occur (ibid: 16; Fegan and Rebouche, 2003; Side, 2006; Smyth, 2006). As a result in NI access to legal abortion is rare, '...with an average 76 women per year being able to access a basic reproductive healthcare service, a service which is widely and freely available throughout the rest of the UK' (FPA et al., 2010:17). Guidance from the Department of Health Social Services and Public Safety is viewed as extremely unclear and subject to varying interpretations leaving women and service providers in an uncertain position. The judiciary's knowledge on abortion is also regarded as flawed (Alliance for Choice, 2010).

The disparity with the rest of the UK appears to be lost within some Westminster departments. In 2009 the Department for International Development (DFID) set out revised guidelines for its work to make abortion safer for women across the developing world. The guidelines stated that DFID sought to improve access to abortion and would support legal and policy reform to do so. As McCann points out the assertion to support reform does not appear to apply to Northern Ireland (McCann, 2009), this is despite the fact that at the time the DFID guidelines were drawn up that the British government held responsibility over the relevant legislation in NI.

With regard to the legislation activists had hoped that the Labour Party would follow through on its policy to reform the law when it came to power in 1997. However the legislation remained unchanged (Side, 2006). After 11 years of a Labour government an opportunity arose in the summer of 2008 to rectify this, when an amendment to the Human Fertilization and Embryology Bill was tabled, calling for the extension of the 1967 Abortion Act to Northern Ireland. The initial proposer, Emily Thornberry MP was summoned by Gordon Brown and warned '... that any move to extend the 1967 Abortion Act to Northern Ireland would put the Stormont administration at risk' (McCann, 2008a:1). Emily Thornberry withdrew her amendment. Diane Abbot MP decided to table the amendment when the HFEB was tabled again in the autumn of 2008. In the days leading up to the Abbot amendment, the threat to the stability of NI administration was also repeated by the then Secretary of State for Health Alan Johnson (Johnson, 2008). The amendment did not reach the debating floor.

The amendment failed to progress due to political manoeuvring by NI politicians. Political opposition to abortion reform in Northern Ireland is on an almost 100% cross party basis. The four main parties resolutely oppose it, as Toynbee (2008) noted 'abortion is one issue that binds Sinn Féin, the DUP, SDLP and Ulster Unionists in an eternal blood brotherhood. Feminists in Northern Ireland refer to the power-sharing government as 'the taliban''.

Only two of the 108 assembly members (MLAs) have shown public support for reform – Dawn Purvis (previously of Progressive Unionist Party now an independent) and Anna Lo (Alliance Party). Quietly others have stated they are in support of reform and that party policy prevents them from speaking out (as related by Purvis, 2010). Commentators noted that in the lead up to the October debate 'Northern Ireland politicians have used all their usual tactics of loud whining, immature grandstanding and – most effective of all – dark threats about imminent constitutional crises to get their own way. With the power-sharing executive at Stormont on the brink, they knew they held the trump card'. (Meredith, 2008)

Toynbee (2008) suggests that the DUP was central to this wrangling:

> despite adamant denials, many are convinced that Labour made a dirty deal with the Democratic Unionists to keep abortion out of Northern Ireland in exchange for votes to squeak through Gordon Brown's 42-day detention bill. The detention bill was regarded as controversial and Brown, uncertain of support from within his own party, needed support from smaller parties to ensure its passing.

Horgan (2008) also points out that in their campaigning on the issue the party political leaders of the four main parties chose to deliberately ignore the fact that 20 women a week leave NI to travel to Britain to have an abortion. In the politicians' view there is no support in NI for abortion rights. The leaders also ignored a petition with 14,000 signatures from NI residents supporting reform of the law (O'Dowd, 2010). In addition support was given from members of all the largest trade unions, and as Horgan (2008: 12) notes

> ... in most cases, this policy has been voted on at branch level and then endorsed by Irish or NI regional conferences – a more democratic approach than that of the political parties who stand for election on sectarian lines and then tell us we've voted for their

position on abortion.

As McCann, (2008b) noted at the time

> the Government, in collaboration with the DUP and with the connivance of the Sinn Fein, Ulster Unionist and SDLP leaderships, has sought to park the issue in the twilight zone.

As the legislation covering abortion remains under criminal jurisdiction the devolution of policing and justice powers to the NI Assembly in 2010 saw responsibility shift to the newly created Department of Justice. However correspondence to Alliance for Choice from the Justice Minister noted that due to the sensitivity of the issue, cross-departmental consideration and assembly wide interest in the debate that 'any changes to the law on abortion would require careful public consideration and would not be just a matter for the Department of Justice' (Ford, 2010:2).

In reflecting on the wider perspective Fegan and Rebouche (2003:222) note:

> politicians, human rights organizations and even some women's rights activists continue to talk about this subject in terms rarely associated with women's rights. In Northern Ireland the debate on abortion is constructed as a profoundly moral issue, invoking deeply held religious views on both sides of the traditional divide.

As a result constructive discussion on women's reproductive rights is largely absent from public debate (ibid: 223). Alliance for Choice has sought to bring a constructive agenda to this debate.

Alliance for Choice

Alliance for Choice first emerged in 1996, following on from the work of the Women's Right to Choose group. The initial aim of Alliance for Choice in the 1990s was to raise awareness about the highly restrictive nature of the availability of abortion in Northern Ireland amongst Labour Party members with a view that when Labour reached power the legislation would be reformed. Although this proved unsuccessful group members remained involved in lobbying in the years that followed, awaiting an opportunity to pursue a change in the legislation. This opportunity arose in mid-2008 when Emily Thornberry's amendment to the HFEB, calling for the extension of the 1967 Abortion Act to NI, was due to be tabled. In the run-up to this activists distributed a briefing on abortion in NI to every MP in the House of Commons and were planning a series of events in the House of Commons on the expected day of the vote in July, but when this fell through, the campaign decided it needed to turn from polite lobbying to 'protests, parades and marches'. As detailed above, MP Diane Abbott subsequently tabled a second amendment to the HFEB. The Bill was due to be debated and voted on in November 2008. Events and activities were centred around Belfast, Lisburn, Derry and London. An overarching group met to co-ordinate the campaign, share experiences and offer advice.

Material circulated by the organization at public events notes that:

> Alliance for Choice is an organization that campaigns for the extension of the 1967 Abortion Act to Northern Ireland. Much of our work has been about making heard the voices of the tens of thousands of women from Northern Ireland who have had abortions in England and elsewhere since 1967 (Alliance for Choice, 2009).

The same document lists a series of key facts about abortion in NI:

- Abortion is legal in Northern Ireland, albeit in very limited circumstances.
- It is estimated that since the introduction of the 1967 Act in Great Britain, over 80,000 women have travelled to England and other European countries to have an abortion.
- Women who wish to have an abortion have to pay up to £2,000. For women on low incomes and women in rural areas, these barriers can have serious implications.
- Women who have been told that the foetus has been diagnosed with severe abnormality are not allowed an abortion in Northern Ireland and have to pay privately for an abortion in Great Britain.
- Women and young girls who get pregnant as a result of incest or rape are not entitled to an abortion in Northern Ireland.
- Women from Northern Ireland are not entitled to a free NHS abortion in England, despite being UK citizens and paying the same taxes as women from the rest of the UK.
- Women and staff who work in this area are continually harassed and intimidated by anti-abortion campaigners.
- Northern Ireland repeatedly violates international law by failing to provide for abortion in Northern Ireland (ibid: 1).

The organization's collective rationale for demanding the extension of abortion legislation is explained in the statement

> ... advocating for abortion in no way interferes with your right to exercise personal conscience at an individual level, but at the public policy level, the focus must be on protecting women who wish to avail of abortion to do so in a safe and secure environment close to home (ibid: 1).

But what of the individual member's rationale for their involvement? In interviews with eight members of the organization a series of themes were identified.

Primary motivations unsurprisingly centred on women's rights and equality with women in the rest of the UK. The activists spoke about the length of their involvement in the campaign, which was seen as a natural continuation of previous engagement on the specific issue of abortion as well as other issues related to equality and human rights.

A sense of injustice over restricted access to abortion was a core motivator for a number of the activists. Some also spoke of their disbelief when they first realized that a woman from Northern Ireland could not have access to a service which was widely available on the NHS in the rest of the UK. One activist related her experience of helping women access support services and how that had influenced her views:

> I became re-engaged with the fight for women's reproductive rights in July 2008 when Diane Abbott MP tabled an amendment to the Human Fertilization and Embryology Bill ... as a student at Queen's University Belfast 18 years ago I was elected to the post of national women's rights officer for the Union of Students in Ireland. In my year in that post I had helped women who for various reasons had found themselves facing a crisis pregnancy, to access terminations in England. The fact that these students had to raise funds, travel to England and rely on support from voluntary groups like the Union of Students in Ireland and the Irish Women's Abortion Support Group appalled me, as I saw the whole process of loans, secrets, lies and hushed phone calls, as adding insult to injury.

A strong feminist voice was evident amongst activists who highlighted the importance of reproductive rights to the cause. Activists spoke of the fundamental right of a woman having control of her body and the positive impact that this had upon the woman.

> As a feminist I firmly believe in the fundamental human right of a woman to control her reproduction. If she is denied this right, she is reduced to her maternal function that is no more than a life support machine for a womb. As trade union activist I know first-hand how important control over reproduction has been in terms of advancing our education, employment, civic and trade union opportunities.

The restriction on reproductive rights was held up as a symbol of the wider anti-women sentiments in society. The feeling of control being held over women, their actions, the opportunities available to them as well as their bodies was something which enraged activists and motivated them to fight against the control,

... this control not only holds women liable for moral degeneracy, but renders invisible the inherent injustices, inequalities and implications many of them experience.

In some instances anti-abortion propaganda reinforced activists' motivations with regard to abortion rights, with one activist commenting:

... I was made to watch SPUC's 'The Silent Scream' in my R.E. class at school. Outraged by this form of sexist propaganda, I had followed and supported campaigns to allow access to free, safe and legal abortions in South American and Southern African countries whilst all the time thinking that such anti-woman sentiment could not possibly be on my doorstep. How wrong was I!

A number of the activists spoke of how their own experiences as mothers had influenced their rationale for supporting reproductive rights.

I firmly believe that children have the right to be loved and cared for. I don't believe that abortion takes away this right. Having made a choice to become a mother for the first time recently, my belief that this is the case has become even stronger. Having a child fundamentally changes your life, being a mother is a huge responsibility and this should not be forced upon anyone. I love my daughter and want her to grow up in a society that values her and respects her human rights.

In terms of asserting reproductive rights Alliance for Choice was viewed by activists as a vehicle to promote such right and in particular to protest about restricted abortion practice, with the HFEB debate providing an initial focus of attention.

... [M]y active involvement with the group began when there was an amendment tabled to the Human Fertilization and Embryology Bill ... Suddenly there was a moment in time where this matter could be resolved! It wasn't. The debate never happened. But, by that point I was too deeply involved with this campaign just to let it lie ... I am part of national and international networks campaigning for abortion rights globally and it is rewarding and frustrating in equal measure. But I cannot let it go now ...

Another activist described how a long term interest in abortion rights coupled with disillusionment in her professional life had influenced her decision to become involved in Alliance for Choice:

I had just completed a Masters in human rights law and my dissertation focused on the silence of abortion in NI – I wanted to use this work and knowledge. I was increasingly frustrated in my day job as everything had become politically 'beige'. There was no energy or desire to challenge anything let alone abortion.

> Everything had to scrutinized beforehand; cleaned up; sanitized to
> the point of why bother!

A lack of voice and representation on the issue of abortion access was a recurring theme amongst interviews with activists. One commented: 'It was [the] first activist-led pro-choice campaign/-organization that I'd heard of and I knew that if I didn't act and become active, I would be without a voice.' Motivating factors additionally included the lack of political leadership and lack of support from within the women's sector:

> I realized that we (women) had become part of the problem as we
> silenced ourselves in relation to abortion – it was almost as if we
> dare not say the word. Alliance for Choice gave a voice to this and a
> loud one at that ...
> The Judicial Review was ongoing; CEDAW [*Committee on the
> Elimination of Discrimination against Women*] and other human
> rights bodies were calling for change; the NI Assembly debates
> were appalling and yet the women's movement remained silent! As
> a feminist in Northern Ireland, finding spaces to express this
> politically is difficult and limited. Having been involved politically
> (Northern Ireland Women's Coalition) and then within the
> women's sector in NI, I found that after a while we had become
> part of the system in many instances invisible. We were happy to
> talk about childcare, employment, representation etc but not about
> our sexuality or reproduction. Given the fundamental nature of
> this to equality and my existence as a woman I became
> disillusioned and frustrated at this lack of recognition.

The conservative nature of Northern Irish society was identified as one of the key barriers to progressing reproductive rights and in turn this was a key motivating factor for activists.

> [This society] continually discriminates against women in terms of
> political representation, pay, access to childcare, domestic
> violence, rape convictions, low paid jobs etc. The Alliance for
> Choice campaign strikes at the very heart of women's inequality;
> the right for her to control her reproduction. It also annoys most of
> the 'pale, male and stale' led political parties in NI ...

Activists also highlighted the issue that their motivation was not to convert the majority to support abortion services but rather to raise awareness and to see a change to the law so that women who did seek an abortion were entitled to do so:

> I do not think for one second that I will change everybody's mind
> on abortion in Northern Ireland, nor would I want to. But I do
> want to change the legislation that discriminates against women
> especially working class women In Northern Ireland. Why can

women in Glasgow and Leeds avail of services that a women in Belfast and Derry cannot, and why must we as a society demonize, victimize and criminalize these women who find themselves faced with a crisis pregnancy. I would however like for those who wish to stop the extension of the 1967 Abortion Act to Northern Ireland to ask themselves honestly, as I have; Who am I to stand in moral judgement of a woman who finds herself with a crisis pregnancy? I know for a fact that the decision to have an abortion is never one taken lightly. I do not know the circumstances in which women find themselves with an unplanned or unwanted pregnancy – so I have no right to stop them. A woman's right to choose means that only the woman who finds herself in this position can decide whether or not to terminate that pregnancy.

The women also spoke of activism enabling them to help other women and learn from them. The informal nature of group meetings was seen as encouraging people to get involved to share skills and work as a collective.

'It's also about giving something back, using your skills, etc. to leave a mark – it's core to feminism – ensuring that you reach back and bring others with you. We all learn from each other.'

The issue of poverty was seen as a key barrier to the need for a campaign to reform the legislation. Activists recounted stories of women living in areas of significant deprivation borrowing money from paramilitaries and having to pay it back at extortionate rates. One activist also alluded to the easier access to abortion services of middle class women, not only in financial terms but the ability to provide a reasonable cover story to explain a short absence away from home.

The Alliance for Choice Campaign

Over the period August 2008 to December 2010 the Alliance for Choice Campaign organized a range of activities to raise awareness and inform the public about abortion rights. This included the use of public meetings, an information and campaigning stall in Belfast and Derry city centres for the weeks leading up to the (non) vote on the HFEB, a public letter writing campaign to Dawn Primarola (the Minister for Public Health at the time that HFEB was to be debated), attendance at trade union conferences, social networking sites, public protests, film nights, liaison with Queen's University students to set up a Pro-Choice Society, writing articles for publication in magazines and newspapers, and participation in a public art project.

Information sharing and promotion of activities took place through email circulation lists and Facebook. The Facebook page started in February 2008 with a few members, growing to over 400 by the end of

2010. This medium was assessed as being particularly useful for promoting events and activities such as campaigning for people to sign the online petition drafted up by the FPA relating to the abortion guidance which garnered thousands of signatures.

Public meetings were held to raise awareness of the issue. These were typically held in city centre hotels or in Queens University Students Union, co-hosted by the inaugural QUB Pro-Choice Society. The public meetings involved a panel of speakers including activists from Alliance for Choice, trade union representatives, FPANI, legal specialists, the Royal College of Midwives, members of the Northern Ireland Assembly (Dawn Purvis, MLA; Anna Lo, MLA); and organizations such as Doctors for a Woman's Choice on Abortion (Professor Wendy Savage, a retired obstetrician and gynaecologist). In terms of impact activists noted that the public meetings attracted different people to the campaign, as well as serving as an opportunity for activists to offer a coherent evidenced based debate. In the lead up to the Westminster vote Alliance for Choice were represented at the Abortion Rights public meeting in the House of Commons.

In the period leading up to the Westminster vote public protests were organized at the City Hall in Belfast, Derry city centre and the Civic Centre in Lisburn. As part of these protests 40 women stood on the steps in front of the buildings, wearing t-shirts (Belfast) sporting masks (Derry) and holding posters and banners. The women's presence on the public stage, campaigning for the extension of abortion rights to Northern Ireland, directly counteracts the main political parties' construction of Northern Irish women as happy with the current situation or – implicitly – as fulfilled by motherhood and domesticity. The protests attracted regional media TV coverage. In the week preceding this, activists also organized regular information and petition stalls in the city centres in Derry and Belfast which attracted a lot of support from the public, in the days preceding the groups' visit to Westminster. They were there almost on a daily basis. The petition collected 14,000 signatures and was presented to Number Ten the day before the vote was to occur. As one activist commented with regard to the support garnered from the public '... I think this is really important as it shows that we are the silent majority'.

The issue of counter protest with the anti-abortion campaign was debated amongst the planning groups on a couple of occasions, specifically with regard to rallies organized by the anti-abortion lobby. The decision was taken not to stage any counter-protest as it could have been counterproductive, portraying Alliance for Choice in a negative manner. Activists also stated that their aim was to engage with political leaders and the wider public to raise awareness of the campaign issues and provide information, engaging with the anti-abortion activists was regarded as largely irrelevant 'their campaign is full of hysteria, misinformation and horrific, totally inaccurate imagery, they have complete tunnel vision, why would we want to engage with them?'.

Political lobbying was initially focused on MPs at Westminster, although local politicians were also lobbied at party conferences. The lobbying of MPs included a letter writing campaign by members of the public which was supported and promoted by Alliance for Choice and visits to Westminster in 2008. A campaign leaflet was produced to use at party political conferences in Northern Ireland. This presented key facts and the arguments for extending the Abortion Act. Alliance for Choice also wrote to the new Minister for Justice in August 2010 asking him to indicate what plans the department had to decriminalize the law on abortion in Northern Ireland and to ensure that Northern Ireland complies with human rights standards. The response, in late November 2010 stated that the issue of abortion legislation was of cross-departmental interest and a matter requiring public consultation. The response fails to provide any detail on if/how/when such changes would be debated (Ford 2010).

Trade Union involvement occurred through public meetings, May Day parades, and planning sessions and was officially ratified through union infrastructures. Trade Union delegates proposed motions to support the campaign at the Women's Conference for the Irish Congress of Trade Unions and Unite UK wide women's conference. Both were overwhelmingly supported by delegates. A speech from a conference delegate highlights the key issues of the Alliance for Choice campaign:

> You would think given the tribal nature of our politics here that certain political parties who wish to 'Defend the Union' with Britain would be on our side of the argument, The Ulster Unionist party and the DUP – but no sisters, when it comes to reproductive rights, they are happy to collude with Sinn Féin and the SDLP to lobby the British government to ensure that the 1967 Abortion Act is not extended to Northern Ireland ... access to abortion in Northern Ireland comes down to a class issue.

To take the campaign to another dimension, activists applied to participate in Anthony Gormley's art exhibit One & Other on the vacant fourth plinth in Trafalgar Square. Running from July to October 2009 the project set out to allow one person every hour get up on the plinth to protest/ celebrate, draw awareness to their cause. Of 35,000 applicants for a place on the plinth 2,400 were chosen. One of these was Goretti Horgan, a member of Alliance for Choice.

Controversy occurred when abortion rights campaigner and comedienne Kate Smurthwaite faked her way onto the plinth, pretending to be Horgan in a protest about lack of abortion access for Northern Irish women: Kate Smurthwaite impersonated her way into quite possibly becoming the world's first living art forgery (Smurthwaite, 2009). The event was seen as symbolic of the efforts of Northern Irish women to access abortion:

> Of course it would take a lot of effort and cost a lot of money for Goretti to come over to be on the fourth plinth – just like the effort and expense incurred by women from Northern Ireland who are forced to travel to England, Wales and Scotland to access abortion services ... so we decided instead that I would go along and impersonate her.

At the appointed hour, having successfully negotiated herself through the identification check, Smurthwaite made her way up to the plinth, where her true identity was revealed when Horgan alerted the media to highlight the ruse. Further controversy followed when the organizers responsible for the webcast of One & Other decided not to upload the video from Smurthwaite's hour onto the project website:

> ... I've asked our local art gallery, which has links with Anthony Gormley, to contact him about the continuing censorship of this hour as I am sure that he would like what we did. There is a long tradition of art that subverts established artistic concepts. In this case, Kate and I subverted the rules of this concept in order to point up the way in which the rules are different for women in Northern Ireland within the UK. Kate pretending to be me also evoked the way in which Irish women often give false names when travelling to Britain for abortions. Hopefully, Gormley will contact them and get them to show it (Horgan, 2009).

The webcast was released five months later after pleas by website visitors, including Horgan.

Alliance for Choice in Derry took part in an International Women's Day art project called 'Bridges' where the group worked on a fabric-based piece about the 'invisible bridges' that women from NI have to cross to get information, support and finance together to get abortions in England or Europe.

An evening of film and discussion was held in Belfast and Derry in October 2009 with the directors of two pro-choice documentary films, Angie Young (The Coat Hanger Project) and Sarah Diehl (Abortion Democracy). In the Belfast session Ann Rossiter, author of Ireland's Hidden Diaspora sat on the panel after the film showing as well as offering a preview of her monologue about abortion rights. Both films place abortion rights firmly within a social justice framework, reflecting on the current law and availability of services in the United States of America (The Coat Hanger Project) and Poland and South Africa (Abortion Democracy).

The Coat Hanger Project draws on interviews with leading academics and activists, who reflect on the historical roots of the pro-choice movement in the United States and focuses on the contemporary context, in areas such as South Dakota which in recent years has sought to place severe restrictions on the availability of abortion in the state. The film outlines the views of activities which successfully campaigned to halt the legislation.

Abortion Democracy poses the question — Why are illegal abortions more accessible in Poland than legal ones in South Africa? The documentary considers the paradox of the implementation of liberal abortion laws in South Africa with Poland's anti-abortion legislation. It highlights how the social and cultural attitudes towards abortion, contraception and reproductive health serve as barriers to accessing abortion in South Africa. In contrast in Poland, despite severe restrictions illegal abortions are available and relatively safe, a legacy of its most recent past and legal abortion, restricted in the 1990s due to pressure from the Catholic Church. The film contains interviews with activists, researchers, health staff, patients and other men and women affected by the restrictions in South Africa and Poland.

The campaign took another direction when, in the lead up to the Westminster elections in Spring 2010 Mark Thomas, comedian and political activist toured the UK in a show which aimed to build a manifesto to improve the UK. During each show the audience were asked to suggest a manifesto item. When the show came to Belfast in early May 2010 as part of the Cathedral Quarter Arts Festival the audience suggested extending the abortion act to NI as a manifesto item, the motion was debated and received support from the audience for the issue to be added to Mark Thomas's manifesto.

Alongside such activities the Alliance for Choice group recognized that a strategic approach was needed. In early July 2010 the planning group approached the Joseph Rowntree Reform Trust Ltd for funding to undertake a feasibility study identifying existing international good practice in relation to information on abortion, taking account of the highly restricted legislative and policy frameworks in Northern Ireland. The project also saw funding for the development of an action plan to take forward next steps, including identification of sources of funding and potential legislative and policy changes. One of the aims of the project was to counteract the reluctance of women's groups as being seen to be too political for fear of losing funding from central government. The submission sets out of the context for the need for the study, the document notes that:

> ... the cultural, political and religious environment in Northern Ireland means that it is difficult to find a safe space for women to outline their views on this issue. Women and young girls attempting to access information services are bullied and harassed by anti-choice groups on a weekly basis and the state does nothing to protect them.

It also noted that, as well as political representatives failing to deal with the issue, the education system was viewed at largely failing young people by providing ineffective sexual health education as well allowing an anti-choice groups to provide false information on abortion.

The organization also responded to DHSSPS Guidelines on the Termination of pregnancy in October 2010 noting that the guidelines contravened Article 10 of the European Convention regarding the provision of information to pregnant women concerning abortion facilities abroad is protected:

> It's hard for Alliance for Choice not to conclude that the Department, backed up by the Judiciary are promoting an anti-choice policy agenda by deliberately threatening those who provide advice and counselling and reinforcing the culture of fear and silence in respect of abortion.

Alliance for Choice working in partnership with the Northern Ireland Women's European Platform and the FPA have compiled evidence to ask the United Nations CEDAW Committee to undertake an Inquiry into abortion services in Northern Ireland under the Optional Protocol Inquiry Procedure under the Convention. The submission, which was sent to the UN in November 2010, was the culmination of over two years of work by each organization. The document sets out the legalistic context, highlights the discrimination and inequality experienced by women in Northern Ireland as well as providing evidence of the systematic nature of human rights violations under CEDAW. The submission also reminds the UN of the failure of the UK Government to respond to the CEDAW Committee's expressed concerns in 1999 and 2008 in relation to the provision of abortion services in Northern Ireland.

Campaign activists have also engaged in a range of other mediums to raise awareness including producing regular articles for *Fortnight*, *Women's News*, the *Morning Star,* and commenting upon related news material in local and national press as well as participating in local radio broadcasts on the issue of access to abortion services. The group also hosted the launch of Ann Rossiter's book *Ireland's Hidden Diaspora*.

The organizations' plans for future activities include hosting a series of events with partner organizations during the week leading up to International Women's Day 2011 and to develop a series of actions based on the feasibility study due to be completed in Spring 2011. It is anticipated this will include the design and delivery of an awareness campaign amongst the women's sector in Northern Ireland.

Conclusion

A woman's right to make her own choices about her body is overwhelmingly supported across the UK and yet it remains criminalized in Northern Ireland. Forty years after the Abortion Act, the overwhelming majority of women in Northern Ireland still do not have that right and many are obstructed from doing so. Alliance for Choice has sought to put abortion on the public agenda, to facilitate wider discussion on abortion rights and to help politicize the debate. The very public nature of the campaign contradicts the assertions of the vast majority of (male) politicians that women in Northern Ireland are not interested in pursuing abortion rights.

The activists involved in Alliance for Choice are passionate about human rights, reproductive rights and feminism. Their campaign has seen them forge links with organizations such as the Belfast Feminist Network, work collaboratively with others including the FPA Advisory Group and Northern Ireland Women's European Platform; and raise awareness of abortion rights using a wide range of mediums including public protest, art and cultural forms, trade union participation and political lobbying.

Alliance for Choice has become a key player in the fight for abortion rights. It has engaged with public institutions with regard to guidelines on the termination of pregnancy and played a pivotal role in the preparation and submission of evidence to CEDAW, highlighting the numerous human rights violations that take place as a result of the restrictive legislation in Northern Ireland. Whilst initial activities centred around the proposed amendment to the HFEB, Alliance for Choice has been central in progressing the campaign to bring the law into line with the needs of women in Northern Ireland. The organization has brought a constructive voice to the debate on abortion rights. Its move from polite lobbying to 'protests, parades and marches' has helped the silent voices of women in NI be heard.

Bibliography

Alliance for Choice *Key Facts on Abortion In Northern Ireland* Information Leaflet (2009).

Alliance for Choice (2009) *Reponses to draft guidelines on abortion* Correspondence provided by J Cross, Alliance for Choice.

Baker, M., 'Restructuring reproduction – International and national pressures' *Journal of Sociology* (2008) 44(1): 65-81.

Best, A., 'Abortion Rights along the Irish-English Border and the Liminality of Women's Experiences' *Dialectical Anthropology,* (2005) 29: 423–437.

Boland, R. and L. Katzive, 'Developments in Laws on Induced Abortion: 1998-2007' *International Family Planning Perspectives,* (2008) 34(3): 110-120.

Center for Reproductive Rights *Abortion and Human Rights* (New York: Centre for Reproductive Rights, 2003).

---, *Women of the World: Laws and Policies Affecting their Reproductive Lives* (New York: Centre for Reproductive Rights, 2004).

Cohen, S., 'Facts and Consequences: Legality, Incidence and Safety of Abortion Worldwide' *Guttmacher Policy Review* (Fall 2009) 12:4.

Cook, R.J. and B.M. Dickens, 'Human rights dynamics of abortion law reform', *Human Rights Quarterly* (2003) 25(1): 1-59.

De Londros, F., 'Ireland is still in denial over abortion', *The Guardian* 16 December 2010.

Department of International Development 'Safe and Unsafe Abortion – Practice Paper' (2010) Available at <http://www.dfid.gov.uk/> [accessed 19th October 2010].

European Parliament *Report on Sexual Health and Rights.* Committee on Women's Rights and Equal Opportunities (2001/2128 (INI) (2002) Available at http://www.europarl.europa.eu/ [accessed 19 October 2010].

Fegan E.V. and R. Rebouche, 'Northern Ireland's Abortion law: The morality of silence and the censure of agency' *Feminist Legal Studies* (2003) 11: 221–254.

FPA (Family Planning Association) Abortion Factsheet. (2010) Available at <http://www.fpa.org.uk/> [Accessed 28 January 2011].

FPA (Family Planning Association) NIWEP (Northern Ireland Women's European Platform) and Alliance for Choice (2010) *Submission of Evidence to the CEDAW Committee Optional Protocol: Inquiry procedure.*

Ford, D., in correspondence to J Cross, Alliance for Choice 30 November 2010.

Gilmartin, M. and A. White, 'Interrogating Medical Tourism: Ireland, Abortion and Mobility Rights' *Signs* (2011) 36(2): 275-280.

Girard, F. and W. Nowick, 'Clear and Compelling Evidence: the Polish tribunal on abortion rights' *Reproductive Health Matters* (2002) 10 (19): 22-30.

Halpern, C.T., E.M.H. Mitchell, T. Farhat, and P. Bardsley, 'Effectiveness of web-based education on Kenyan and Brazilian adolescents' knowledge about HIV/AIDS, abortion law, and emergency contraception: Findings from TeenWeb' *Social science and medicine* (2008) 67(4): 628-637.

Hanafin, P., 'Refusing disembodiment Abortion and the paradox of reproductive rights in contemporary Italy' *Feminist Theory,* (2009): 10(2) 227-244.

Hashiloni-Dolev, Y. and N. Weiner, 'New reproductive technologies, genetic counselling and the standing of the fetus: views from Germany and Israel' *Sociology of health and illness* (2008) 30(7): 1055-1069.

Hessini L., L. Hays, E. Turner and S. Packer, 'Abortion Matters to Reproductive Justice' in *SisterSong, Reproductive Justice Briefing Book* (2008).

Horgan G., 'Abortion – Is This The Moment for Northern Ireland?' *Fortnight Magazine*, August 2008.

Horgan, G., Comment section, <http://www.webarchive.org.uk/> (2009)

IFPA (Irish Family Planning Association) Abortion - Statistics. Available at <http://www.ifpa.ie/> [Accessed 28th January 2011].

Johnson, A., Personal correspondence to author, 18 September 2008.

Kramer, A., 'Defending Biomedical Authority and Regulating the Womb as Social Space Prenatal Testing in the Polish Press', *European Journal of Womens Studies,* (2010) 17(1): 43-59.

---, 'The Polish Parliament and the Making of Politics through Abortion' *International Feminist Journal of Politics,* (2009) 11(1), 81-101.

Lamas, M., 'The Abortion Issue in the Development Agenda of Latin America' *Perfiles Latinoamericanos,* (2008) 16(31): 65-93.

Lee-Rife, S.M., 'Women's empowerment and reproductive experiences over the lifecourse' in *Social science and medicine,* (2010) 71(3): 634-642.

Manuel, P.C. and M.N. Tollefsen, 'Roman Catholicism, secularization and the recovery of traditional communal values: The 1998 and 2007 referenda on abortion in Portugal', *South European Society and Politics,* (2008) 13(1): 117-129.

McCann, E., 'Why Northern Ireland women need their own Abortion Act' Belfast Telegraph, 17 July 2008.

Meredith, F., 'Over the sea and unheard', *The Guardian*, 20 October 2008.

Mishtal, J.Z., 'Matters of "Conscience": The Politics of Reproductive Healthcare in Poland', *Medical Anthropology Quarterly* (2009) 23(2): 161-183.

Mueller, C., 'Participation and protest: Women and politics in a global world', *Journal of Women Politics and Policy* (2006) 28(2): 127-129.

Mullally, S., 'Gendered Citizenship: Debating Reproductive Rights in Ireland', *Human Rights Quarterly* (2005) 27(1): 78-104.

Munson, Z., 'Mobilizing on Campus: Conservative Movements and Today's College Students', *Sociological Forum* (2010) 25(4): 769-786.

O' Dowd, K., interview with author, 17 November 2010.

Patel, C.J. and T. Kooverjee, 'Abortion and Contraception: Attitudes of South African University Students' in *Health Care for Women International,* (2009) 30(6): 550-68.

Purvis, D., interview with author 19 January 2011.

Rapp, L., D.M. Button, B. Fleury-Steiner, and R. Fleury-Steiner, 'The Internet as a Tool for Black Feminist Activism: Lessons From an Online Antirape Protest' *Feminist Criminology* (2010) 5(3): 244-262.

Reitsma-Street, M., 'Radical Pragmatism: Prevention and Intervention with Girls in Conflict with the Law', *Child and Youth Services* (2004) 26(2): 119-137.

Rossiter, A., *Ireland's Hidden Diaspora: the 'abortion trail' and the making of a London-Irish underground,1980-2000* (IASC Publishing, London, 2009).

Scott, J., 'Generational changes in attitudes to abortion: A cross-national comparison', *European Sociological Review* (1998) 14(2): 177-190.

Side, K., 'Contract, charity, and honorable entitlement: Social citizenship and the 1967 abortion act in Northern Ireland after the Good Friday Agreement', *Social Politics* (2006) 13(1): 89-116.

Smyth, L., 'Feminism and abortion politics: Choice, rights, and reproductive freedom' *Women's Studies International Forum* (2002) 25(3): 335-345.

Smyth, L., 'The cultural politics of sexuality and reproduction in Northern Ireland' *Sociology-the Journal of the British Sociological Association,* (2006) 40(4): 663-680.

Smurthwaite, K., (2009) 'Kate on Fourth Plinth in abortion access protest' <http://www.thefword.org.uk/blog/2009/10/kate_on_fourth>

Somma, N.M., 'How do Voluntary Organizations Foster Protest? the Role of Organizational Involvement on Individual Protest Participation', *The Sociological Quarterly* (2010) 51(3): 384-407.

Toynbee P., 'Labour's stitch-up will deny women fundamental rights', *Guardian* 21 October 2008.

United Nations *Report of the International Conference on Population and Development, Cairo, 5–13 September 1994.* A/CONF/171/13. (1994) Available at <http://www.un.org/>. [Accessed 12 December 2010].

United Nations *Fourth World Conference on Women: Action for Equality, Development and Peace, Beijing Declaration and Platform for Action, Beijing, 4–15 September 1995.* A/CONF.177/20. Available at <http://www.un.org/>. [Accessed 12 December 2010].

Vilar, D., 'Abortion: the Portuguese case' *Reproductive health matters,* (2002) 10(19) 156-161.

Notes on Contributors

Fiona Bloomer completed a PhD. in Psychology at University of Ulster, and is now a Research Associate with the University's Institute for Research in Social Sciences. She specializes in research in community relations and a broad range of equality issues.

Megan Buckley is a Doctoral Teaching Fellow in the Department of English at the National University of Ireland, Galway. Her work has appeared in publications such as *Doing Family* (LIT Verlag, November 2010), *Emerging Voices: Gender & Sexuality in Irish Criticism* (2009), and the *European English Messenger* (2009). She also teaches seminars on Victorian women's poetry.

Jacinta Byrne-Doran is a lecturer in Psychology at Waterford Institute of Technology where she teaches on undergraduate programmes in Psychology and Social Care, and on the MA in Social Studies. She is also involved in research supervision at Doctorate level. She holds a Ph.D. from the University of Leicester, where her research explored the lived experience of working mothers in Ireland. She is a registered psychologist with the Psychological Society of Ireland and a graduate member of the British Psychological Society. As a working mother of three young teens her research interests lie specifically in the area of women, motherhood and work. She has made conference presentations at national and international level on the topics of 'Home Education in Ireland' and 'Analyses of the Healthy Organization, Employment and Psychoanalytic Theory'.

Alyson Campbell is a lecturer in Theatre Studies at Brunel University London, and a director. She is co-convenor of the International Federation of Theatre Research's new Queer Futures working group and was founder and director of the Queer at Queen's research and performance programme as part of the annual OUTburst Queer Arts

Festival in Belfast. Her research, practice and teaching share a focus on gender and queer theories and performance practices, experiential theatre, affect in theatre, dramaturgy and contemporary performance analysis.

Mary Caulfield is an adjunct lecturer of English and Drama at SUNY Farmingdale. She has just received her PhD from the School of Drama at the University of Dublin, Trinity College. Her research uncovers the neglected plays of Constance Markievicz, and looks to controversial women in Ireland's past who combine the political and the performative to assert their own public positions while promoting women's agency and visibility. Also a practicing actor, she has published articles on her research, most recently in *Theatre Research International*, and she is currently co-editing a collection entitled *The Rest is History: Ireland, Performance and the Historical Imagination*.

John Countryman is Director of Theatre at Berry College. He is a member of ACIS, CAIS, and IASIL as well The Literary Managers and Dramaturgs of the Americas. His articles have appeared in *Theatre Journal, NUA, Irish Studies Working Papers, Theatre Symposium* and the *Irish Literary Supplement*. He is the editor of *Theatre and Politics in the Twentieth Century*, published by the University of Alabama press, and is a contributing co-editor of the forthcoming volume *Country of The Young* to be published by Four Courts Press. In addition to acting in film and theatre, he produced the American premiere of Northern Ireland playwright John Boyd's *The Flats*, and is the recipient of the Kennedy Center Medal of Excellence in College and University Theatre, and two American College Theatre Association awards for directing. He is currently working on a history of the Druid Theatre Company in Galway.

Brenda Donohue is a PhD student in the Dept. of Italian in Trinity College Dublin. She is in the final year of her research, which is funded by the School of Languages, Literatures and Cultures. Her thesis focuses on the themes of death and feminism in the work of two contemporary female playwrights, Marina Carr and Emma Dante. Her research interests include feminism, Irish and Italian theatre and translation for theatre. Brenda has a forthcoming publication entitled 'Liminality in Carr and Dante', which will be published in *Focus: Papers in English Literary and Cultural Studies*. She is a member of the Irish Society for Theatre Research and Sibèal Irish Postgraduate Feminist & Gender Network.

Lisa Fitzpatrick lectures in Drama at the University of Ulster. She has published widely on contemporary women's writing, violence on stage, and Irish and Canadian theatre. She is the editor of *Performing Violence in Contemporary Ireland* and her current research is on the staging of sexual violence.

Charlotte Headrick is a professor of Theatre Arts at Oregon State University, where she has been a faculty member since 1982. She has been recognized with a number of awards for excellence in teaching. She has directed many Irish plays including the American Premieres of several including Charabanc's *Lay Up Your Ends*, Gemma O'Connor's *SigNora Joyce*, Elizabeth Kuti's *Treehouses*, Declan Hughes's *Love and a Bottle,* and Nicola McCartney's *Heritage*; in 1999, she directed Patricia Burke Brogan's *Eclipsed* at Western Kentucky University and the University of Illinois and in that same year she directed *Tea in a China Cup* at the University of Central Oklahoma; in 2006, she directed Frank McGuiness's *Observe the Sons of Ulster Marching Toward the Somme* at Berry College. In 2012, she will direct Elizabeth Kuti's award-winning *The Sugar Wife* at Oregon State. She is widely published in the field of Irish Drama and has also presented her research nationally and internationally on Irish women dramatists. Twice a fellow at the Center for the Humanities, she is the co-editor with Eileen Kearney of *Women of Ireland*, an anthology of Irish Women dramatists in press at Syracuse University.

Sara Keating completed her PhD at the Samuel Beckett Centre, Trinity College, Dublin. She has taught courses on contemporary Irish drama at New York University, Trinity College, and UCD. She writes about theatre for various national publications, including the *Irish Times*, the *Sunday Business Post*, and *Irish Theatre Magazine*, and has published essays on Tom Murphy, Martin McDonagh, and Samuel Beckett, amongst others, in various academic books and journals.

Aideen Kerr is a third year PhD candidate in the Department of Drama in Trinity College researching Oscar Wilde under the supervision of Brian Singleton. She has a BA degree in English Literature, Drama and Sociology (UCD) and a MA degree in Anglo-Irish Literature and Drama, also from UCD. Aideen is a teaching assistant in Trinity's Drama Department and she co-founded and edited Trinity's theatre magazine *The Player* 2010-11. She has been published in the UCD EGS journal and has further publications in the pipeline. Aideen has also had a selection of poetry exhibited in various Dublin galleries and published in Trinity College's staff and student creative writing journal *College Green*. She is currently working on a novel.

Mária Kurdi teaches in the Institute of English Studies at the University of Pécs, Hungary. Her main fields of research are modern Irish literature and English-speaking drama. Her books include a survey of contemporary Irish drama in Hungarian (1999), a volume of essays entitled *Codes and Masks: Aspects of Identity in Contemporary Irish Plays in an Intercultural Context* (Peter Lang, 2000), a collection of interviews made with Irish playwrights (2004), and *Representations of Gender and Female Subjectivity in Contemporary Irish Drama by Women*, published by Edwin Mellen Press in 2010. With Donald E. Morse and Csilla Bertha she co-edited the book *Brian Friel's Dramatic Artistry: 'The Work Has Value'*, published by Carysfort Press, Dublin, in 2006. In 2009 also Carysfort Press brought out her edited volume *Literary and Cultural Relations: Ireland, Hungary, and Central and Eastern Europe*.

Tom Maguire is a Senior Lecturer in Theatre Studies at the School of Creative Arts of the University of Ulster. He teaches and researches in the areas of contemporary British and Irish theatre, Theatre for Young Audiences, applied theatre, and storytelling. *Theatre for Young Audiences: a critical handbook* which he has edited with Karian Schuitema will be published by Trentham Books in 2012. He is a member of the Editorial Board for *About Performance* and Chair of the Board of Big Telly Theatre Company, Northern Ireland. He is a free-lance theatre critic contributing to *Irish Theatre Magazine* and BBC Radio Ulster's *Arts Extra*.

Lisa McGonigle is a PhD candidate in the Irish Studies programme, University of Otago, New Zealand, where her doctoral research is focused on how 'the scandals' in the Catholic Church are represented in Irish literature and popular culture. She also holds a BA (Hons) in English Studies from Trinity College, Dublin and an MLitt in Irish-Scottish Studies from the University of Aberdeen. She has published several articles and chapters on various topics within Irish Studies.

Suzanne Patman has been involved in gay and lesbian activism since the early days of the LGBT rights movement in Tasmania, Australia. She has worked and published in the field of education since 1995 and collaborated with Alyson Campbell on a variety of performance projects in Australia and the UK. She is currently pursuing studies in horticulture.

Carole-Anne Upton is Professor of Drama in the School of Creative Arts at the University of Ulster, where her main research interests are in the areas of contemporary theatre practice, particularly in Northern Ireland; translation for performance, directing and mise en scène. Recent work has examined documentary theatre, and performance and 'the real' in Northern Ireland. She has previously published on modern Irish drama, and postcolonial anglophone and francophone theatre in Africa and the Caribbean. She is principal editor of *Performing Ethos: An international journal of ethics in theatre and performance.* She published *Moving Target: Theatre Translation and Cultural Relocation* with St Jerome Press and has subsequently developed work on the translator as metteur-en-scène.

Julia Walther completed her dissertation on 'Feminist book publishing in Ireland' at the National University of Ireland, Galway in 2010. She now lives and works in Germany as an independent scholar and translator.

S. E. Wilmer is Professor of Drama and Head of the School of Drama, Film and Music at Trinity College Dublin. He is the author of *Theatre, Society and the Nation: Staging American Identities* (Cambridge University Press, 2002) and (with Pirkko Koski) *The Dynamic World of Finnish Theatre* (Like Press, 2006). Books that he has edited or co-edited include (with Audrone Zukauskaite), *Interrogating Antigone in Postmodern Philosophy and Criticism* (Oxford University Press, 2010); *Native American Performance and Representation* (Arizona University Press, 2009); (with Anna McMullan) *Reflections on Beckett* (University of Michigan Press, 2009); *National Theatres in a Changing Europe* (Palgrave Macmillan, 2008); (with Pirkko Koski) *Humour and Humanity* (Like Press, 2006); (with John Dillon) *Rebel Women: Staging Ancient Greek Drama Today* (Methuen, 2005); and *Writing and Rewriting National Theatre Histories* (Iowa University Press, 2004). He has served as a Visiting Professor at Stanford University and UC Berkeley. He is also a playwright, a member of the Executive Committee of the International Federation for Theatre Research, and formerly the Chair of the Publications Committee and member of the Executive Committee of the American Society for Theatre Research.

INDEX

Carysfort Press was formed in the summer of 1998. It receives annual funding from the Arts Council.

The directors believe that drama is playing an ever-increasing role in today's society and that enjoyment of the theatre, both professional and amateur, currently plays a central part in Irish culture.

The Press aims to produce high quality publications which, though written and/or edited by academics, will be made accessible to a general readership. The organisation would also like to provide a forum for critical thinking in the Arts in Ireland, again keeping the needs and interests of the general public in view.

The company publishes contemporary Irish writing for and about the theatre.

Editorial and publishing inquiries to:
Carysfort Press Ltd.,
58 Woodfield,
Scholarstown Road,
Rathfarnham,
Dublin 16,
Republic of Ireland.

T (353 1) 493 7383
F (353 1) 406 9815
E: info@carysfortpress.com
www.carysfortpress.com

HOW TO ORDER

TRADE ORDERS DIRECTLY TO:
Irish Book Distribution
Unit 12, North Park, North Road,
Finglas, Dublin 11.

T: (353 1) 8239580
F: (353 1) 8239599
E: mary@argosybooks.ie
www.argosybooks.ie

INDIVIDUAL ORDERS DIRECTLY TO:
eprint Ltd.
35 Coolmine Industrial Estate,
Blanchardstown, Dublin 15.
T: (353 1) 827 8860
F: (353 1) 827 8804 Order online @
E: books@eprint.ie
www.eprint.ie

FOR SALES IN NORTH AMERICA AND CANADA:
Dufour Editions Inc.,
124 Byers Road,
PO Box 7,
Chester Springs,
PA 19425,
USA

T: 1-610-458-5005
F: 1-610-458-7103

The Art Of Billy Roche: Wexford As The World

Edited by Kevin Kerrane

Billy Roche – musician, actor, novelist, dramatist, screenwriter – is one of Ireland's most versatile talents. This anthology, the first comprehensive survey of Roche's work, focuses on his portrayal of one Irish town as a microcosm of human life itself, elemental and timeless. Among the contributors are fellow artists (Colm Tóibín, Conor McPherson, Belinda McKeon), theatre professionals (Benedict Nightingale, Dominic Dromgoole, Ingrid Craigie), and scholars on both sides of the Atlantic.

ISBN: 978-1-904505-60-0   €20

The Theatre of Conor McPherson: 'Right beside the Beyond'

Edited by Lilian Chambers and Eamonn Jordan

Multiple productions and the international successes of plays like *The Weir* have led to Conor McPherson being regarded by many as one of the finest writers of his generation. McPherson has also been hugely prolific as a theatre director, as a screenwriter and film director, garnering many awards in these different roles. In this collection of essays, commentators from around the world address the substantial range of McPherson's output to date in theatre and film, a body of work written primarily during and in the aftermath of Ireland's Celtic Tiger period. These critics approach the work in challenging and dynamic ways, considering the crucial issues of morality, the rupturing of the real, storytelling, and the significance of space, violence and gender. Explicit considerations are given to comedy and humour, and to theatrical form, especially that of the monologue and to the ways that the otherworldly, the unconscious and supernatural are accommodated dramaturgically, with frequent emphasis placed on the specific aspects of performance in both theatre and film.

ISBN: 978 1 904505 61 7 €20

The Story of Barabbas, The Company

Carmen Szabo

Acclaimed by audiences and critics alike for their highly innovative, adventurous and entertaining theatre, Barabbas The Company have created playful, intelligent and dynamic productions for over 17 years. Breaking the mould of Irish theatrical tradition and moving away from a text dominated theatre, Barabbas The Company's productions have established an instantly recognizable performance style influenced by the theatre of clown, circus, mime, puppetry, object manipulation and commedia dell'arte. This is the story of a unique company within the framework of Irish theatre, discussing the influences that shape their performances and establish their position within the history and development of contemporary Irish theatre. This book addresses the overwhelming necessity to reconsider Irish theatre history and to explore, in a language accessible to a wide range of readers, the issues of physicality and movement based theatre in Ireland.

ISBN: 978-1-904505-59-4 €25

Irish Drama: Local and Global Perspectives

Edited by Nicholas Grene and Patrick Lonergan

Since the late 1970s there has been a marked internationalization of Irish drama, with individual plays, playwrights, and theatrical companies establishing newly global reputations. This book reflects upon these developments, drawing together leading scholars and playwrights to consider the consequences that arise when Irish theatre travels abroad.

Contributors: Chris Morash, Martine Pelletier, José Lanters, Richard Cave, James Moran, Werner Huber, Rhona Trench, Christopher Murray, Ursula Rani Sarma, Jesse Weaver, Enda Walsh, Elizabeth Kuti

ISBN: 978-1-904505-63-1 €20

What Shakespeare Stole From Rome

Brian Arkins

What Shakespeare Stole From Rome analyses the multiple ways Shakespeare used material from Roman history and Latin poetry in his plays and poems. From the history of the Roman Republic to the tragedies of Seneca; from the Comedies of Platus to Ovid's poetry; this enlightening book examines the important influence of Rome and Greece on Shakespeare's work.

ISBN: 978-1-904505-58-7   €20

Polite Forms

Harry White

Polite Forms is a sequence of poems that meditates on family life. These poems remember and reimagine scenes from childhood and adolescence through the formal composure of the sonnet, so that the uniformity of this framing device promotes a tension as between a neatly arranged album of photographs and the chaos and flow of experience itself. Throughout the collection there is a constant preoccupation with the difference between actual remembrance and the illumination or meaning which poetry can afford. Some of the poems 'rewind the tapes of childhood' across two or three generations, and all of them are akin to pictures at an exhibition which survey individual impressions of childhood and parenthood in a thematically continuous series of portraits drawn from life.

Harry White was born in Dublin in 1958. He is Professor of Music at University College Dublin and widely known for his work in musicology and cultural history. His publications include "Music and the Irish Literary Imagination" (Oxford, 2008), which was awarded the Michael J. Durkan prize of the American Conference for Irish Studies in 2009. "Polite Forms" is his first collection of poems

ISBN: 978-1-904505-55-6   €10

Ibsen and Chekhov on the Irish Stage

Edited by Ros Dixon and Irina Ruppo Malone

Ibsen and Chekhov on the Irish Stage presents articles on the theories of translation and adaptation, new insights on the work of Brian Friel, Frank McGuinness, Thomas Kilroy, and Tom Murphy, historical analyses of theatrical productions during the Irish Revival, interviews with contemporary theatre directors, and a round-table discussion with the playwrights, Michael West and Thomas Kilroy.

Ibsen and Chekhov on the Irish Stage challenges the notion that a country's dramatic tradition develops in cultural isolation. It uncovers connections between past productions of plays by Ibsen and Chekhov and contemporary literary adaptations of their works by Irish playwrights, demonstrating the significance of international influence for the formation of national canon.

Conceived in the spirit of a round-table discussion, *Ibsen and Chekhov on the Irish Stage* is a collective study of the intricacies of trans-cultural migration of dramatic works and a re-examination of Irish theatre history from 1890 to the present day.

ISBN: 978-1-904505-57-0   €20

Tom Swift Selected Plays

With an introduction by Peter Crawley.

The inaugural production of Performance Corporation in 2002 matched Voltaire's withering assault against the doctrine of optimism with a playful aesthetic and endlessly inventive stagecraft.

Each play in this collection was originally staged by the Performance Corporation and though Swift has explored different avenues ever since, such playfulness is a constant. The writing is precise, but leaves room for the discoveries of rehearsals, the flesh of the theatre. All plays are blueprints for performance, but several of these scripts – many of which are site-specific and all of them slyly topical – are documents for something unrepeatable.

ISBN: 978-1-904505-56-3   €20

Synge and His Influences: Centenary Essays from the Synge Summer School

Edited by Patrick Lonergan

The year 2009 was the centenary of the death of John Millington Synge, one of the world's great dramatists. To mark the occasion, this book gathers essays by leading scholars of Irish drama, aiming to explore the writers and movements that shaped Synge, and to consider his enduring legacies. Essays discuss Synge's work in its Irish, European and world contexts – showing his engagement not just with the Irish literary revival but with European politics and culture too. The book also explores Synge's influence on later writers: Irish dramatists such as Brian Friel, Tom Murphy and Marina Carr, as well as international writers like Mustapha Matura and Erisa Kironde. It also considers Synge's place in Ireland today, revealing how *The Playboy of the Western World* has helped to shape Ireland's responses to globalisation and multiculturalism, in celebrated productions by the Abbey Theatre, Druid Theatre, and Pan Pan Theatre Company.

Contributors include Ann Saddlemyer, Ben Levitas, Mary Burke, Paige Reynolds, Eilís Ní Dhuibhne, Mark Phelan, Shaun Richards, Ondřej Pilný, Richard Pine, Alexandra Poulain, Emilie Pine, Melissa Sihra, Sara Keating, Bisi Adigun, Adrian Frazier and Anthony Roche.

ISBN: 978-1-904505-50-1   €20.00

Constellations - The Life and Music of John Buckley

Benjamin Dwyer

Benjamin Dwyer provides a long overdue assessment of one of Ireland's most prolific composers of the last decades. He looks at John Buckley's music in the context of his biography and Irish cultural life. This is no hagiography but a critical assessment of Buckley's work, his roots and aesthetics. While looking closely at several of Buckley's compositions, the book is written in a comprehensible style that makes it easily accessible to anybody interested in Irish musical and cultural history.   *Wolfgang Marx*

As well as providing a very readable and comprehensive study of the life and music of John Buckley, Constellations also offers an up-to-date and informative catalogue of compositions, a complete discography, translations of set texts and the full libretto of his chamber opera, making this book an essential guide for both students and professional scholars alike.

ISBN: 978-1-904505-52-5   €20.00

'Because We Are Poor': Irish Theatre in the 1990s

Victor Merriman

"Victor Merriman's work on Irish theatre is in the vanguard of a whole new paradigm in Irish theatre scholarship, one that is not content to contemplate monuments of past or present achievement, but for which the theatre is a lens that makes visible the hidden malaises in Irish society. That he has been able to do so by focusing on a period when so much else in Irish culture conspired to hide those problems is only testimony to the considerable power of his critical scrutiny." Chris Morash, NUI Maynooth.

ISBN: 978-1-904505-51-8   €20.00

'Buffoonery and Easy Sentiment':
Popular Irish Plays in the Decade Prior to the Opening of The Abbey Theatre

Christopher Fitz-Simon

In this fascinating reappraisal of the non-literary drama of the late 19th - early 20th century, Christopher Fitz-Simon discloses a unique world of plays, players and producers in metropolitan theatres in Ireland and other countries where Ireland was viewed as a source of extraordinary topics at once contemporary and comfortably remote: revolution, eviction, famine, agrarian agitation, political assassination.

The form was the fashionable one of melodrama, yet Irish melodrama was of a particular kind replete with hidden messages, and the language was far more allusive, colourful and entertaining than that of its English equivalent.

ISBN: 978-1-9045505-49-5   €20.00

The Fourth Seamus Heaney Lectures, 'Mirror up to Nature':

Ed. Patrick Burke

What, in particular, is the contemporary usefulness for the building of societies of one of our oldest and culturally valued ideals, that of drama? The Fourth Seamus Heaney Lectures, 'Mirror up to Nature': Drama and Theatre in the Modern World, given at St Patrick's College, Drumcondra, between October 2006 and April 2007, addressed these and related questions. Patrick Mason spoke on the essence of theatre, Thomas Kilroy on Ireland's contribution to the art of theatre, Cecily O'Neill and Jonothan Neelands on the rich potential of drama in the classroom. Brenna Katz Clarke examined the relationship between drama and film, and John Buckley spoke on opera and its history and gave an illuminating account of his own *Words Upon The Window-Pane*.

ISBN 978-1-9045505-48-8   €12

The Theatre of Tom Mac Intyre: 'Strays from the ether'

Eds. Bernadette Sweeney and Marie Kelly

This long overdue anthology captures the soul of Mac Intyre's dramatic canon – its ethereal qualities, its extraordinary diversity, its emphasis on the poetic and on performance – in an extensive range of visual, journalistic and scholarly contributions from writers, theatre practitioners.

ISBN 978-1-904505-46-4 €25

Irish Appropriation Of Greek Tragedy

Brian Arkins

This book presents an analysis of more than 30 plays written by Irish dramatists and poets that are based on the tragedies of Sophocles, Euripides and Aeschylus. These plays proceed from the time of Yeats and Synge through MacNeice and the Longfords on to many of today's leading writers.

ISBN 978-1-904505-47-1 €20

Alive in Time: The Enduring Drama of Tom Murphy

Ed. Christopher Murray

Almost 50 years after he first hit the headlines as Ireland's most challenging playwright, the 'angry young man' of those times Tom Murphy still commands his place at the pinnacle of Irish theatre. Here 17 new essays by prominent critics and academics, with an introduction by Christopher Murray, survey Murphy's dramatic oeuvre in a concerted attempt to define his greatness and enduring appeal, making this book a significant study of a unique genius.

ISBN 978-1-904505-45-7 €25

Performing Violence in Contemporary Ireland

Ed. Lisa Fitzpatrick

This interdisciplinary collection of fifteen new essays by scholars of theatre, Irish studies, music, design and politics explores aspects of the performance of violence in contemporary Ireland. With chapters on the work of playwrights Martin McDonagh, Martin Lynch, Conor McPherson and Gary Mitchell, on Republican commemorations and the 90th anniversary ceremonies for the Battle of the Somme and the Easter Rising, this book aims to contribute to the ongoing international debate on the performance of violence in contemporary societies.

ISBN 978-1-904505-44-0 (2009) €20

Ireland's Economic Crisis - Time to Act. Essays from over 40 leading Irish thinkers at the MacGill Summer School 2009

Eds. Joe Mulholland and Finbarr Bradley

Ireland's economic crisis requires a radical transformation in policymaking. In this volume, political, industrial, academic, trade union and business leaders and commentators tell the story of the Irish economy and its rise and fall. Contributions at Glenties range from policy, vision and context to practical suggestions on how the country can emerge from its crisis.

ISBN 978-1-904505-43-3 (2009) €20

Deviant Acts: Essays on Queer Performance

Ed. David Cregan

This book contains an exciting collection of essays focusing on a variety of alternative performances happening in contemporary Ireland. While it highlights the particular representations of gay and lesbian identity it also brings to light how diversity has always been a part of Irish culture and is, in fact, shaping what it means to be Irish today.

ISBN 978-1-904505-42-6 (2009) €20

Seán Keating in Context: Responses to Culture and Politics in Post-Civil War Ireland

Compiled, edited and introduced by Éimear O'Connor

Irish artist Seán Keating has been judged by his critics as the personification of old-fashioned traditionalist values. This book presents a different view. The story reveals Keating's early determination to attain government support for the visual arts. It also illustrates his socialist leanings, his disappointment with capitalism, and his attitude to cultural snobbery, to art critics, and to the Academy. Given the national and global circumstances nowadays, Keating's critical and wry observations are prophetic – and highly amusing.

ISBN 978-1-904505-41-9 €25

Dialogue of the Ancients of Ireland: A new translation of Acallam na Senorach

Translated with introduction and notes by Maurice Harmon

One of Ireland's greatest collections of stories and poems, The Dialogue of the Ancients of Ireland is a new translation by Maurice Harmon of the 12th century *Acallam na Senorach*. Retold in a refreshing modern idiom, the *Dialogue* is an extraordinary account of journeys to the four provinces by St. Patrick and the pagan Cailte, one of the surviving Fian. Within the frame story are over 200 other stories reflecting many genres – wonder tales, sea journeys, romances, stories of revenge, tales of monsters and magic. The poems are equally varied – lyrics, nature poems, eulogies, prophecies, laments, genealogical poems. After the *Tain Bo Cuailnge*, the *Acallam* is the largest surviving prose work in Old and Middle Irish.

ISBN: 978-1-904505-39-6 (2009) €20

Literary and Cultural Relations between Ireland and Hungary and Central and Eastern Europe

Ed. Maria Kurdi

This lively, informative and incisive collection of essays sheds fascinating new light on the literary interrelations between Ireland, Hungary, Poland, Romania and the Czech Republic. It charts a hitherto under-explored history of the reception of modern Irish culture in Central and Eastern Europe and also investigates how key authors have been translated, performed and adapted. The revealing explorations undertaken in this volume of a wide array of Irish dramatic and literary texts, ranging from *Gulliver's Travels* to *Translations* and *The Pillowman*, tease out the subtly altered nuances that they acquire in a Central European context.

ISBN: 978-1-904505-40-2 (2009) €20

Plays and Controversies: Abbey Theatre Diaries 2000-2005

Ben Barnes

In diaries covering the period of his artistic directorship of the Abbey, Ben Barnes offers a frank, honest, and probing account of a much commented upon and controversial period in the history of the national theatre. These diaries also provide fascinating personal insights into the day-to- day pressures, joys, and frustrations of running one of Ireland's most iconic institutions.

ISBN: 978-1-904505-38-9 (2008) €20

Interactions: Dublin Theatre Festival 1957-2007. Irish Theatrical Diaspora Series: 3

Eds. Nicholas Grene and Patrick Lonergan with Lilian Chambers

For over 50 years the Dublin Theatre Festival has been one of Ireland's most important cultural events, bringing countless new Irish plays to the world stage, while introducing Irish audiences to the most important international theatre companies and artists. Interactions explores and celebrates the achievements of the renowned Festival since 1957 and includes specially commissioned memoirs from past organizers, offering a unique perspective on the controversies and successes that have marked the event's history. An especially valuable feature of the volume, also, is a complete listing of the shows that have appeared at the Festival from 1957 to 2008.

ISBN: 978-1-904505-36-5 €20

The Informer: A play by Tom Murphy based on the novel by Liam O'Flaherty

The Informer, Tom Murphy's stage adaptation of Liam O'Flaherty's novel, was produced in the 1981 Dublin Theatre Festival, directed by the playwright himself, with Liam Neeson in the leading role. The central subject of the play is the quest of a character at the point of emotional and moral breakdown for some source of meaning or identity. In the case of Gypo Nolan, the informer of the title, this involves a nightmarish progress through a Dublin underworld in which he changes from a Judas figure to a scapegoat surrogate for Jesus, taking upon himself the sins of the world. A cinematic style, with flash-back and intercut scenes, is used rather than a conventional theatrical structure to catch the fevered and phantasmagoric progression of Gypo's mind. The language, characteristically for Murphy, mixes graphically colloquial Dublin slang with the haunted intricacies of the central character groping for the meaning of his own actions. The dynamic rhythm of the action builds towards an inevitable but theatrically satisfying tragic catastrophe. ' [The Informer] is, in many ways closer to being an original Murphy play than it is to O'Flaherty...' Fintan O'Toole.

ISBN: 978-1-904505-37-2 (2008) €10

Shifting Scenes: Irish theatre-going 1955-1985

Eds. Nicholas Grene and Chris Morash

Transcript of conversations with John Devitt, academic and reviewer, about his lifelong passion for the theatre. A fascinating and entertaining insight into Dublin theatre over the course of thirty years provided by Devitt's vivid reminiscences and astute observations.

ISBN: 978-1-904505-33-4 (2008) €10

Irish Literature: Feminist Perspectives

Eds. Patricia Coughlan and Tina O'Toole

The collection discusses texts from the early 18th century to the present. A central theme of the book is the need to renegotiate the relations of feminism with nationalism and to transact the potential contest of these two important narratives, each possessing powerful emancipatory force. Irish Literature: Feminist Perspectives contributes incisively to contemporary debates about Irish culture, gender and ideology.

ISBN: 978-1-904505-35-8 (2008) €20

Silenced Voices: Hungarian Plays from Transylvania

Selected and translated by Csilla Bertha and Donald E. Morse

The five plays are wonderfully theatrical, moving fluidly from absurdism to tragedy, and from satire to the darkly comic. Donald Morse and Csilla Bertha's translations capture these qualities perfectly, giving voice to the 'forgotten playwrights of Central Europe'. They also deeply enrich our understanding of the relationship between art, ethics, and politics in Europe.

ISBN: 978-1-904505-34-1 (2008) €20

A Hazardous Melody of Being:
Seóirse Bodley's Song Cycles on the poems of Micheal O'Siadhail

Ed. Lorraine Byrne Bodley

This apograph is the first publication of Bodley's O'Siadhail song cycles and is the first book to explore the composer's lyrical modernity from a number of perspectives. Lorraine Byrne Bodley's insightful introduction describes in detail the development and essence of Bodley's musical thinking, the European influences he absorbed which linger in these cycles, and the importance of his work as a composer of the Irish art song.

ISBN: 978-1-904505-31-0 (2008) €25

Irish Theatre in England: Irish Theatrical Diaspora Series: 2

Eds. Richard Cave and Ben Levitas

Irish theatre in England has frequently illustrated the complex relations between two distinct cultures. How English reviewers and audiences interpret Irish plays is often decidedly different from how the plays were read in performance in Ireland. How certain Irish performers have chosen to be understood in Dublin is not necessarily how audiences in London have perceived their constructed stage personae. Though a collection by diverse authors, the twelve essays in this volume investigate these issues from a variety of perspectives that together chart the trajectory of Irish performance in England from the mid-nineteenth century till today.

ISBN: 978-1-904505-26-6 (2007) €20

Goethe and Anna Amalia: A Forbidden Love?

Ettore Ghibellino, Trans. Dan Farrelly

In this study Ghibellino sets out to show that the platonic relationship between Goethe and Charlotte von Stein – lady-in-waiting to Anna Amalia, the Dowager Duchess of Weimar – was used as part of a cover-up for Goethe's intense and prolonged love relationship with the Duchess Anna Amalia herself. The book attempts to uncover a hitherto closely-kept state secret. Readers convinced by the evidence supporting Ghibellino's hypothesis will see in it one of the very great love stories in European history – to rank with that of Dante and Beatrice, and Petrarch and Laura.

ISBN: 978-1-904505-24-2 €20

Ireland on Stage: Beckett and After

Eds. Hiroko Mikami, Minako Okamuro, Naoko Yagi

The collection focuses primarily on Irish playwrights and their work, both in text and on the stage during the latter half of the twentieth century. The central figure is Samuel Beckett, but the contributors freely draw on Beckett and his work provides a springboard to discuss contemporary playwrights such as Brian Friel, Frank McGuinness, Marina Carr and Conor McPherson amongst others. Contributors include: Anthony Roche, Hiroko Mikami, Naoko Yagi, Cathy Leeney, Joseph Long, Noreem Doody, Minako Okamuro, Christopher Murray, Futoshi Sakauchi and Declan Kiberd

ISBN: 978-1-904505-23-5 (2007) €20

'Echoes Down the Corridor': Irish Theatre - Past, Present and Future

Eds. Patrick Lonergan and Riana O'Dwyer

This collection of fourteen new essays explores Irish theatre from exciting new perspectives. How has Irish theatre been received internationally - and, as the country becomes more multicultural, how will international theatre influence the development of drama in Ireland? These and many other important questions.

ISBN: 978-1-904505-25-9 (2007) €20

Musics of Belonging: The Poetry of Micheal O'Siadhail

Eds. Marc Caball & David F. Ford

An overall account is given of O'Siadhail's life, his work and the reception of his poetry so far. There are close readings of some poems, analyses of his artistry in matching diverse content with both classical and innovative forms, and studies of recurrent themes such as love, death, language, music, and the shifts of modern life.

ISBN: 978-1-904505-22-8 (2007) €25 (Paperback)
ISBN: 978-1-904505-21-1 (2007) €50 (Casebound)

Modern Death: The End of Civilization

Carl-Henning Wijkmark. Trans: Dan Farrelly

Modern Death is written in the form of a symposium, in which a government agency brings together a group of experts to discuss a strategy for dealing with an ageing population.

The speakers take up the thread of the ongoing debates about care for the aged and about euthanasia. In dark satirical mode the author shows what grim developments are possible. The theme of a 'final solution' is mentioned, though the connection with Hitler is explicitly denied. The most inhuman crimes against human dignity are discussed in the symposium as if they were a necessary condition of future progress.

The fiercely ironical treatment of the material tears off the thin veil that disguises the specious arguments and insidious expressions of concern for the well-being of the younger generation. Though the text was written nearly thirty years ago, the play has a terrifyingly modern relevance.

ISBN: 978 1 904505 28 0 (2007) €8

Brian Friel's Dramatic Artistry: 'The Work has Value'

Eds. Donald E. Morse, Csilla Bertha and Maria Kurdi

Brian Friel's Dramatic Artistry presents a refreshingly broad range of voices: new work from some of the leading English-speaking authorities on Friel, and fascinating essays from scholars in Germany, Italy, Portugal, and Hungary. This book will deepen our knowledge and enjoyment of Friel's work.

ISBN: 978-1-904505-17-4 (2006) €25

The Theatre of Martin McDonagh: 'A World of Savage Stories'

Eds. Lilian Chambers and Eamonn Jordan

The book is a vital response to the many challenges set by McDonagh for those involved in the production and reception of his work. Critics and commentators from around the world offer a diverse range of often provocative approaches. What is not surprising is the focus and commitment of the engagement, given the controversial and stimulating nature of the work.

ISBN: 978-1-904505-19-8 (2006) €30

Edna O'Brien: New Critical Perspectives

Eds. Kathryn Laing, Sinead Mooney and Maureen O'Connor

The essays collected here illustrate some of the range, complexity, and interest of Edna O'Brien as a fiction writer and dramatist. They will contribute to a broader appreciation of her work and to an evolution of new critical approaches, as well as igniting more interest in the many unexplored areas of her considerable oeuvre.

ISBN: 978-1-904505-20-4 (2006) €20

Irish Theatre on Tour

Eds. Nicholas Grene and Chris Morash

'Touring has been at the strategic heart of Druid's artistic policy since the early eighties. Everyone has the right to see professional theatre in their own communities. Irish theatre on tour is a crucial part of Irish theatre as a whole'. Garry Hynes

ISBN 978-1-904505-13-6 (2005) €20

Poems 2000-2005 by Hugh Maxton

Poems 2000-2005 is a transitional collection written while the author – also known to be W.J. Mc Cormack, literary historian – was in the process of moving back from London to settle in rural Ireland.

ISBN 978-1-904505-12-9 (2005) €10

Synge: A Celebration

Ed. Colm Tóibín

A collection of essays by some of Ireland's most creative writers on the work of John Millington Synge, featuring Sebastian Barry, Marina Carr, Anthony Cronin, Roddy Doyle, Anne Enright, Hugo Hamilton, Joseph O'Connor, Mary O'Malley, Fintan O'Toole, Colm Toibin, Vincent Woods.

ISBN 978-1-904505-14-3 (2005) €15

East of Eden: New Romanian Plays

Ed. Andrei Marinescu

Four of the most promising Romanian playwrights, young and very young, are in this collection, each one with a specific way of seeing the Romanian reality, each one with a style of communicating an articulated artistic vision of the society we are living in. Ion Caramitru, General Director Romanian National Theatre Bucharest.
ISBN 978-1-904505-15-0 (2005) €10

George Fitzmaurice: 'Wild in His Own Way', Biography of an Irish Playwright

Fiona Brennan

'Fiona Brennan's introduction to his considerable output allows us a much greater appreciation and understanding of Fitzmaurice, the one remaining under-celebrated genius of twentieth-century Irish drama'. Conall Morrison

ISBN 978-1-904505-16-7 (2005) €20

Out of History: Essays on the Writings of Sebastian Barry

Ed. Christina Hunt Mahony

The essays address Barry's engagement with the contemporary cultural debate in Ireland and also with issues that inform postcolonial critical theory. The range and selection of contributors has ensured a high level of critical expression and an insightful assessment of Barry and his works.

ISBN: 978-1-904505-18-1 (2005) €20

Three Congregational Masses

Seoirse Bodley

'From the simpler congregational settings in the Mass of Peace and the Mass of Joy to the richer textures of the Mass of Glory, they are immediately attractive and accessible, and with a distinctively Irish melodic quality.' Barra Boydell

ISBN: 978-1-904505-11-2 (2005) €15

Georg Büchner's Woyzeck,

A new translation by Dan Farrelly

The most up-to-date German scholarship of Thomas Michael Mayer and Burghard Dedner has finally made it possible to establish an authentic sequence of scenes. The wide-spread view that this play is a prime example of loose, open theatre is no longer sustainable. Directors and teachers are challenged to "read it again".

ISBN: 978-1-904505-02-0 (2004) €10

Playboys of the Western World: Production Histories

Ed. Adrian Frazier

'The book is remarkably well-focused: half is a series of production histories of Playboy performances through the twentieth century in the UK, Northern Ireland, the USA, and Ireland. The remainder focuses on one contemporary performance, that of Druid Theatre, as directed by Garry Hynes. The various contemporary social issues that are addressed in relation to Synge's play and this performance of it give the volume an additional interest: it shows how the arts matter.' Kevin Barry

ISBN: 978-1-904505-06-8 (2004) €20

The Power of Laughter: Comedy and Contemporary Irish Theatre

Ed. Eric Weitz

The collection draws on a wide range of perspectives and voices including critics, playwrights, directors and performers. The result is a series of fascinating and provocative debates about the myriad functions of comedy in contemporary Irish theatre. Anna McMullan

As Stan Laurel said, 'it takes only an onion to cry. Peel it and weep. Comedy is harder'. 'These essays listen to the power of laughter. They hear the tough heart of Irish theatre – hard and wicked and funny'. Frank McGuinness

ISBN: 978-1-904505-05-1 (2004) €20

Sacred Play: Soul-Journeys in contemporary Irish Theatre

Anne F. O'Reilly

'Theatre as a space or container for sacred play allows audiences to glimpse mystery and to experience transformation. This book charts how Irish playwrights negotiate the labyrinth of the Irish soul and shows how their plays contribute to a poetics of Irish culture that enables a new imagining. Playwrights discussed are: McGuinness, Murphy, Friel, Le Marquand Hartigan, Burke Brogan, Harding, Meehan, Carr, Parker, Devlin, and Barry.'

ISBN: 978-1-904505-07-5 (2004) €20

The Irish Harp Book

Sheila Larchet Cuthbert

This is a facsimile of the edition originally published by Mercier Press in 1993. There is a new preface by Sheila Larchet Cuthbert, and the biographical material has been updated. It is a collection of studies and exercises for the use of teachers and pupils of the Irish harp.

ISBN: 978-1-904505-08-2 (2004) €35

The Drunkard

Tom Murphy

'The Drunkard is a wonderfully eloquent play. Murphy's ear is finely attuned to the glories and absurdities of melodramatic exclamation, and even while he is wringing out its ludicrous overstatement, he is also making it sing.' The Irish Times

ISBN: 978-1-90 05-09-9 (2004) €10

Goethe: Musical Poet, Musical Catalyst

Ed. Lorraine Byrne

'Goethe was interested in, and acutely aware of, the place of music in human experience generally - and of its particular role in modern culture. Moreover, his own literary work - especially the poetry and Faust - inspired some of the major composers of the European tradition to produce some of their finest works.' Martin Swales

ISBN: 978-1-9045-10-5 (2004) €25

The Theatre of Marina Carr: "Before rules was made"

Eds. Anna McMullan & Cathy Leeney

As the first published collection of articles on the theatre of Marina Carr, this volume explores the world of Carr's theatrical imagination, the place of her plays in contemporary theatre in Ireland and abroad and the significance of her highly individual voice.

ISBN: 978-0-9534257-7-8 (2003) €20

Critical Moments: Fintan O'Toole on Modern Irish Theatre

Eds. Julia Furay & Redmond O'Hanlon

This new book on the work of Fintan O'Toole, the internationally acclaimed theatre critic and cultural commentator, offers percussive analyses and assessments of the major plays and playwrights in the canon of modern Irish theatre. Fearless and provocative in his judgements, O'Toole is essential reading for anyone interested in criticism or in the current state of Irish theatre.

ISBN: 978-1-904505-03-7 (2003) €20

Goethe and Schubert: Across the Divide

Eds. Lorraine Byrne & Dan Farrelly

Proceedings of the International Conference, 'Goethe and Schubert in Perspective and Performance', Trinity College Dublin, 2003. This volume includes essays by leading scholars – Barkhoff, Boyle, Byrne, Canisius, Dürr, Fischer, Hill, Kramer, Lamport, Lund, Meikle, Newbould, Norman McKay, White, Whitton, Wright, Youens – on Goethe's musicality and his relationship to Schubert; Schubert's contribution to sacred music and the Lied and his setting of Goethe's Singspiel, Claudine. A companion volume of this Singspiel (with piano reduction and English translation) is also available.

ISBN: 978-1-904505-04-4 (2003) €25

Goethe's Singspiel, 'Claudine von Villa Bella'

Set by Franz Schubert

Goethe's Singspiel in three acts was set to music by Schubert in 1815. Only Act One of Schuberts's Claudine score is extant. The present volume makes Act One available for performance in English and German. It comprises both a piano reduction by Lorraine Byrne of the original Schubert orchestral score and a bilingual text translated for the modern stage by Dan Farrelly. This is a tale, wittily told, of lovers and vagabonds, romance, reconciliation, and resolution of family conflict.

ISBN: 978-0-9544290-0-3 (2002) €14

Theatre of Sound, Radio and the Dramatic Imagination

Dermot Rattigan

An innovative study of the challenges that radio drama poses to the creative imagination of the writer, the production team, and the listener.
"A remarkably fine study of radio drama – everywhere informed by the writer's professional experience of such drama in the making...A new theoretical and analytical approach – informative, illuminating and at all times readable." Richard Allen Cave

ISBN: 978- 0-9534-257-5-4 (2002) €20

Talking about Tom Murphy

Ed. Nicholas Grene

Talking About Tom Murphy is shaped around the six plays in the landmark Abbey Theatre Murphy Season of 2001, assembling some of the best-known commentators on his work: Fintan O'Toole, Chris Morash, Lionel Pilkington, Alexandra Poulain, Shaun Richards, Nicholas Grene and Declan Kiberd.

ISBN: 978-0-9534-257-9-2 (2002) €12

Hamlet: The Shakespearean Director

Mike Wilcock

"This study of the Shakespearean director as viewed through various interpretations of HAMLET is a welcome addition to our understanding of how essential it is for a director to have a clear vision of a great play. It is an important study from which all of us who love Shakespeare and who understand the importance of continuing contemporary exploration may gain new insights." From the Foreword, by Joe Dowling, Artistic Director, The Guthrie Theater, Minneapolis, MN

ISBN: 978-1-904505-00-6 (2002) €20

The Theatre of Frank Mc Guinness: Stages of Mutability

Ed. Helen Lojek

The first edited collection of essays about internationally renowned Irish playwright Frank McGuinness focuses on both performance and text. Interpreters come to diverse conclusions, creating a vigorous dialogue that enriches understanding and reflects a strong consensus about the value of McGuinness's complex work.

ISBN: 978-1904505-01-3. (2002) €20

Theatre Talk: Voices of Irish Theatre Practitioners

Eds Lilian Chambers, Ger Fitzgibbon and Eamonn Jordan

"This book is the right approach - asking practitioners what they feel." Sebastian Barry, Playwright "... an invaluable and informative collection of interviews with those who make and shape the landscape of Irish Theatre." Ben Barnes, Artistic Director of the Abbey Theatre

ISBN: 978-0-9534-257-6-1 (2001) €20

In Search of the South African Iphigenie

Erika von Wietersheim and Dan Farrelly

Discussions of Goethe's "Iphigenie auf Tauris" (Under the Curse) as relevant to women's issues in modern South Africa: women in family and public life; the force of women's spirituality; experience of personal relationships; attitudes to parents and ancestors; involvement with religion.

ISBN: 978-0-9534257-8-5 (2001) €10

'The Starving' and 'October Song':

Two contemporary Irish plays by Andrew Hinds

The Starving, set during and after the siege of Derry in 1689, is a moving and engrossing drama of the emotional journey of two men.

October Song, a superbly written family drama set in real time in pre-ceasefire Derry.

ISBN: 978-0-9534-257-4-7 (2001) €10

Seen and Heard: Six new plays by Irish women

Ed. Cathy Leeney

A rich and funny, moving and theatrically exciting collection of plays by Mary Elizabeth Burke-Kennedy, Síofra Campbell, Emma Donoghue, Anne Le Marquand Hartigan, Michelle Read and Dolores Walshe.

ISBN: 978-0-9534-257-3-0 (2001) €20

Theatre Stuff: Critical essays on contemporary Irish theatre

Ed. Eamonn Jordan

Best selling essays on the successes and debates of contemporary Irish theatre at home and abroad. Contributors include: Thomas Kilroy, Declan Hughes, Anna McMullan, Declan Kiberd, Deirdre Mulrooney, Fintan O'Toole, Christopher Murray, Caoimhe McAvinchey and Terry Eagleton.

ISBN: 978-0-9534-2571-1-6 (2000) €20

Under the Curse. Goethe's "Iphigenie Auf Tauris", A New Version

Dan Farrelly

The Greek myth of Iphigenie grappling with the curse on the house of Atreus is brought vividly to life. This version is currently being used in Johannesburg to explore problems of ancestry, religion, and Black African women's spirituality.

ISBN: 978-09534-257-8-5 (2000) €10

Urfaust, A New Version of Goethe's early "Faust" in Brechtian Mode

Dan Farrelly

This version is based on Brecht's irreverent and daring re-interpretation of the German classic. "Urfaust is a kind of well-spring for German theatre... The love-story is the most daring and the most profound in German dramatic literature." Brecht

ISBN: 978-0-9534-257-0-9 (1998) €10